With the Lapps in the High Mountains

this first English translation
supported by a grant from
Figure Foundation

With the Lapps in the High Mountains

A Woman among the Sami, 1907–1908

Emilie Demant Hatt

Edited and translated by Barbara Sjoholm

THE UNIVERSITY OF WISCONSIN PRESS

The University of Wisconsin Press
1930 Monroe Street, 3rd Floor
Madison, Wisconsin 53711-2059
uwpress.wisc.edu

3 Henrietta Street
London WC2E 8LU, England
eurospanbookstore.com

Printed in the United States of America

Library of Congress Cataloging-in-Publication Data
Hatt, Emilie Demant, 1873-1958.
[Med Lapperne i højfjeldet. English]
With the Lapps in the high mountains : a woman among the Sami,
1907–1908 / Emilie Demant Hatt ; edited and translated by Barbara Sjoholm.
p. cm.
Originally published in Sweden as Med lapperne i hojfjeldet, copyright 1913.
Includes bibliographical references.
ISBN 978-0-299-29234-8 (pbk. : alk. paper) — ISBN 978-0-299-29233-1 (e-book)
1. Sami (European people)—Sweden. 2. Hatt, Emilie Demant, 1873–1958—Travel.
3. Lapland—Description and travel. I. Sjoholm, Barbara, 1950– II. Title.
DL641.L35H3818 2013
305.89′4570485—dc23
2012032682

Grateful acknowledgment is made to the following publications, which first
published excerpts from *With the Lapps in the High Mountains: Two Lines*
(spring 2007), *Antioch Review* (spring 2008), *Orion Magazine* (July 2008,
web edition), and *Natural Bridges* (fall 2008).

Contents

Foreword by Hugh Beach   vii

Acknowledgments   xi

Introduction   xiii

Translator's Notes   xxxvii

With the Lapps in the High Mountains   3

Notes   155

Further Reading about the Sami and Sápmi   163

Foreword

No one wishing to know anything about the Sami reindeer herding people of northern Fennoscandia can fail to encounter the name of Emilie Demant Hatt, a name forever associated with that of Johan Turi and his book *Muitalus sámiid birra*. *Muitalus* appeared in English in 1931 as *Turi's Book of Lappland*, the first book by a Sami author, but it is also very much Emilie's book. She was its original translator and editor, as well as its promoter. As a young person growing up in America, I, like so many others, fell under its spell, and it fueled my dream of joining the reindeer herders. Remarkably, youthful dreams often do come true (perhaps because they are so many!), and I have had the pleasure to spend many years living with Sami herders in northern Sweden and in time to study their changing way of life as a professional anthropologist.

I encountered Emilie a second time when reading *With the Lapps in the High Mountains*, first published in 1913, but by then I had already spent some years with the herders myself, and my relation to it was therefore unlike that of so many others. These circumstances made this book all the more special to me, for I became amazed not so much by the material I read about the Sami, but rather by the kindred soul who had seen things so sharply and described them so lovingly. Yes, the book contains much of ethnographic value and provides a historic snapshot to academicians, but more than that, it is a riveting story filled with personal adventure and learning and yet entirely free of pretentiousness. In Emilie's hands the Sami she meets come to life as human persons and are not simply objects of study or informants. Ironically, it is probably her lack of contemporary academic anthropological training, which frees her account from the contrivances of social theory of the times and concepts of the evolution of superior races, that makes her story timeless and brings it so much in line with the best of so-called postmodern anthropology.

It is often the simplest things that bring us together across the years. How well I appreciate her account of seeking relief from an overly smoke-filled tent by opening a makeshift vent hole in the tent cloth, lying with face turned outward to clear the eyes and gasp for fresh air, only to be forced in again soon by the cold. There is hardly a page that does not instill in me a sense of familiarity rather than exoticism, and I feel I know her herding friends rather well through many of the characteristics I have encountered among my own. This is not a communality she has spun in me simply through the similarities of our experiences; I think it is basically a matter of tone. She tells things as they are; she makes no attempt to be an observing scientist "fly on the wall," but is an active agent and companion in the life of her hosts; she is a humanist. Most importantly, she did not set herself apart but wished to live among the Sami she visited as one of them, to learn from them and to pitch in with the work wherever she could.

With the Lapps is intimately related to Turi's book about the Sami, but it is also entirely different. This is Emilie's own account of her travels with the reindeer herding nomads of northern Sweden. Thanks to Barbara Sjoholm it now appears for the first time in English translation. While Turi's book attained relatively swift international acclaim, *With the Lapps* has remained a little known gem. Assuredly it did stimulate a couple of past generations of Scandinavians to learn about the Sami and some perhaps to visit Sápmi, but even for its limited readership the book has been out of print for decades. For a long time now it has held a place mainly in the hearts of scholars interested in the Sami and the north.

Barbara Sjoholm complements her translation with a biographical introduction. I find this facet of Sjoholm's work every bit as meritorious as the translation itself. She has brought Emilie to life in all her complexity and freed her at last from the grudging fetters that have continually surrounded the importance of her contributions. To achieve her goals, Emilie had to negotiate them constantly with those of other strong-willed partners and benefactors. She was under pressure, for example, to bend the thrust of her work to substantiate the theoretical standpoint of her publisher, Hjalmar Lundbohm, regarding the proper education for Sami children. She must have been a superb diplomat, for in the end she always did as she wanted while maintaining good favor and respect.

Moreover, it cannot be denied that Emilie's sizeable contributions to the spread of knowledge about and sympathy for Sami lifeways and culture, along with her appreciation of Sami people as equals to any others, has often been belittled by assertions of Sami cultural nationalism that occasionally have been misdirected. There are those who feel that Emilie's light cannot shine too brightly lest it diminish the glow of Johan Turi's as the first Sami author. She has therefore at times been portrayed as little more than a maid in his service to cook and wash while he wrote. Sjoholm's exhaustive research through Emilie's personal correspondence and that of those with whom she communicated reveals the many layers of Emilie and Johan's intense relationship and her essential part in the course of forming *Muitalus* even if Johan did all the writing. Thanks to Sjoholm, readers should come to appreciate them both more as individuals and also to sense the real wonder of what they were able to accomplish together.

Returning now to *With the Lapps* after so many years, I appreciate it all the more in a professional capacity as well. The recent emphasis on hermeneutics and awareness of the biases of interpretation within the anthropological discipline has caused modern researchers to realize the confines of their gender perspectives—and equally important, the gendered perspectives of the people around them. As a woman, Emilie could interrelate with women and children in the Sami camps in a way that a man never could. Our knowledge of Sami life would be impoverished without her voice, and the Sami have been fortunate to have had such a person among them to tell about their daily lives. Her writing is easily accessible to all, laymen and professional anthropologists alike. Because of her personal qualities, her sex, her artistic bent, freedom from schooled ethnographic aspirations, and her unusual pleasure in nomadic camp life which most women with her background shunned as an extreme discomfort, Emilie has given us a book of immense anthropological value far ahead of its time. She must be considered one of the earliest female ethnographers in a period when this was almost unheard of, and she was not only early, she was also remarkably modern.

Having been with the Sami in the high mountains myself, my only regret when rereading *With the Lapps* now in Sjoholm's translation is that I will never be in person with Emilie in the high mountains. Then again, in another sense and thanks to Sjoholm all of us can join Emilie on her adventures and get to know her herding companions while at the same time enjoying the pleasure of her own company.

HUGH BEACH

Professor of Anthropology, Uppsala University, Sweden, and author of
A Year in Lapland: Guest of the Reindeer Herders

Acknowledgments

Thanks are due the following people for help with the translation and my research on Emilie Demant Hatt's life and work over the years: in Denmark, Lis Bruselius, Mette Dyrberg of the Skive Art Museum, John Fellow, and Rolf Gilberg and Jesper Kurt-Nielsen of the National Museum of Denmark's Ethnographic Collection; in Norway, Cathrine Baglo, Harald Gaski, John Gustavsen, Hans-Ragnar Mathisen, Ragnhild Nilstun, Dikka Storm, and Mikael Svonni; in Sweden, the staffs of the Nordiska Museet's archives and library and Marie Tornehavn of the museum's picture department. I am particularly grateful to Carl-Henrik Berg, a Swedish librarian whose research on my behalf has been invaluable.

The Danish Arts Council gave me a welcome stipend to work on the translation in Denmark. The American-Scandinavian Foundation also provided me with a generous travel grant that allowed me to spend time at Lake Torneträsk and to follow Demant Hatt's route, albeit more comfortably, from Karesuando to Tromsdalen.

I've appreciated all the efforts on the book's behalf from the hard-working staff at the University of Wisconsin Press.

I'd like to thank my partner, Betsy Howell, who, as a wildlife biologist, takes more than the average interest in reindeer and wolves; Hugh Beach, a long-time supporter of the project, whose translation suggestions and insight into Sami cultural history have been enormously helpful; Tom DuBois, for his efforts updating the Sami words and for valuable feedback; Eva Silvén of the Nordiska Museet, a clear-eyed advisor and friend; Henrik Gutzon Larsen, for help with Danish translations and for his important work on Gudmund Hatt; and Katherine Hanson, who has so generously assisted with knotty translation issues. Katherine taught me how to become a translator long ago and still remains an inspiration.

Introduction

In the summer of 1908, a small item appeared in a newspaper in Tromsø, Norway, under the title "A Danish Lapp-Lady." A Miss Demant was to be found not far from town in Tromsdalen—a valley that served as a summer home for the Sami pastoralists who followed their reindeer herds in an annual migration from Sweden.

> She has spent a whole year with a Lapp family, has dressed herself in Lappish costume, and lives in the family's tent. Together with the Lapps she has wandered over the mountains from Torneträsk Lake in Sweden to Tromsdalen. She is doing well and has only praise for the Lapps.[1]

Thirty-five-year-old Emilie Demant, later Demant Hatt, had indeed been living with the Sami, known then as the Lapps, for over a year.[2] The Copenhagen artist had originally visited Lapland with her sister Marie in the summer of 1904. On a train through the mountains, Emilie and Marie happened to meet Johan Turi (1854–1936), a Sami wolf-hunter who dreamed of writing a book someday about his people. A few days later Turi rowed the sisters over Lake Torneträsk to visit the summer encampment of his extended family at Laimolahti. Demant Hatt was so intrigued by Turi and his community that she resolved to live with them if she could, to speak their language, and to learn their customs.

Emilie Demant Hatt (1873–1958) eventually made the Sami and Sápmi a large part of her life's work as an ethnographer, writer, and visual artist.[3] On her return to Copenhagen, she kept in touch with Turi and found a way to study the Sami language at the University of Copenhagen with the philologist and specialist in Finno-Ugric languages, Vilhelm Thomsen. Three years after her first visit as a tourist, in June of 1907, Demant Hatt traveled back to

Northern Fennoscandia

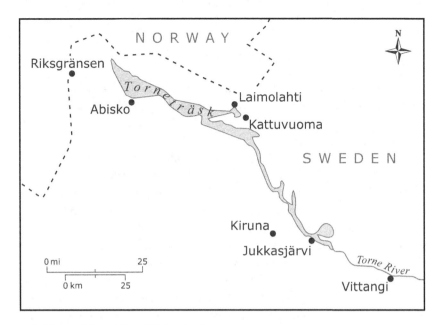

Lake Torneträsk and Swedish Lapland

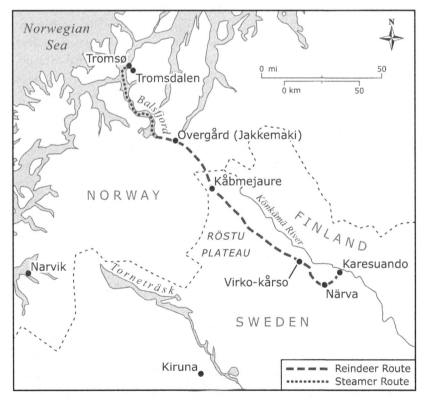

Spring migration route of the Karesuando Sami to Tromsdalen, 1908

northern Sweden with the aim of immersing herself in the daily life of a Sami family. When the opportunity presented itself the following spring of traveling with another group of Sami on their annual reindeer migration from Sweden to Norway, she took it.

After returning to Sweden from Norway in July 1908, Demant Hatt stayed a few months longer to work with Johan Turi on the notebooks that would eventually become the basis for his manuscript. In these notebooks Turi wrote histories, folktales, and practical information about everything from reindeer herding to medical matters. Back in Denmark that October, Demant transcribed, translated, and shaped Turi's writing into a full-length narrative, the first literary work by a Sami author. *Muitalus sámiid birra/En bog om lappernes liv* appeared in a bilingual Sami–Danish edition in 1910 and was an immediate sensation. It was soon translated into German, then Swedish, and eventually into English as *Turi's Book of Lappland*.[4] Demant Hatt continued to do fieldwork in Sweden in 1910 and 1911; in 1913 she published her own narrative, *With the Lapps in the High Mountains*.[5] In 1911 she had married a young Danish scholar, Gudmund Hatt (1884–1960), and together they returned to Lapland almost yearly through 1916, gathering data for a proposed book of their own about the Sami and collecting artifacts for the National Museum of Denmark. Demant Hatt edited another manuscript by Johan Turi and his nephew Per, *Lappish Texts*, and compiled a collection of Sami folktales, *By the Fire*, illustrated with her own block prints.

Near the end of her life Demant Hatt told an interviewer about the moment in 1907 when she tried to understand what she should do with her growing knowledge of Sami life: "I was no ethnographer and wasn't going to 'study the Lapps.' I'd only had since childhood an almost mystical longing to live with the mountain people."[6] Yet she went on to contribute significantly to the ethnography of the Swedish Sami through fieldwork, collaborative ethnography, and material collections for the National Museum of Denmark. Her work as the editor and translator of *Muitalus sámiid birra* and her own book of travel and ethnography, *With the Lapps in the High Mountains*, along with her public stance as a supporter of Sami rights, made her a recognizable figure in Danish public life.

With the Lapps in the High Mountains is, in part, an ethnographic study of two *siidas* or communities of Sami families with their primary residence in Sweden. One *siida*, residing around and south of Lake Torneträsk, were Talma Sami. Another *siida*, whose winter home was near Karesuando and whose summer camp was on the Norwegian coast, were Karesuando or Könkämä Sami. But the book is also the tale of a grand adventure, full of events, anecdotes, and striking descriptions of a landscape and a largely vanished way of life. Academically untrained as an ethnographer, Demant Hatt brings an artist's eye and a writer's narrative skill to her story of living and traveling with the Sami during the first decade of the twentieth century.

With the Lapps in the High Mountains begins with Demant Hatt's arrival at the *siida's* summer camp on Lake Torneträsk in June of 1907, while there is still snow in the mountains. The earliest chapters relate to the often idyllic days of boating on the lake, children's play, and the courting of young couples. She describes work that happens inside the tent—cooking, sewing, and caring for children—and outside it—chopping wood, hauling water, building fires, and culling the herds. As the days grow shorter, the *siida* leaves its lakeside encampment and begins to follow the reindeer in their search for forage. Demant Hatt writes about taking down the tents and packing everything up, and about the *siida's* migration to the late fall and winter quarters in the forest at a lower elevation. With the arrival of colder weather more of the action takes place within the family tent. The family that Demant Hatt portrays most vividly is that of Johan Turi's brother Nikki (a pseudonym for Aslak Turi), his wife Sara (Siri), and their five children, four of whom were still living at home: grown son Biettar (Per); seventeen-year-old Inga (Ristina); eleven-year-old Elle (Anne); and ten-year-old Nilsa (Andaras).

In late November Demant Hatt accompanies Nikki on a hair-raising journey, driving her own sled, to the village of Jukkasjärvi near Kiruna for the yearly Saint Andrew's Market and sleeps in a bed for the first time in months. Christmas back in the tent is a slightly dismal affair, with the temperature stalled far below freezing and cheer at the minimum, due to Sara's strict religious views. Sara, like many of the local Talma Sami and the Finnish settlers, is a member of the Laestadian church, a Lutheran sect. After the New Year, the *siida* travels to its midwinter quarters in Vittangi. Demant Hatt falls ill and recuperates slowly in the home of Finnish settlers with the help of medical attention. But by March she's eager to explore more of Sápmi and particularly to find a way to cross over the high mountains between Sweden and Norway with the Sami and their reindeer. Her migration on foot and by sled takes her on a trek of over two hundred kilometers to the green valley of Tromsdalen on the Norwegian coast.

With the Lapps in the High Mountains is constructed like a traditional traveler's tale, beginning with an arrival and ending near her departure for home a year later. The daily life of the Sami is set against a background of seasonal change, from the snowy June of 1907 to the warm summer of July 1908. As the months go on, she participates in most aspects of life with the Turi family; she cooks, stretches hides, and makes herself Sami clothing from reindeer skin. She gathers wood, learns to pack up the reindeer, and walks on migrations from the high summer camp to the lower forests and marshes en route to Vittangi. She spends time with the children, teaching Elle to draw and observing (and sometimes participating in) their games. Demant Hatt tells us about reindeer marking and slaughtering, about food preparation and tent construction. She invites us into the tent to explain about bedding and sleeping arrangements. She allows us to witness a revival meeting of ecstatic Laestadians. She lets us see her making social mistakes and being firmly but gently corrected. As the narrative progresses, Demant Hatt takes on more challenges—driving her own sled through the forest to the fair at Jukkasjärvi and crossing a high mountain range on foot in the company of nomads and their reindeer and dogs.

As a narrative, the story is highly satisfying, full of humor and human interest, but also thrills and plenty of chills, with a few villains (Norwegian farmers demanding "hay damages") and many heroes, including Demant Hatt herself. Her powers of visual observation, honed by years of studying and making art, enabled her to call up striking descriptions of the landscape, notable for their attention to color and to mood:

> Already in August we had snow squalls, but the approach of winter wasn't seriously apparent until September, when the snow could linger several days and the ice on the lakes and marshes was quite thick. Of course that alternated with splendid days of sunshine and the mountain forests were a marvel of color. The birch's shiny gold coins fell down on the reddest of red ground. The lower slopes of the mountains were golden; further up, violet. On top lay new snow and above that a high radiant blue September sky. When it grew dark the Northern Lights fanned out and waved under the stars. One evening there was a golden gateway to the south, and to the north sharp bright rays shot like bundles of rockets up under all the stars, as if from the top of Ripanen. The tents glowed like small volcanoes; out of the open cone poured a column of fire—red smoke and sparks, which climbed and died out in the darkness above.

Demant Hatt describes weather and snow conditions; landscapes of rivers, forests, mountain plateaus, and marshes; the passing of the seasons. Some of the most dramatic descriptions come in the last chapters of *With the Lapps in the High Mountains* as she writes of crossing ice bridges and traveling with pack reindeer along precipitous cliffs. Just as memorable are the scenes of descent from the mountains into the Norwegian valleys, with soft moss underfoot, flowers, and the smell of salt water as they come to "the Sea Kingdom."

From an ethnographic point of view *With the Lapps in the High Mountains* is remarkable for the amount of detail it gives about the lives of children and women. Many of the men were out with the herds during the first summer she spent in Lapland, and Demant Hatt spent most of her time in and around the tent. Demant Hatt describes the children of the community playing at being reindeer together and supplies many details about Sami child-raising, from birth to bathing to education. She gives information about courtship, engagements, and marriage. She portrays women's work as core to Sami life, and, indeed, it could be said that that women are the central characters of *With the Lapps in the High Mountains*. She admires their graceful movements in a small space, their strength, their aesthetics, and in the case of Sara, their judiciousness and equanimity.

Although Johan Turi was a crucial source of information on many aspects of reindeer herding and hunting and on spiritual and healing practices, it was Sara whom Demant Hatt depended on, as a friend and teacher, over the many months that she lived in the tent. It is Sara's wisdom that permeates much of *With the Lapps in the High Mountains*; it is Sara who teaches her guest how to sit, how to observe tent etiquette, how to sew a dress of tanned reindeer skin, and most importantly, how to have a conversation. Although Demant Hatt had studied Sami and arrived in Lapland with a large Norwegian–Sami dictionary, she soon found that the dialect spoken among her new community was markedly different from what she had learned from Professor Thomsen at the University of Copenhagen. She said that Sara taught her the names of objects in the tent and in the natural world by the time-honored method of pointing and repeating.

With the Lapps in the High Mountains is full of lively anecdotes about the family she lived with and about their larger social networks, including the Finnish settlers in the area who are also followers of the Laestadian faith and with whom the Sami sometimes boarded in winter or when ill. Her descriptions of the Turi family are grounded in warm affection. Here she is on Sara: "In spite of her age, near sixty, she was straight-backed and graceful, as almost all Lapp women are. She was especially beautiful in her golden *dorka* (inner fur) with white leather gloves, and a tall white stand-up collar that attractively framed her intelligent brown face with the lively eyes and the loose black hair under the red cap." And on ten-year-old Nilsa looking for his cap in the morning: "It was particularly difficult for Nilsa to find his cap. Often he was almost at the point of tears from rage, knocking dogs out of his way, overturning all the bedclothes, shoving pokers around to get more light. Kidding and good advice rained down him: *Čana gitta go gávnnat.* 'Hold it tight when you find it.' Or, *Leagos dus gáhpir oppanassii?* 'Do you even have a cap?'"

Some of the scenes are frankly funny—as when she describes sparks from the fire setting people's hair alight, or a dog being put in its place by a reindeer, or herself attempting to stay in her sled as a reindeer dashes headlong forward. Demant Hatt has a knack for creating character with just a few words—the daughter of the family, Inga, for instance, coming into the tent after being out all night in below freezing weather guarding the reindeer; or Nikki unconcernedly cleaning his rifle in the tent as the Laestadians pray all around him. She notes the family's words in Sami and translates them into Danish. Lines of fresh and sometimes mordant dialog pepper the narrative.

Demant Hatt herself is often unobtrusive in the stories—unobtrusive but not invisible. We see her crouching with Inga in some bushes, hiding from a couple of sweethearts who are searching for them; we see her visiting Elle and a friend on the rock where they have laid out their dolls and stones representing reindeer; we see her skiing slowly by herself on Christmas morning and hearing the murmuring of the "underground beings" below the snow. We feel her exhaustion at times and also her intense sense of well-being. Indeed, it's a sense of joyfulness that most often pervades this book, a tremendous ease with what is a physically demanding life.

If Demant Hatt's long stay with the Turi family in their tent was unheard of for the time, her decision to accompany the Karesuando Sami on their spring migration was even more daring for a woman in 1908. The Tromsø newspaper spoke of her "wandering" over the mountains from Torneträsk. In fact the pastoralist Sami did not wander, but moved purposefully from their traditional "winterlands" to "summerlands" and back again, herding and protecting their reindeer as the animals followed traditional migration routes in search of seasonal pasturage. Some Sami didn't make lengthy cross-country migrations—for instance, the Turi family. But Demant Hatt was determined to have a longer and perhaps more dangerous "nomadic" experience. Friends in Kiruna helped her to get to Karesuando for the well-known Easter services, and there she found a family willing to let her accompany them on the migration to Norway's Tromsdalen. She may have partly chosen this family because they were part of a group whose end point was just outside Tromsø. From there Demant Hatt would be able to take the steamer south to Narvik and board the train heading back over the mountains to Kiruna.

Demant Hatt began her strenuous new journey in April of 1908 in the area around Närva, a winter grazing area that was a staging ground for a number of *siidas* gathering for the migration to Norway. The Karesuando Sami were divided into districts according to the routes they took from Sweden to Norway and back again and by their camps in summer and winter. The 9th district, which moved from Närva to the Troms Peninsula (*Tromshalvøya* or *Stuoranjárga* in Sami), was further broken down into four groups, depending on their final destination. The 9th district consisted of around three hundred individuals and some four thousand reindeer.[7] Although the *siida* was a collective group and herding work was handled jointly, the principle of ownership was observed. For instance, Demant Hatt's hosts on the trip were relatively poor with only twenty reindeer, while the foreman of the *siida*, Anders Omma, owned some seven hundred reindeer.[8]

The females of the reindeer herd had been separated out at the beginning of April and had already moved over the high mountains to calve. The male herd was now on its way, with groups of Sami following in caravans of reindeer, called strings, which included the load-bearing sledges and individual sleds. The sledges carried tent poles and coverings, fur sleeping bags, bags of sugar, coffee, and meal, and all the family's kitchen supplies, not only for making food en route, but for setting up a whole household when they would arrive in Tromsdalen in two months.

Demant Hatt left Närva with her hosts: Gate, her husband Heikka, and their young daughter Rauna (their real names were Anne, Jounas, and Margreta Rasti). After some days they arrived in an area Demant Hatt called Virkokårso, most likely Vuoggásgorsa or Vuoggáscearru from the description. Here, surrounded by four "bald mountains," and not far from the Könkämä River, which forms the border between Sweden and Finland, was a forest of scrub birch and heather, with plenty of forage for the reindeer, an important consideration as the Sami waited for the weather to warm so that they could begin their trek into high altitudes.[9] During the spring migrations the Sami preferred to keep to the mountain ranges so as to avoid the shrubbery and insects of the valleys below; yet it was important that the high plateaus and ridges not be entirely covered with snow and ice, so that the reindeer could find food.

Finally, around the end of May, the weather was deemed suitable, and the group set off in a caravan, ascending to the Röstu, a high plateau that extends all the way to the mountain peaks between Sweden and Norway. Demant Hatt's account is short on place names, but it's likely that they followed the traditional paths that trended west and north, over the plateau. She records the weather and a wealth of detail about the migration and the people and animals. They often traveled at night though it was still daylight, because the colder temperatures made the snow and ice more stable. The terrain is sometimes smooth-going and sometimes rough, broken by gorges and rivers in melt:

> Then suddenly our voices drowned in a crashing thunder from a river. When we came right up to it, we could barely shout to each other. How were we going to cross this foaming, roaring monster, rushing white deep down between two sheer boulder walls? The women went a distance along the bank until they found a passable snow bridge, the kind formed in winter from snow and frozen spray. In spring the water wears the bridge thin. I shuddered at the thought of going over a not very wide bridge, which looked anything but solid. Under it the river boiled at furious speed. The delicate woman now began to relate every possible story she knew of death and disaster in these parts. It wasn't exactly cheering and I asked her to stop. We had a great deal of trouble with the puppies. When the woman grew tired of carrying them on her back or in her arms in a sack, they were placed on one of the reindeer, but naturally they cried and barked and frightened the reindeer, so once more they had to be carried. They certainly tried to walk for very short stretches, but at that pace we didn't get far, so they were stuffed into the sack again.

Eventually the nomads reached Kåbmejaure or Ghost Lake, and from there they crossed the border into Norway and began a long series of descents into the fjord valleys. Demant Hatt made the decision to go with a group taking a shorter but more strenuous route down, and these are some of the most nerve-wracking moments, for Demant Hatt and for the reader. Eventually the group arrived in Overgård (which Demant Hatt calls Jakkemaki). Here Demant Hatt was able to observe first-hand the conflicts between the farmers and the reindeer herds. These valleys, which had been used by the reindeer and their hunters and later herders for thousands of years, were increasingly owned by Norwegians, many of whom had moved up to the far north from southern Norway, spurred by generous offers of land from the government.

The reindeer herds continued overland onto the Troms Peninsula, accompanied by the herders, who still had almost another hundred kilometers to go before reaching the summer residence in Tromsdalen. But for Demant Hatt, the spring migration was over. Along with some of the other women and children, she walked a country road to Nordsjøbotn on the Balsfjord and boarded a steamer for Tromsø. Arriving in the town on June 27, she posted a long letter to her sister, written over the course of the migration. After a few days, she took a small ferry to the Troms Peninsula and made her way to the permanent turf huts of the *siida's* summer camp. There she spent the next two weeks.

The last chapter of *With the Lapps in the High Mountains*, describing the end of the trek and life in the encampment, is short and perhaps the most politically charged section of the book. It was here in Tromsdalen, after months of living with and identifying with the Sami, that Demant Hatt felt the discomfort of seeing how her friends and companions were treated by the Norwegian farmers and the local government. Although the Sami had many individual friendships with local people and engaged in trade that helped the local economy, they often found themselves on the wrong side of the law, made to pay the costs of real or invented damage to fields or crops that reindeer had trampled. Demant Hatt found it particularly painful to see the tourists arrive by horse and buggy from Tromsø, a popular stop on the cruise route up to the North Cape. Here at a touristy reindeer corral set up by the Sami, the foreigners snapped photographs and bought Sami handicrafts:

> When the tourists gather around the corral, taking photographs and gesticulating, the atmosphere seems filled with exclamation marks. The whole business is a repellant marketplace. The Lapps go around with small bundles of wares; bargaining and buying goes on while the reindeer stand there drowsy and hungry after having run themselves ragged around the corral, frightened of the confusion and all the strange people.
>
> The children, who look like miniature adults, enthrall the tourists, who feed them candy and give them money. It's remarkable that so-called cultivated people can't conduct themselves with more dignity and true understanding. It's as if, for the tourists, the Lapps are only a flock of curious and "sweet" animals.

∾

With the Lapps in the High Mountains is based partly on journal entries and on letters that Demant Hatt wrote to her family during her year and a half in

Sápmi in 1907–8. Her intent from the beginning was to keep a clear record of what she was experiencing, and her thirty-odd letters, long and faithfully scribbled on thin paper in pencil or ink that has now gone greenish, form a continuous record of her life that she was able to draw on to write her book several years later. She was somewhat less successful in managing to keep a regular diary. Although she enthusiastically begins her personal journal on June 21, 1907, with her arrival in Torneträsk, "This *is* a fairytale, and it's a fairytale kingdom I find myself in," her entries begin to peter out by the end of the summer. It could not have been easy to find time to write regularly given the nature of her active life, the lack of light in the winter, and the general smokiness of the tent. Later, she used this journal to record stories from some of the rest of her trip the following year. In addition to the letters and journals, Demant Hatt kept some very small notebooks of her expenses, which yield some interesting information—for instance, how much she paid Aslak Turi monthly to live with the family and what she also contributed to the larder when able to shop in Kiruna.

A sense of excitement, curiosity, and joy run through many of these letters and longer journal entries. They contain little in the way of methodical note-taking. Demant Hatt was content to live immersed in Sami daily life, recording with a keen ear and observant eye the new world in which she found herself. The narrative and descriptive passages of *With the Lapps in the High Mountains* are what give the book its immediacy and vibrancy. The letters, of course, also show a more complex and varied response to some of what Demant Hatt was experiencing. Her description, in a letter to her family, of her first days in Tromsø, is markedly different from what she describes in *With the Lapps in the High Mountains*, for it includes visiting the dentist, getting her boots repaired, and giving in to the temptation to buy a light linen dress with money sent by her family. She records some late nights in the company of the agreeable sister of the captain of the Balsford steamer. Yet she also mentions a sense of indignation at the way people stare at her and her Sami friends in town. Rumors had preceded her arrival: she was a Swedish spy or the daughter of the Lapp king or a distinguished Danish baroness.[10]

Demant Hatt had brought a camera and some art supplies with her to Lapland, and her photographs (many of which illustrate the original *With the Lapps in the High Mountains*) supplement her descriptions of places and people. Photographic representation of the Sami has a long and contested history, given that many Sami were photographed by tourists or by scientists to illustrate racial theories prevalent in Sweden and Germany from the late nineteenth century through the 1930s. Demant Hatt's photographs instead capture a small group of Sami at work and at play; there is often an unstudied, intimate air to the photos that is revealing of her close relationships with the children and adults. During her time in Sápmi, Demant Hatt painted no full-size oil canvases, but she made a number of pencil and pen-and-ink sketches and watercolors in her sketchbooks. Few are highly finished, but they show life in the tent—from bathing babies, to cooking, to smoking pipes. She particularly enjoyed drawing children at play: skiing, tobogganing, and throwing snowballs.

In *With the Lapps in the High Mountains* Demant Hatt doesn't attempt to cover everything that she saw and experienced during her time in Lapland. The compression and artful details are, from a literary standpoint, strengths of the book, but they can also lead to a portrait of the Sami as romantic nomads outside modern life. She was specifically interested in the mountain Sami and tended not to mention the fact that not all Sami were primarily reindeer pastoralists who undertook migrations with their herds. Many *siidas* in Sápmi had long combined farming, fishing, and reindeer herding. The coastal or sea Sami of Norway as well as Sami living along the rivers and lakes of Sweden, Finland, and Russia had been skilled boat builders, trappers, and fishers for hundreds of years. In later fieldwork Demant Hatt visited Sami in different areas of Sweden and Norway and made notes on their ways of life, but her heart seems to have always been with "the mountain people," and that is certainly expressed in *With the Lapps in the High Mountains*.

In terms of reindeer herding itself, Demant Hatt doesn't clearly explain the difference between intensive and extensive herding practices. In the former, prevalent in southern Sápmi, the Sami had fewer reindeer but tended to domesticate them for purposes of food and milk, and for creating objects of utility and trade. With extensive herding, common in the north of Sápmi and a practice brought to the districts around Jukkasjärvi by reindeer owners who came from elsewhere (including the Turi family), the Sami were encouraged to allow their herds to increase; wealth was in numbers. The Swedish government was moving slowly to define the rights of Sami citizens in regard to reindeer husbandry, but in doing so, it was defining away the identity of Sami who didn't engage in reindeer husbandry. As the twentieth century progressed, these non–reindeer herders grew to be 90 percent of the Sami population all over the north of Fennoscandia. By the 1930s, traditional nomadism was on the wane. It didn't resume fully after the German occupation of Norway from

1940–45, which closed the border with Sweden. The Germans had destroyed much of the far north of Finland and Norway, including Sami homes and farms; some Sami emigrated away or voluntarily assimilated; others were more forcibly encouraged to adapt.[11] The situation in neutral Sweden was different during and after the war, but in that country too, traditional reindeer pastoralism gradually took on a more legislated and geographically confined aspect, far different from the "nomad life" that Demant Hatt celebrated.

The notion of being a nomad had drawn her since childhood, and her passionate stance on many issues pertaining to the Sami came in part from a clinging to a dream of a people apart and untouched by some of the problems of Western Civilization. Demant Hatt often contrasts and favorably compares Sami communal and individual conduct with that of European society. She tends to be selective about how much information she allows into her story regarding the modern world's proximity to the traditional life of the Sami community. She never refers to the railway that connects Sweden and Norway through the mountains or to the coastal steamer from Tromsø to Narvik. She simply appears at Torneträsk one day and she leaves the reader in Tromsdalen at the end. Yet in addition to taking trains to and from Denmark to northern Sweden, it's certain that Demant Hatt availed herself of the railway during the second half of her long stay in the mountains, if only to travel to Kiruna and Abisko. The Sami themselves used the train for travel; that's how she originally met Johan Turi in 1904. Kiruna, the fast-growing town built near traditional Sami winter grazing grounds, figures little in her narrative. Only once does she mention seeing the lights of the iron ore mine and hearing the dynamite blasts.

Yet unlike many who described the Sami at the turn of the century and first decades of the twentieth century, Demant Hatt's view of this people is nuanced, detailed, and respectful. In contrast, much of what was written about the Sami during the same time period, both by casual tourists to Lapland and by those who had or would have a larger forum as ethnographers, was often condescending. Gerda Niemann, an employee of the Swedish Tourist Association (STF), described seeing Sami for the first time during a train stop in 1903: "At Kaisepakte station waited some of these proud mountain-born masters, the small crooked-legged Lapps, and they, like the children we'd passed on the train platforms, were instinctively drawn toward the dining car, where they were offered small treats."[12] In 1907, the same summer Demant Hatt was living at Laimolahti, Ellen Kleman, the editor of the feminist journal *Dagny*, visited the Sami camp of Pålnoviken across the lake from Abisko's tourist station: "The children of the wilderness are perhaps still talking for a while there, in their own speech, about the foreign guests, and perhaps we'll become a memory in their lives, just as incomprehensible to them as they are for us. Because we scarcely know about and understand these large children, who live their lives in Lapland's wild places in their short, light, wonderfully colorful summer and their long winter's dark night."[13]

K. B. Wiklund, a professor of Finno-Ugric at the University of Uppsala, whose "schoolbooks for nomad children" would influence several generations of Sami and who was one of the Swedish state's most trusted advisors on Sami issues, would eventually come to play a role in Demant Hatt's professional life.[14] In 1903, in its annual yearbook, STF published a lecture given by Wiklund at the organization's annual meeting the previous year. Wiklund encouraged readers to come north not just for the animals, plants, and mountains, but to study the lives of the Lapps. He particularly recommends visiting the Sami in winter. The lecture glides smoothly from topic to topic as he brings his readers into a Sami tent, describing the smells of food cooking, the smoke, the reindeer hides on the twigs that formed the flooring. Yet even as he speaks of the need to get to know the Sami, "to see that they are human beings," he doesn't mention any individuals by name or give a sense of relationship or interaction. The lecture, in fact, seems to suggest a man not very comfortable in his surroundings. Describing waking up after a freezing cold night in a tent, he writes, "When morning breaks, pale and dreary, one sits silent and frozen around the fire and looks at it with washed-out, fixed eyes. One's hair hangs in one's face, one's nose is soot-filled, one's cheeks dirty and flaccid. No one says anything, not even the coffee has any effect."[15]

A young man who became Denmark's best-known explorer and ethnographer, Knud Rasmussen, visited northern Sweden and spent time with the Sami in 1901. His dispatches, appearing initially in the *Berlingske Tidende*, were published as *Lapland* in 1907, after Rasmussen had become famous for his first expedition to the north of Greenland. Rasmussen, with his language skills and knowledge of Greenlandic society, was able to also collect stories, folklore, and myths from the Inuit. These he published in two popular volumes, *New People* in 1905 and *Under the Lash of the North Wind* in 1906. It's very likely that Demant Hatt read these two books in between her first journey to Lapland as a tourist in 1904 and her return in 1907; she may also have attended the popular lectures Rasmussen gave in Denmark after his return from the Greenland expedition.

What is certain is that she did read Knud Rasmussen's book on Lapland, which she found in a Tromsø bookshop in 1908. She stayed up most of one night to peruse it and was disappointed. By this time she had lived a year with the Sami in two different *siidas*; she spoke the language and was deeply immersed in the lives of the Sami and aware of their struggles to keep their culture intact and to maintain their legal rights in several countries. In a letter home she wrote, "Oh, Lord, how thin it is in pages and superficial, he lies regularly—from ignorance. It's so irritating."[16] Although Rasmussen's views were to become more complex, in his earlier work he tended to describe indigenous people as "nature's children" and see their fate as sealed. Addressing Silock, a Sami man he has met, he writes,

> The reindeer herds will disappear, and your friends will die along with their wilderness. Silock, your people are sentenced to death.
> There is a war now in the Lapmark, and those fighting are two cultures. And the new one must be victorious, because it bears the future within itself.
> But each victory walks over corpses. The Lapps will be oppressed in their own land and give way with the quiet resignation of those sentenced to death to the new people, those who charge ahead with their trains and dynamite.
> And they will die as quietly and unnoticed as they always have lived up here.[17]

According to Rasmussen, in the meeting of the primitive with the civilized, civilization would always prevail and "nature's children" would always lose. Demant Hatt had a very different view of the people whose resilience she respected and whose rights she defended in *With the Lapps in the High Mountains*: "the Lapps won't go under because they're a primitive people with an innate lack of vigor. All things considered, it appears that the theory of primitive people dying out doesn't hold up. There are large numbers of primitive people who to this very day steadily live on, even though for a hundred years they've been sentenced to death."

Demant Hatt's year of immersion in the life of Sami was followed by several months of work with Johan Turi on what was to become *Muitalus sámiid birra*. The two were given the use of rooms in a mining shack near the Torneträsk railway station from around August of 1908 into October. The fifty-four-year-old Turi, a bachelor who had never quite fit into traditional Sami society and who had long dreamed of writing a book about his people, finally set to work, with Demant Hatt's encouragement and suggestions for topics, to put down his memories and knowledge of Sami traditions, including information about medicine, religion, hunting, and courtship.[18]

Working with Turi that fall, listening to his stories and encouraging him to write in depth about things that she was curious to know about herself, gave Demant Hatt a greater understanding of the world that she'd been inhabiting for over a year. Their joint work, an early example of collaborative ethnography, enriched both their manuscripts and give them a complementary feel. Unlike many ethnographers at the turn of the century, Demant Hatt never thought of publishing Turi's stories as her own or making him a coauthor of his own narrative. She was clear from the beginning that *Muitalus sámiid birra* would be his achievement, though in later years she was able to acknowledge how much of her own time and labor the project had taken.

The effort of first transcribing Turi's book in the original Sami and then translating it into Danish consumed the next year of Demant Hatt's life back in Denmark. She worked with a former fellow student, Anders Pedersen, to decipher and clarify the words and meaning and to find equivalents in Danish, and then, with their former professor, Vilhelm Thomsen, to settle on an orthography. Demant Hatt also became the managing editor of the project responsible for seeing the manuscript typeset in Copenhagen and then printed. The publisher was Hjalmar Lundbohm, the wealthy director of the Kiruna mine, an art collector, a self-identified supporter of the Sami, and a friend to both Johan Turi and Demant Hatt. Demant Hatt and Lundbohm had met by chance in Jukkasjärvi in November of 1907 (Demant Hatt describes the market in *With the Lapps in the High Mountains* but not meeting Lundbohm). The two began a friendship that led to a close working partnership and lasted until Lundbohm died in 1926. When Lundbohm financially backed the production of *Muitalus sámiid birra* in 1910, he made it the first in a series, "The Lapps and Their Land," which came to consist of some ten titles and included *With the Lapps in the High Mountains*.

It was Lundbohm who encouraged Demant Hatt to write her own book. As early as March 14, 1908, he wrote her, "It's too bad if at least some part of what of you know now didn't become accessible to others, it would be almost immoral to keep it for yourself. Bear in mind that *no one* for many years has lived through what you are witnessing now, and I believe that your observations are more valuable than others because you've observed with kindly eyes and not with the prying and distorted eyes of the tourist or the dry and tedious eyes of the researcher. If one should draw people correctly it doesn't hurt to have sympathy."[19]

Five years later, on January 5, 1913, after having read the manuscript of *With the Lapps in the High Mountains,* he praised her work unreservedly: "The depiction throughout is captivating and full of interest, the style is simple and fine, free of studied, unnecessary ornamentation, which is the worst thing I know." Lundbohm wrote in the same letter that he hoped Demant Hatt's "book's central point will perhaps become the expression of the Lappish question," meaning that Demant Hatt would address the political questions of the day about Sami rights.[20] There are indeed times, particularly toward the end of *With the Lapps in the High Mountains,* that Demant Hatt turns her thoughts to the situation of the reindeer herders, in particular the conflicts between the farmers and settlers and the pastoralist Sami. Yet for Demant Hatt, who had observed the conflicts firsthand, little was ever theoretical. For her, there was no dry "Lappish question," there were only individual Sami and their joys and struggles. Initially Demant Hatt seems to have worried about writing her own book about the Sami. Her reservations are apparent in this letter from Hjalmar Lundbohm, "I understand the reluctance you feel to go in search of which the Lapps themselves would like to have concealed and to make a book of that. But you don't need to do that. Just write what you yourself feel and what you have gotten to know and experience without thinking of the public, write it as a journal or a letter, it doesn't matter."[21]

Demant Hatt felt a responsibility to the Sami to portray them with affection and respect and to explain, as best she could, their way of life. She may have felt that it was Johan Turi's book that, naturally enough, captured Sami life from the inside. Yet she may have also realized it was precisely her position as a privileged outsider that could help shape interest in the Sami and an understanding of their place in the world, not only to her Danish readership but to the larger Fennoscandian public and governmental authorities engaged in deciding the fate of the Sami in terms of land, education, and their roles in civic life. In the end, Demant Hatt perhaps wisely left out long explanations of Sami history and politics, and told her story personally. The book reads the better for her warm portraits of those she lived with and the many details of their lives.

～

Demant Hatt felt the need for a better grounding in anthropology after she returned home from her year and a half in northern Sweden. She met her husband-to-be, eleven years younger, when a friend introduced them. In the fall of 1909 Gudmund Hatt began to tutor her informally, using his own studies in anthropology as a guide. Gudmund had spent two years in the United States, including one summer with family friends at a mission in Oklahoma, among the Cherokee. He had studied anthropology for a year at Harvard with Roland B. Dixon and was now a graduate student in geography at the University of Copenhagen under H. P. Steensby, who had written extensively on the Inuit of Greenland.

In addition to her studies in Copenhagen, Demant Hatt returned to Sweden twice on her own to do fieldwork among the Sami. In 1910 she spent two months living with an elderly couple, Märta and Nils Nilsson, in their tent in Glen in southern Sápmi (Jämtland). Märta was a rich source and Demant Hatt was later to write a manuscript, "Long Ago," about her time with Märta and Nils, using her field notes as a source.[22] Demant Hatt also returned to Kiruna in 1910 and 1911 (as well as in 1916 with Gudmund) to work with Johan Turi on another project that would eventually become *Lappish Texts*, which would include more of what Turi considered sacred and secret information about the Sami.[23]

Gudmund and Emilie's marriage in 1911 led to almost a decade of cooperative projects. Her passionate interest in the Sami encouraged his choice of research subjects for some years, while his scholarly bent influenced Demant Hatt's method of gathering information and its presentation. Some of the original lengthy endnotes to *With the Lapps in the High Mountains* bear the hallmarks of Gudmund's more academic approach to research. The couple traveled in early 1912 to Stockholm, Helsinki, and Saint Petersburg, where Gudmund visited museums in search of objects to describe and compare for his eventual dissertation in 1914, and Demant Hatt drew beautifully precise pen and ink drawings to accompany his text.[24]

In the summer of 1912 they trekked, by foot and horse, to a remote area of the southernmost edge of Sápmi, near Idre in Dalarna, where Gudmund spent days out in the mountains with local reindeer herders, and Demant Hatttook notes on her conversations and observations. From Gudmund's hands-on experience and intensive reading on northern Scandinavian and Siberian pastoralism came a substantial paper, "Notes on Reindeer Nomadism," published in Danish and American journals.[25] Gudmund also wrote articles about varieties of Sami sleds and the artificial head-molding of Sami infants. In his published work on the Sami, Gudmund was careful, even enthusiastic, to cite Emilie's research and writing. The Hatts also began to collect artifacts on this trip; on subsequent trips they gathered many more objects for the National Museum of Denmark and for their own studies.[26]

All of Demant Hatt's work during the years 1908 to 1913, translating and editing Johan Turi's book, lecturing about her travels and the Sami, as well as her continuing ethnographic studies and fieldwork in Lapland, enriched the story she would eventually tell in *With the Lapps in the High Mountains*. Her reputation in ethnographic circles for *Muitalus sámiid birra* as well as her connection with Gudmund and other colleagues in Sweden and Denmark doubtless helped with the reception of her book when it was published. Ole Olufsen, the editor of the journal of the Royal Danish Geographical Society, *Geografisk Tidsskrift*, and an explorer and ethnographer of Central Asia, called it "a superb, lively, and detailed description of everyday life among the Lapps all through the seasons . . . one reads the nineteen chapters with pleasure and enjoyment." H. P. Steensby wrote in *Berlingske Tidende*, "For Lappish ethnography and cultural history, the book is of great and lasting worth." She was also called "an adventurer, who is a courageous, first-rate scholar" in *Politiken*, another of Denmark's important newspapers. In Sweden, K. B. Wiklund noted that the book was "not only a desirable complement to Turi's book, but also a work that both in the depiction of people and in ethnographic description rises high above the existing literature on the subject."[27]

Demant Hatt and her husband continued to work together on the Sami for some years more, supported, most likely, from Demant Hatt's bequest from an uncle and Gudmund's part-time work. They may also have had financial support from Hjalmar Lundbohm. With a grant from the American-Scandinavian Foundation for Gudmund to study, they traveled to the United States and Canada for a year, 1914–15, which included some months in New York, Washington, D.C., and Ottawa. In New York, Gudmund studied anthropology and archeology with Franz Boas and other professors at Columbia University. Demant Hatt, who knew little English when she arrived, attended basic lectures on American Indian culture and helped Gudmund with his studies on clothing and footwear. According to Gudmund, Boas was familiar with Demant Hatt's work with Turi through the German translation of *Muitalus sámiid birra*, and Boas and his wife, Marie, extended several dinner invitations to the Hatts. Gudmund, whose English was excellent, showed Emilie's slides and spoke about the Sami at a presentation to the Ethnological Society at the American Museum of Natural History in early 1915. He noted he was then considered the expert on Sami culture though it should have been Emilie who received the credit.[28]

Gudmund Hatt was offered a job in 1919 at the National Museum of Denmark as a curator, which at that time consisted largely of registering and preserving Denmark's prehistoric sites. Hatt's interest turned to archeology and human geography, and he became a professor of geography at the University of Copenhagen in 1929. He later made a name for himself with his books on the archeology of the Iron Age, as well as his writings and talks on geopolitics in the 1930s.[29] The Hatts had traveled twice more to different parts of Sápmi after their return from North America, collecting artifacts and filling field notebooks with folklore, phrases, and definitions. The visit to old friends in Torneträsk and Tromsdalen in 1916 was something of a homecoming for Emilie and the last time she and Gudmund would travel north. Their proposed book on the Sami never came to fruition, and Demant Hatt gradually turned her attention away from ethnography and back to her art career. Although she continued to give the occasional interview and to write popular articles about the Sami through the 1920s and 1930s, most of her love for Sápmi could be seen in the paintings she produced in great numbers throughout the 1930s and 1940s. These striking landscapes of glacier-blue mountains, ice bridges, and forests, with reindeer and figures in harmony with their wintery environment were admired for their color and vision. Demant Hatt contributed frequently to juried exhibits and had several one-woman shows. One art critic proposed, "In Emilie Demant Hatt, Danish Expressionism possesses one of its most original and significantly gifted persons. . . . Here we're not talking of ethno- or geographical pictorial views, but purely and simply about pictures whose genesis is the result of amazing painterly experiences."[30] While much of Demant Hatt's art work remains in Denmark, the so-called Lapland paintings are owned by the Nordiska Museet in Stockholm, along with her field notebooks, photographs, and original correspondence with Johan Turi, which she donated with the encouragement of Ernst Manker, the first curator of the museum's new Sami department.

Demant Hatt's work with Johan Turi, while important, has led over the last hundred years to her public identification with *Muitalus sámiid birra* to the exclusion of her own writing and fieldwork. She has been called his muse, his secretary, or his housekeeper, and her significant achievement as an early woman ethnographer has been diminished or rendered invisible.[31] In Sweden, where the tradition of "studying the Lapps" goes back several centuries, Demant Hatt's reputation, tied to her work with Johan Turi, is better established than in Denmark. While gender naturally plays a role in the erasure of Demant Hatt's place in Danish anthropology, so does the fact that she was a self-educated ethnographer who published relatively little of her research.

Ethnography, the province of travelers and explorers at the turn of the century, had assumed a more academic status by the 1920s and 1930s, and

Denmark's ethnographic society was extremely narrow and all male. The department of geography at the University of Copenhagen employed at first only one professor and then a second—Gudmund Hatt—during much of Demant Hatt's lifetime. Until 1945 there was no separate anthropology department at the university. Most would-be ethnographers came from different disciplines and were attached in some way to the National Museum of Denmark. Greenland, Central Asia, and North Africa were the favored choices for Danes doing ethnography, and no one but Demant Hatt ever studied the Sami.[32] There would have been no professional place for Demant Hatt, even had she chosen to try to pursue an academic career. That she didn't choose to continue her ethnographic research and writing and instead returned to painting may say more about her abilities and dreams as an artist than about her obstacles or failures as an ethnographer. No one who has ever had the pleasure of looking at her paintings, particularly the many landscapes with their blue and white mountains, frozen lakes, reindeer herds, and figures in bright blues and reds, can fail to understand how her years in Sápmi influenced her imagination.

Of the many tourists and ethnographers who have written articles or books about the Sami, Emilie Demant Hatt is one of the few to be remembered positively by the Sami themselves. Part of the reason for her continued importance in the growing field of Sami studies is the role that she played in editing and translating Johan Turi's book and helping make the voice of the Sami people heard. But many of those who now study Sami cultural history have found in Demant Hatt's writing a great deal of useful information on many aspects of domestic life. Demant Hatt, along with Knud Rasmussen, was one of the few early Scandinavian ethnographers to speak and read the language of the people she studied. Her long stays in Sápmi, her close observations, and her focus on the lives of women and girls give her writings particular significance.

Although her section on migrating with the Sami is relatively brief, it is one of the only accounts written by a Sami-speaking outsider who made the journey from Sweden to Norway. Her chapter on Tromsdalen is remarkable in the way she uses her position as an insider to explain how the Sami view their traditional "summerland," and as an outsider, a privileged Dane, to speak up in anger at the way the Sami are treated. While many of Demant Hatt's attitudes were unusual for her time, she was not outside her era. Both perspectives, that of the honest, curious, observer-participant, and that of the outsider in love with the romance of nomadism, are valuable and may help to illuminate some of the paradoxes of anthropology. *With the Lapps in the High Mountains* is an important work of ethnography. But, most of all, the book enchants as an adventure story, a personal journey of independence and community above the Arctic Circle, told in a warm, humorous, and passionate voice that still speaks to us today.

Translator's Notes

Translating a book published in 1913 has particular challenges. The language is more formal at times than contemporary Danish and certainly American English. I've tried to retain some of the flavor of Demant Hatt's Danish sentences, with their somewhat Germanic habit of keeping the meaning until the end and their wry sense of humor, embedded in the syntax. At the same time I've sometimes broken up long paragraphs with many semicolons and paragraphs that run on for several pages, with a view to making reading easier.

In terms of other language issues, Demant Hatt incorporates a number of Northern Sami words and expressions to give flavor to her narrative. In almost all cases, she translates the words or phrases into Danish. In some cases she has singled out the expression and provides a longer explanation in her notes. In general I've simplified this process so as not to slow the reader down and merely include a brief gloss in the text of a word such as *árran*—hearth—the first time it's used, after which I use the English word, except in a few cases where there's no single translation for an expression such as *joik* (a form of music) or *siida*, a community of reindeer pastoralists, but also a concept with multiple meanings.

The Northern Sami orthography that Demant Hatt employed in her book was correct for the time period, but most of the Sami languages (there are nine living languages, five of them in Sweden and Norway and the others in Finland and Russia) now use modern spellings. The Northern Sami words and sentences have been updated to the current orthography by Thomas A. DuBois, Olivia Lasky, John Prusynski, and Mikael Svonni, and I appreciate their help greatly. On Professor DuBois's suggestion, I've left the place names as Demant Hatt spelled them. A few can be found on current maps, spelled in different ways.

Demant Hatt uses a variety of measurements, including older Danish words, *alen* (two feet) and *mil* (the Danish mile, which is approximately 7.5 American miles). She also uses metrics, however, and in the interests of consistency I've put all measurements into centimeters, kilometers, and meters. All temperatures in the book are given in Celsius.

Notes

The original version of *With the Lapps in the High Mountains* contains almost eighty endnotes, a number of them very long (altogether the notes comprise forty pages of the original two-hundred-page book). The extensive, detailed notes are a sign that her original intention to tell the story of her travels expanded as she began to move in more ethnographic circles. It's likely the notes were composed at the instigation of her husband, Gudmund Hatt, who was by that time familiar with academic research and its requirements. Hatt may have edited some notes, and he contributed at least one (a long signed article on the artificial shaping of the heads of Sami infants). Two other long notes, on earmarking reindeer calves, were contributed by J. Hultin and by K. B. Wiklund, the professor of Finno-Ugric at the University of Uppsala. Wiklund is cited in the notes elsewhere, as is Johan Turi and his book *Muitalus sámiid birra*. Finally, some of Demant Hatt's additional information in the notes, as in her text, comes from research she undertook in 1910–12 in other parts of Sápmi. While the notes can be drier in tone and more detailed than her narrative voice, the style is generally recognizable as her own.

Many of the notes have to do with Sami material culture and reindeer herding in the early twentieth century, and as such they are valuable for scholars. Those who read a Scandinavian language will be glad to know that the original Danish edition of *Med lapperne i højfjeldet* has been digitized by the Internet Archive and the edition includes all the notes. For the general reader, some of the more detailed information she conveys in the notes will be of less interest, and some of it is already available elsewhere in English (diagrams of a Sami tent and examples of calf earmarks, for instance). At the same time there are other instances where Demant Hatt may not clarify enough or where she counts on the Danish reader to know more than a contemporary English reader would understand easily.

Thus, for the general reader, I've provided a smaller number of notes, the majority of which I've written, condensing some of Demant Hatt's ideas but using more current definitions and incorporating some Sami words. The notes are there to assist where the meaning is not completely sufficient or clear in the text or to comment on word choice. I have also translated a select number of Demant Hatt's original notes where they offer insights or more narrative information (for instance, note 13 on the *joik*). Her words are italicized.

Sami and Lapp

While *Sami* is the name that the Sami people have historically used for themselves, to much of the rest of the world they have been *Lapps* or *Laplanders*. The word *Lapp*, while once used by the Sami themselves in writing in or speaking a Nordic or other language, gradually fell out of use over the course of the twentieth century. As early as 1918, the Sami titled a new periodical *Samefolkets Egen Tidningen* (The Sami People's Own Journal). Sami (the word is both noun and adjective, singular and plural; it has had a variety of spellings) was accepted as the official nomenclature of state and local governments in Fennoscandia in the early 1970s and is now used worldwide. Lapp now falls into the same category as other earlier nomenclature for indigenous people, such as *Eskimo*, which has now been supplanted by *Yupik* and *Inuit*. Lapp has also at times in the past and even in the present been a pejorative term.

In speaking to her Sami friends in their language, Demant Hatt would have certainly referred to them as "Sami"; but in writing about them in Danish, she chose the word they were known by to her readers, as well as to scholars. Writing home to her parents she sometimes playfully signs herself "Lappflicka" (Swedish for "Lapp Girl") or mentions that people (Swedes and Finns) sometimes call her "Lappfröken" or "Lapp Miss." In all her correspondence, the people she lived with are "Lapps"; it was natural for her to employ "Lapps" in her book title and throughout her narrative. Late in her endnotes (22; original, 67), she writes, almost as an afterthought to another note, "Among themselves they don't call themselves Lapps but *sápmelaččat* or *sámit* (in the singular, *sápmelaš* or *sámi*)." By the early 1950s, however, she was using "samme" and "samerne" in her writing (for instance in her guide to the photographs that she gifted to the Nordiska Museet).

It would have been possible to change "Lapp" throughout my translation to "Sami," but to do so would change the reality that *With the Lapps in the High Mountains* is a historical document from the early twentieth century and valuable for that reason. We wouldn't republish or retranslate the books of the early Arctic explorers and substitute "Inuit" for "Eskimo." Scholars, translators, and publishers would instead endeavor to use "Inuit" in all contextual writing, such as introductions, notes, and jacket covers. For that reason I've given this book a subtitle, "A Woman among the Sami, 1907–8." When the

voice is mine, I use "Sami." Otherwise I faithfully translate Demant Hatt's
lapper as "Lapps."

Photographs

Over the course of her travels in Lapland in 1907 through 1916, Demant Hatt
took some 350 photographs (prints exist in the Nordiska Museet archives in
Sweden and in the Danish National Archives). They were most likely taken
with a small box camera, perhaps a Brownie, which would have been light
and portable. Most of the black and white photographs are from her time in
1907–8 and are particularly valuable because they show the people she was
writing about in *With the Lapps in the High Mountains*. A number of these
photographs were included in her book in 1913; she also used a few photographs by the great Swedish photographer who lived in Kiruna, Borg Mesch.
In her book, the captions are brief, and none of those photographed are iden-
tified by name. Johan Turi's unmistakable portrait, for instance, is titled "Lapp
in Winter Dress."

Several decades later, when Demant Hatt was preparing material to gift
to the Nordiska Museet, she typed up a guide to her prints, now mounted
in scrapbooks. This guide identifies all the people in the photographs, particularly the families she lived and traveled with. It also describes places and
activities. In some cases she provides ages and information about those in
the pictures (marriages and deaths). The photographs lack the clarity and
composition of those by a professional (the weather and difficult travel conditions also played a role), but they capture a place and time and, most important, informal scenes among the people whose company she so enjoyed.
Demant Hatt had strong graphic skills and a masterly sense of color; she later
used some of the photos as aide-mémoire for painting. The photographs are
important on their own, however, as historical representations, and a small
selection of them are published here with captions identifying the people in
them. There is also one Demant Hatt didn't include in her book: the photo-
graph of her standing with Sara/Siri, wearing traditional Sami clothes. It is
one of my favorites.

With the Lapps in the High Mountains

I

JUNE 8, AND THERE'S SNOW EVERYWHERE! That means experiencing spring twice this year. At home in Denmark, in Jutland, the fjords already wore their summer colors, and when I traveled through the moors between Viborg and Langå on the night of May 28, the dark hills lay breathing in the white night, under a moon ringed with green, while flocks of birds flew north. Here, even though snow covers everything, the ptarmigans are playing, their brown summer plumage has almost returned. Yesterday a snowstorm; today it's warm as summer and heavy thunderclouds draw close, growling. The sun doesn't sleep at night and doesn't allow anyone else to, either. The snow melts with astonishing speed. Water comes and goes in every direction and on its way gives life to everything. It nurses plant roots, so buds and shoots come forth in the sun. It throws itself out over ledges and blows in the wind like gray hair. It murmurs and moans. It gurgles and soughs and fills the air with its nuisance and noise. The cuckoo calls day and night, the fine wet birch leaves sparkle with brilliant light. Gray reindeer flock between the skinny, white-spotted trunks; in their velvet-covered, blood-filled new antlers throbs the passionate pulse of spring. Down in a little dark brook rustles a plump lemming, which resembles a yellow duckling. Large, brown-striped bumblebees hum in the warm air. They say that the ice on Torneträsk Lake is a meter thick, but so brittle that you can step through it. Still, the Lapps and Finns ski back and forth over the lake. Last year the lake was free of ice by the 18th of June. If we don't get a storm soon, it will be later this year.

On June 20, the storm came; the lake grew flecked with blue, and the ice drifted over to Tarrakoski. The day after, Johan Turi turned up in a boat to fulfill his promise to take me to the Lapps.

It was past midnight before we set out. During the summer light the Lapps never pay attention to whether it's day or night; they travel when they're ready, midday or midnight. That evening the sun was covered with soft gray clouds and the water was still, slightly misty; far out a loon cried into the rain. After we'd eaten and drunk coffee on the other side of the lake, Turi put out our small fire on the beach and, around two in the morning, we set off with the bags on our backs up through the forest over the low mountains to Kattuvuoma. It was now raining, steadily and heavily, but Turi said it meant good luck when it rained the first time you came to a new place.

Toward early morning, around four o'clock, we could see from a high ridge the five small gray Finnish farms and behind them a few Lapp tents.

"We'll sleep here for an hour," decided Turi. It was too early to visit people. Without more ado, he lay down and pulled his thin, shabby outer fur over his head to keep off the mosquitoes. The air was gray with swarms of mosquitoes. He gave me an old scrap of linen for the same purpose. The thick moss was wet through and through and so was I—though warm. When, after an hour, we continued down the side of the mountain, smoke rose in thin columns from the short granite chimneys of the small farms below. They were up and about, having coffee. We stepped over the foot-high threshold into the main room of the Finnish settlers.

The room was large, and in one corner a fire burned in the wide, open fireplace. Beds and settles were arranged all around the rough-hewn planked walls, and in them slept children of all sizes, with their clothing on. Under one of the windows the housewife sat at the table drinking her morning coffee. She was scrawny and her skin resembled a dingy linen rag that sun and rain had bleached; she looked as if she had faded almost to her soul. Her bare legs stuck out of a skimpy gray skirt, and the loose cotton bodice was unbuttoned at the breast. A pair of half-grown girls were also up. One stood at the table eating cold cooked fish in this manner: she took the whole fish in her hand, picked at it with her fingers, and left only the bones, which she sucked clean and then put on the window sill. The second girl set the coffee pot on the fire to reheat for us, and then picked up the smallest crying child from the cradle, a Lappish *gietkka* that hung from the ceiling, and gave it to her mother. The little one had on nothing but a clean cotton dress. The mother pulled out an indescribable breast that quickly stilled the thirst and tears. When it had been satisfied, the little one was handed back to the half-grown girl. Shortly afterward the milk, in a different condition, flowed out of the child, over the girl's hands and onto the floor. So the child was put in the bed of a little sister, and the girl with the wet hands started grinding coffee beans. She offered us a cup and we enjoyed it in the dairy room, which was also full of sleeping children.

Turi took me later to the outermost and smallest farm. There the housewife was pretty and clean and quite young, so the horde of children—five girls—hadn't yet spread to the dairy room. I was given a settle all to myself in that small room and had enough quiet for a few hours of sleep.

I'd never seen such an abundance of children before as here in Kattuvuoma. They swarmed everywhere like lemmings. There were five families and almost all the women were pregnant, but brimming with health, except for the first woman I visited. The men were tall and heavy, with gloomy faces and something unyielding in their expression.

At one of the farms were lodged two old Lapp women who couldn't keep up with the hard life outdoors year round. They looked like fairy-tale witches, when they came hobbling along with their staffs, with knives and keys at their belts and wearing old patched furs with the skin side out. Their eyes were deeply sunken, and the skin of their faces and hands looked like a ploughed field. Clearly, water hadn't touched it in a long time. For the most part, they sat by the fire in the low dark room, submerged in the bitter silence of the deaf, with hands fumbling at their naked chests. In a corner of the room stood a small, brightly painted chest, and a sled serving as a bed, with an old reindeer hide and some rags. The narrow, tarred sled, at least a meter long, made quite a roomy bed for such a tiny little crumpled-up old Lapp lady.

The Lapps' tents lay some distance away from the farms on the other side of the brook.[1] Since they would soon be moving on, they were very busy getting things ready for summer. Near the farms stood their storehouse, where they kept flour and butter, coffee, rice and sugar, clothes, and everything they didn't have use for every day. The Lapps often had errands to the storehouse, during which time they visited the farms and drank coffee. The Finns were their fellow believers in the Laestadian church.[2]

The first time I met Sara and Nikki, my prospective hosts, Sara asked in a kindly way if I didn't feel alone here among strangers in a strange land. Her friendliness and motherly manner did me good, as I had been otherwise steadily subjected to common curiosity from all the others.

My nomad life, as was to be expected, began with a departure; from Kattuvuoma we headed to Laimolahti on the evening of June 25. There was a great deal to haul down from the tent site to the boats: flour sacks, dried meat, cooking pots, skins, bedclothes, and so on. The two long boats were loaded to the brims and on top of the baggage sat the dogs. The sun was low, the lake was still; the contours of the green mountain shadows trembled faintly. Cold water sprayed out like a blue fan behind the boat; the fine ribs of the fan ended in a soft frizzle. One of the boats was rowed by the grown son, Biettar, while Sara sat astern and steered with the wide, short steering oar. All the red and yellow trim on their faded blue tunics or *koftas* glowed in the sun, just like the colors on their warm brown skin.[3] The second heavily laden boat was rowed by their seventeen-year-old daughter Inga, and Nikki steered. Into Laimolahti came strong winds from the "big lake"—Torneträsk. The waves and wind were against us, but the girl pulled just as steadily and calmly on the oars as a man. She was warm and had shoved her little embroidered hat back on her neck, so the wisps of hair fell free on the round, light brown forehead. Her skin was pure and golden from the sun; white strong teeth shone between the full, prettily formed lips. Her cheeks were rounded, red and plump, so they smoothed the transition from the wide cheekbones to the narrower jaw. Her blue *kofta* barely reached below her knees; its sleeves were narrow and much too short, a girl growing out of her clothes. When we came to shore, Nikki went up into the forest to look for suitable wood for tent poles. Sara took the coffee things and made a fire. The children, ten-year-old Nilsa and eleven-year-old Elle, ran off on their own while we carried the things up from the beach to the *luovvi*, or storehouse, still standing from the summer before. Inga's strength and stamina were amazing. She could lie on her back over a huge load, pull the straps over her shoulders, and get up. She pointed to a heavy sack and wanted me to do the same, but that wasn't possible.

Sara's fire burned red, and when the coffee was ready we all gathered around the flames. The children had also joined us; they didn't work, but ran around and took possession of the settlement, greeting their old play areas, trees, and stones. They tested how deep the brook was and began exploring, as is the custom with Lapp children after every move to a new place. The sun had gone behind a mountaintop in the north, but shone over the snow on the far peaks. We sat in the twilight's blue haze in the birch wood and drank reviving coffee with a snack of dried reindeer meat. After coffee Sara looked for a new tent site, but when she didn't find anything better she chose the old one from the year before. We swept away last year's twigs, so the spot was completely clean. The twigs were taken a short distance away and burned (Lapps don't have piles of refuse—trash isn't allowed to pile up anywhere). Everyone took hold of the thin birch trunks Nikki had brought, to peel their bark off. It came off easily—a cut along the trunk and you could pull off the bark in big pieces. The children joined in of their own free will. They enthusiastically licked the sweet juice they found between wood and bark.

Inga went into the forest with a sharp ax stuck in her belt and a length of reindeer leather over her shoulders. A while later she came back like a walking green tree. She carried on her back, with a rein like a shoulder strap, an enormous bundle of fresh birch twigs, which completely covered her head and back. The twigs were to be used for flooring in the tent. She threw the burden off and went back into the forest, and when she returned she had the trunk of a hefty birch over her shoulder. Its big green crown trailed behind. There was something primeval about this healthy girl with the ax in her belt, something of a young animal in the calm, lithe movements, in the way in which she worked.

Sara and her son Biettar raised the tent, and when that was done, Sara covered the earth inside with a mat of fresh birch twigs a foot thick. They were laid, one by one, with root ends down, so they made an elastic but secure carpet. The placing of the twigs began in the back part of the tent and stopped a little before the door. Then stones were carried in for the *árran* or hearth; the stones were laid in a circle in the middle of the tent and the fire was lit. Chopped logs were brought in and placed from the fire circle to the door, on either side, partly to keep the root ends of the floor branches down and partly to keep the entrance free and make room for the fire. For those who sit in the tent, it's convenient to have wood there, where you can just reach over and take it; and for those who carry the wood, it's also convenient merely to open the door flap and toss it in. But the passage in and out is certainly impeded; it can be hard enough for adults but much worse for small children and puppies.

When the tent was finished, the bedding was brought in; the bedclothes for two people were rolled up in a reindeer skin, which was used as padding underneath. The bedding was placed on the twigs, right up next to the tent walls; that gave a solid, cozy back support for sitting. The coffee kettles were placed in the *boaššu*, or kitchen space, along with the little round willow basket with the cups, the red cotton bag containing a chunk of sugar, and some sacks with, respectively, flour, rice, and unroasted coffee beans.[4] The sacks are sewn from goatskin with the hairy side out and an opening of tanned reindeer skin. A copper kettle with fresh water from a nearby brook or spring has its place in the middle of the kitchen, and in front of that is a large black stew pot. Additionally, there are a couple of wooden ladles, wooden salt flasks, a pair of butter boxes, and the large wooden bowl, where dough is kneaded, and from which the family eats reindeer meat. All the wooden objects are painstakingly crafted and tastefully decorated with carvings and engraved patterns. From one of the hooks in the kitchen space hung a Mauser rifle. Two kettle chains were fixed to the sooty pole over the fire. Sara hung the stew pot above the flames and put a little salt in the water. Nikki cut up some rather old reindeer meat and put it in the pot. The large tree that Inga had dragged home was placed outside the tent as a chopping block, a *smáhkkomuorra*. Its crown, with the branches gone, was placed against the earth; the root end was placed at a suitable height in the intersection of two crossed birch supports underneath. Here is where all the wood is chopped.

The flames burned brightly and shone through the tent cloth; from outside, the tent glowed like a colored lamp against the violet mountain where the snow lay in long strips. Inside burned the fire that I'd longed for, for so many years. The reality far exceeded my dreams. I went in and sat down on the fragrant birch leaves. The pale tent poles that the smoke hadn't yet darkened smelled of the forest and were moist to the touch. The fire warmed my face and scorched the nearest birch leaves. The stew pot bubbled; steam and sparks rose up through the smoke opening at the tent peak.

I was sitting at my future place to the right of the door, almost in the middle of the *loaidu*, a work space during the day and sleeping area at night. On the same side, up near the kitchen space, sat Biettar, together with his dog, Čæppe. While Biettar ate, the dog stood behind him with his front paws on his owner's shoulders and his mouth placed in the immediate vicinity of Biettar's. His eyes followed every bite from hand to mouth; naturally, so much persistence was rewarded with a taste now and then. For the Lapps, it's a virtue when the dogs beg while people are eating. It shows they have a healthy appetite and the energy to feed themselves—that is to say, vigor.

On the other side of the fire sit the master and mistress of the tent. The housewife's place is always nearest the kitchen on the left side of the tent; the children and servants have their places closer to the door.

After the meat was cooked, it was taken out of the pot and placed into two wooden bowls. The largest bowl was placed on the twigs in the middle of the *loaidu* on the left side, and the family ate together, as many as could fit around the bowl. Biettar, Inga, and I divided the contents of the smaller bowl. The left hand holds the meat; the right cuts it with a knife, which everyone, down to the children, carries in a sheath. The sliced-off mouthful is set on the tip of the knife and dipped in the extra fat that's in a little ladle next to the bowl.

When dinner was over, the bed was made ready and this didn't take long. A reindeer hide was laid over the twigs, then a large pillow or in many cases just a sack stuffed with old pieces of cloth or the like. For a cover was a wool blanket or two (the bed is the same both winter and summer, but in winter you have a thick sheep or reindeer skin over you, along with a wool blanket on top). Over the bed a *rákkas* was slung up to protect against the mosquitoes. When that was done, everyone took their shoes off and spread out to dry the hay that had been inside the shoes. After which we sat for a quarter of an hour and warmed our bare feet, chatting comfortably. No one removed their clothes. If you had on two tunics, you took off the outermost one, but you always set the belt aside (if you don't take off the belt, it's said, jokingly, Stallo will come in the night and lift you up with it).[5] When we'd lain down, the dogs sniffed around for leftover scraps. The shadows of the flames shone through the thin linen walls of the mosquito tenting; the dogs' large shadows came and went. The fire died down, and the sun grew strong; the birds came and perched on the tent poles up in the *reahpen* or opening. It was hard to sleep through such a light night out in nature.

II

THE EVENING AFTER, ALL THE OTHER TENTS moved from Kattuvuoma to Laimo. It was a large community, or *siida*, but spaced out.[6] When families stayed together, the groups made up two or three tents. It grew lively when the others arrived, for they had cows and goats with them. Bells tinkled, dogs barked and fought, the Lapps shouted and laughed. Everyone was busy. The fires were lit all around, the tents raised, the long brown boats rowed back and forth to fetch and unload. The forest and mountains suddenly came alive with people cutting wood and carrying water. The children scurried around and looked after themselves. Everyone was in a holiday mood. It was summer now, time to rest. For a couple of months you could forget winter's exertions and burdens. Now everything was warm, green, and bright for the mountain folk. With their cheerful colors and good humor they resembled large flowers in the landscape.

A couple of days later, Turi came unexpectedly and it turned into quite a party in the tent that evening. He'd brought wheat bread to treat everyone, along with little gifts for the girls, a pair of ordinary safety pins they use to fasten together their neckerchiefs (now that, according to the opinion of the Laestadians, it is "sinful" to wear silver jewelry), and a piece of hand soap that Inga, however, didn't want if it was *haksesáibbo* (perfumed soap). Perfume smelled abominable to their unspoiled senses. Nor did Turi forget the foreigner; for me he had a box of good cigarettes. We amused ourselves looking at maps. This is something the Lapps understand and enjoy. They know immediately whether a map is up or down. It's also easy for them to draw maps in rough outline over the area they travel. They know the landscape down to the smallest detail.

Turi had come to participate in the marking of the reindeer calves, which would take place on a little island nearby. The next morning, when we rowed over, the herd was already gathered. There were probably two or three thousand reindeer with their small calves. They came racing down through the valley to a large open place where the marking was going to take place. The well-known creaking sound in the reindeer's legs could be heard here, where there were so many reindeer in motion, rather like thunderous rain on large leaves or a violent hailstorm. There's something strongly stirring about the sound and about the sight of the light-footed animals that run in gray waves. Those who see a large herd of reindeer for the first time can't but feel shivers, thrilling to the excitement. The Lapps themselves experience a sort of intoxication at the sight of the herd.

When the storm had calmed and a certain quiet prevailed, the calves and mothers called and answered each other unceasingly; *nau, nau*—*øh, øh, høh*, and the long drawn-out *jah, jah*. The collective noise was reminiscent of a crowd of shouting, talking people in the distance. Suddenly the whole herd set itself in motion and then it rumbled, like thunder coming from the underworld. The Lapps ran and cast their lassos among the animals. The red tassels of their red caps flashed everywhere. The rope whirred through the lasso's bone-ring with a shrill whistle; it flew over all that aliveness and in a flash descended around the neck of a small dark calf or around a leg, whatever it met with. Quickly the loop was untied, the calf laid down; the Lapp held it with his legs while he pulled the knife from his belt and, with a couple of quick but precise incisions, cut marks in the reindeer's ear (he puts one of the small hairy ear slices in his mouth each time while he's marking, until he has his hands free and can put it in an inner chest pocket; afterward the small lumps of skin are pulled through a sinew thread and counted, so they have a count of all the marked calves). After that, the reindeer was let go; it ran with its little bleeding ear back to its mother. It didn't show the slightest sign of pain. Around the herd the dogs trotted, to keep watch, or they perched on something high, so they had an overview of the scene.

It was overcast, light gray and quiet. Some of the reindeer stood peacefully and grazed, while others lay down and chewed their cud. But suddenly the whole herd sprang into motion as if by command, rumbling and thundering, and the Lapps shouted and the dogs barked. In the course of a short time, peace was restored and the marking continued. When, some hours later, I was again home in the tent, I was told to keep an eye on the herd when it came by our tents on its way up over the mountains. This was so I could see the reindeer swimming through the river, Ripasasjokk.

It wasn't until afternoon that the doors of the tents were torn open to the call, *Eallu boahtá!* "The herd is coming!" We'd already heard the sound, and right afterward the animals came across the open space and through the forest back to the mountains. Everyone who could get to their feet went out to enjoy the sight of this living property. With necks stretched out, the hair on their chests flying, heads thrown back, and the small white tail stump in the air, they raced like a vision over the moorland. The dogs bayed; men and women ran. Over by the tents, people recognized individual reindeer with glad cries and pointed fingers. Wives who stood there weren't going with the herd, but rejoiced in the sight. When the thunderous beauty had passed, when every last reindeer and every red-tasseled cap had disappeared between the birches, the women went back to their small children and housekeeping—to everyday tasks—but their thoughts and sharp ears followed the herd. They were with them in spirit, doing the work that belonged to their youth.

Up in an open space in the forest the ear-marking of the reindeer continued for another hour. Then both people and reindeer rested a good while, before the swimming across the river began. It was the first time that the small calves would test the cold water, which flowed down from snow and ice, and the current was strong. A boat rowed the whole time out by the mouth of the river, where it flowed into Torneträsk, in order to be ready to save the calves taken by the current. Such a shouting, leaping, and racing—all to get every animal across. The calves were afraid of the water and ran away, their mothers after them, and after them a Lapp or a dog, until they were captured and chased into the water. Reindeer cows and calves ran around looking for each other, but finally every one of them was out in the river. The river was white froth from the movement of thousands of animals swimming; like a living carpet the many gray-brown backs glided under a forest of antlers over to the other side. As quickly as the reindeer came up on land, they shook themselves and a halo of water droplets flew off the soaking wet fur.

Now, in great haste, we got in the boats, with the dogs after us, the aim being to cross quickly and to round up the herd before they took flight. The marking continued the rest of the day on a very large wet bog up under the mountains. The men and boys marked the calves; the girls and dogs kept the animals together. Each girl had her post at the edge of the herd.

While rain now poured from the sky, we ran, soaked through, between unstable tussocks, between knee-high willows, over rocks and holes, often in water over our ankles. It's no easy thing to keep several thousand semi-wild animals together in a relatively small area. The girls directed the dogs with the musical command-words that the Lapps use in reindeer herding. The dogs streaked out in every direction, but if one did something wrong or sowed confusion in the herd, it was called back with a yell that could wake the dead. When you've heard the Lapps work with the herd, you can well understand why they often have such weak, hoarse voices in ordinary speech. It's because they use them to their full capacity in reindeer herding, when the dogs are ordered off and called back. The voice has to cut through a long distance and an unbelievable din. (Perhaps they also save their voices half unconsciously for the times when they truly need them). In addition, those who work with reindeer must be lightening quick in thought and action. Even if the herd is in flight, they must seize the moment and let the lasso fly if they've glimpsed an animal to be captured. The rope is cast and then coiled up, ready for the next throw. They also need to keep a sharp eye on the dogs, and scout out particular reindeer in the swarming confusion. A bad or untrained dog can cause a great disturbance when, in mistaken zeal, he charges barking into the middle of the herd, which then spreads out like chaff in the wind. Angry words rain down upon the dog; he slinks off in shame, followed by the fiercest curses and furious looks. When there's time, he also gets a beating if he's done something truly wrong. Yet the Lapps have a rule that you shouldn't strike and scold at the same time, only one thing at a time. That's because you need to be careful not to insult the dog. If an otherwise competent dog feels affronted by someone who, in his opinion, has treated him too roughly, it can happen that the dog suddenly sits down and looks at things without budging, however much his master commands. Only kind words and friendliness can soften him up so that he'll take up his work again, though a sit-down strike can last as long as a whole day. Some dogs are lazy and can only be bothered to jump in a pinch. Others are all excitement, with shining eyes, and each muscle tensely following the movements of the reindeer, and woe betide the reindeer that breaks away from the herd. That reindeer has a panting dog at its heels, a dog that keeps up until he sees his chance, and cuts in front of the reindeer and forces it back. Often the reindeer itself abandons its flight and returns to the herd. More or less serious quarrels occur between the reindeer and the dogs.

I saw such a small clash between Benno and a large male reindeer. Benno belonged to our neighbor's tent; he was blind in one eye, deaf as a post, stump-tailed, toothless, and very old, but was he a dog! And although he had only one eye, he had that one; he didn't need to hear. Benno knew his work and needed no commands. He was on the go from morning until night, even though it was hard on the old legs. He chose his post at a spot high enough that he could oversee the section of the herd that lay within his ability to reach. He worked on his own without a master, and the reindeer had respect for him (the reindeer recognize the dogs and have varying degrees of respect for them depending on how skillful they are). But one time things went wrong for Benno. A large bull reindeer had broken out of the circle and Benno had brought it back, but in his zeal to serve he kept barking and nipping at it until they returned to the herd. At that, the reindeer grew insulted and whipped around, got the dog under him, and thrashed his old body so you could hear the blows. Proudly the bull returned to the herd. Benno didn't make a sound, but limped quietly over to his post. A little while later he was at work again and probably had forgotten the ignominious scene. In his younger days Benno wasn't for sale for love or money; such a dog outweighs the work of several people.

When the marking was finished, the herd rested and grazed; afterward they migrated toward the Norwegian border, followed by the herders and dogs that would guard the herd this summer over in Norway.

III

Now it grew quiet in the camp with the men and boys away and some of the young girls too; in other words, all the reindeer herders. Only the housewives, children, and old people stayed behind. The women quickly took up the various summer tasks, and they had a great deal to do.

It's a pleasure to see Lapp women active in the tent, their movements balanced and supple. When they go out or in, they hold their clothes together around the knees, so as not to touch or overturn anything. They're calm and dignified no matter what they undertake. Their hand gestures and movements are beautiful, whether they weave ribbons or scrape guts. It's certainly difficult working in a cramped tent with unstable flooring; it has promoted women's gracefulness, along with skiing and a life in the open air. The Lapps are lithe, particularly the women; flexibility develops naturally and is maintained by the sitting position in the tent. In the North, men and women don't sit alike. The men have their legs crossed under them. A woman never takes that position—it wouldn't be good form. She sits with a leg to each side, bent at the knees, with the feet turned outwards, resting on her seat, a position that demands such great flexibility that it can only be acquired after generations. A Lapp woman can sit in this way for hours without tiring. She can also sit with one leg placed under her, or normally, on her seat, with both legs stretched out. Generally, however, she sits in the position mentioned above, where you can see a small, elegantly shaped foot poking out on each side under the dress, a position she finds comfortable, and from which she can easily rise. In the south of Lapland women sit in the same manner as the men.

The Lapp women aren't idle. They take care of their homes and their children with the same solicitude as any other conscientious housewife. First come the daily tasks such as wood chopping, water carrying, coffee making, and food preparing; then there's tanning, needlework, and spinning sinew. For the housewife who has young children, it's hard to manage without a servant girl. A family that can afford it keeps a maidservant, but the girl also participates in reindeer herding when necessary.

Wood chopping is no small task; like water carrying, it's usually the responsibility of servants or the older children. Birches need to be cut down, often from quite a long ways off, and dragged home to the tent, where they're chopped on the *smáhkkomuorra*. Whenever the Lapps have had long residence in the birch forest, it's naturally very thinned out. The old Germanic custom of cutting the tree "belt high" particularly disfigures the forest. You must not blame them too much, when the Lapps, in this case as in so many others, are simply following ancient Germanic cultural practices.

Besides, they're not wasteful with their firewood, like people in other forests that Lapps don't enter and where trees lie rotting in large numbers. They take all the firewood home with them, and in summer they burn only dry wood, painstakingly gathered. But here at Laimo little dry wood was to be found, and that's why they chopped down the birches in the forest. It's said the Lapps are wasteful with fire, but that's not correct. Everyone understands that in winter a strong fire is necessary if people are going to be living on the snow under a more or less open sky in all kinds of weather nine months of the year. Despite this, they don't waste their firewood any place they've found that's not destroyed. They don't have a fire at night, and often the fire is quite minimal, even completely out, for several hours during the day. If someone comes into the tent, he often says, *Vuoi, dolahis goahti dego jámeha goaht.*

"A tent without heat is a death-tent." For the Lapp, the fire is absolutely indispensable, even apart from the benefit of warmth. The fire is the only thing that creates a cozy atmosphere in such poverty-stricken circumstances. Its lively sound and flickering light makes it entertaining: "The fire is like a good companion," say the Lapps.

Food and preparing food is fairly monotonous. Large and small get coffee on an empty stomach (without bread) as far as the kettle stretches—two or three cups for the adults and one for the children. And in the morning, when hunger strikes, everyone eats separately when and what he likes of what is available. If there's leftover meat from the previous evening, the stew pot is hung from the fire and warmed up. The children have the right to it, though, for the leftover meal is seldom large.

Otherwise the day's small meals during summertime consist of sun-dried reindeer meat, whose fatty ribs are much enjoyed. They put a rib or two on the fire, so the topmost layer of fat is heated; with a knife they cut off the fat and meat and eat it down to the point where the bone is so polished that the dogs will scarcely look at it. Before or after the meal but not with it, they eat buttered bread (the butter is usually rancid, since it can only be bought once a year). They spread quite a thick layer on the bread with their thumbs. The bread is unfermented; flour and water are sloshed together in a large round wooden bowl, then shaped into balls of dough the size of a fist. The ball is pressed out into a thick pancake that, back in the wooden bowl, is further shaped by hand to become round and quite thin. It's then pricked like a biscuit either with the tip of a birch twig or with the ends of a bundle of bird feathers. The cake is laid on a hot iron frying pan, or when that's missing, directly on the embers. It's turned a couple of times, until it's toasted on the outside; then it's placed on the hearthstone or on a piece of wood near the fire, until it's baked completely through. Such bread tastes quite wonderful, especially when it's fresh. If the household is large, bread is baked nearly every day. The Lapps say jokingly that those who eat the first-baked cake will be poor and those who eat the last baked will be rich; this is similar to the proverb that says he who's greedy for fat and greasy food will become a reindeer thief.

Throughout the day they alternate in this way between small meals and coffee; only in the evening is the large stew pot hung over the fire. Every second evening we had cooked reindeer meat, with grease for dipping; and on the other evenings, gruel. For this meal, the meat was cut into small pieces and cooked in water with a cup of rice and, if we were lucky, a handful of raisins. It could well be that the meat had to be scraped for maggots before it was put in the kettle, but meat can be like that in summer. The whole winter it's been frozen and is only taken out in spring and isn't completely fresh. It's what the Lapps call *goastebiergu* (old meat).

This applies, of course, only to cooked meat, for example, the neck meat saved from the winter food. The true *goikebiergu* or jerky, which is dried in the sun, is quite fresh and tasty. As soon as the months of August and September arrive, they begin gradually to butcher, and after that there's fresh reindeer in the stew pot again. In summertime, food is always simple among the Lapps, now that the intensive milking of reindeer has ceased.[7] Some fresh fish can bring a little change once in a while, but fish is a more usual food in winter. If a mountain Lapp fishes a bit in summer, then the fish is salted and put by for the coming winter, when it will be ordinary midday food or a between-meal snack in place of the summer's jerky.

Food preparation isn't, however, what takes the Lappish housewife the most time, since all the grown people in the tent from the husband down to the servants and six- and seven-year-old children have access to all the food and prepare for themselves their small meals depending on their taste and appetite. "I can't make food for you," said Sara, when, out of misguided humbleness, I asked her to give me whatever I was supposed to eat. "How can I know when you are hungry and what you'd like to eat?" The main meal of the day, in the evening, is usually prepared by the male of the household. He carves the meat and places it in the stew pot. In older times, food preparation was completely the man's job, at least as far as the meat went.

But even without much food preparation, the Lapp women are busy working. Small children need watching, and the whole household must be clothed, both family and servants (whose wages, up in the North, consist only of reindeer and clothes). And since most of the clothes are made of skin, tanning is a lot of work. For tanning they use mainly willow bark, but for tanning tent cloth and rough skin such as cowhides, birch bark is used. They buy cowhides from the farmers, and they only use them for the sole of the summer shoe, because the hides are particularly strong. But for everything else they use reindeer skin. They use sinew thread exclusively to sew the many skin garments and other leather things. It's also the woman's work to spin sinew thread. The dried sinews are beaten with the back of an ax, if they're from an old reindeer and hard. Afterward, they're split by tearing with the hands into coarse strands. Now the real spinning begins. The sinews are divided further, moistened with saliva, and pulled with the teeth into suitably fine strips. Then they're twisted by hand against the thigh and the thread lengthens, until it's long enough, after which the single thread is doubled against the cheek with the right hand. It can be spun fine and white as a silk thread and thick and coarse as sailcloth thread. The coarsest thread can be used for the sewing and patching of shoes.

In spring when the bark is easy to loosen, they lay the roughly separated tendons in a small case of bark, which is taken from a thick willow trunk. Inside it's kept suitably moist (later, when no bark cases are available, the tendon thread is moistened with water and placed in a cloth). Eventually as the threads are spun, they're looped around the bark case. The supply of spun sinew thread is stored in the skin of a loon. They use a great deal of sinew thread, and it's woman's work in "free" hours, when they go visiting each other and on rainy days, when there's nothing else to be done (in somewhat older times, women spun much sinew thread while watching the reindeer).

A rainy day can be cozy; as long as you're sitting there nice and snug, it's pleasant listening to the rain patter on the tent cloth. The smoke opening is closed up tight, so the fire keeps going, and that makes for a comfortable half-darkness, not without a certain charm. Less charming, of course, is the smoke. When it settles as a matter of course in the tent, everyone weeps and coughs. Neighbor women come for a visit with their sinew thread and remain sitting for a while; the coffee pot is kept hot and the chat is lively. The women are quick and witty when they talk among themselves. They all have senses of humor and snappy comebacks, just like the children. In contrast, they're quieter when the men are around.

But as the day progresses and the rain continues, the coziness disappears. The visitors cease. Everyone has to take care of themselves and their homes as much as possible. The fire sputters and smokes without burning; the coffee pot hangs cold and empty in the kitchen space; the witty remarks are used up. The tent cloth no longer keeps out the water. It hangs heavy and wet from the tent poles and drips mercilessly over everything. Only the patch you sit on is dry. It's impossible to work anymore; everything is wet and dark. The birch-twig flooring glistens with moisture; there's a puddle of rainwater in the stew pot; the bedclothes behind you grow wet. Drop after melancholy drop trickles down your neck to your back.

Yet the weather shifts unbelievably quickly up here. One day it was suffocatingly hot, but toward evening, it turned suddenly cold and the whole landscape changed. We were completely surrounded by clouds, big thick clouds in all shapes and unearthly colors, swelling and smoldering, as if boiling up from a dreadful kettle. The tent and the immediate surroundings were clearly and sharply outlined in all this thick vapor, like an oasis in hell. Hell came to mind since it was near sunset and clouds took on a burning glow from the sun. They glided over and under and behind each other, changing from black and gray to the wildest fire red. It was as if you looked out over an endless swamp and down into a bottomless abyss and the fire was everywhere. It could make you grow uneasy, standing on your small patch of ground—as if you inhabited an extinct world, where, at the same time, evil was on the move.

IV

Not until July was the tent moved to a more sheltered spot. You had to be prepared well in advance for the autumn storms. In particular, everyone built a hedge of birch trees around their tent, a couple of meters off, a sort of fence of trunks and branches almost as tall as the tent itself. Although the fence gave protection, it had been prettier to see the gray tent up against the mountains. The clumsy rough fence hid the tent, with the exception of a wide entrance in front of the door. The fence was also used to hang all manner of things upon. When it wasn't raining, they set out their bedding there every morning and took it in every evening before sunset.

The Lapps air out their bedding every day year round, when it's not actually storming. In the winter you often have to knock the snow off the bedclothes before you bring them in. The bedding is therefore always fresh, which the Lapps greatly value (in addition, the winter airing is also helpful in that the prospective "inhabitant," that is, a flea or louse, freezes to death). All during their youth they sleep as reindeer herders out in the open air, and in the tent the ventilation is excellent. Their sense of smell is fine, and bad smells bother them a great deal. This sounds perhaps like an odd assertion when you're always hearing about "Lapp smell," and how the air is poisoned wherever they enter. What they smell of is train oil, boiled down from whale or seal blubber, which they smear on their furs, and the coal tar oil they use on their shoes. In the tent you don't notice that oily smell as much because the air is steadily replaced, but in a closed room it can become quickly unpleasant, so that even the Lapps themselves are bothered by it. One day I heard a Lapp woman saying she couldn't eat boiled herring, because the smell reminded her far too vividly of the grease used on skins.

Nor is it correct when it's said Lapps are dirty, both in terms of their person or their food. The biggest complaint about their food is that you find reindeer hair in everything you're served in a Lapp tent, in bread and coffee, not to mention meat, blood sausage, and the like. But those who know a little about the conditions know how unavoidable reindeer hair is. Everyone is dressed in fur, and reindeer hair sheds easily; you find hair everywhere. On that point there's nothing else to do but say, as do the Lapps: "Reindeer hair isn't dirty; everything about a reindeer is clean."[8]

The Lapps find dog or human hair in food just as distasteful as we do. If a Lapp housewife goes to knead dough, she always washes her hands first. To compare their cleanliness with ours obviously doesn't do; it's considered clean, for example, each time you've finished eating to rinse the wooden bowl with a crooked index finger and lick it clean, so no bit of food remains. This is similar to our peasants licking their spoons after meals and placing them up on the leather strap on the wall. The Lapp tucks his licked spoon in his chest pocket. The stew pot is cleaned, however, in boiling water before everyday use, and in summer the cups and so on are washed in warm water. In winter, when it's many degrees below zero and water freezes between your fingers, you can understand skimping on a wash more often than the usual sense of hygiene finds advisable.

Personal cleanliness is also greatest in summer, yet no one neglects it—summer or winter—as much as most people believe. All the younger Lapps gladly wash their faces, necks, and hands once a day, and always with warm water and soap. As a washcloth they use any rag at hand or the corner of their neckerchief. Generally, they wash in the middle of the day. When they wash in the evenings, "the hare comes and licks you in the night" (the white polar hare is a symbol of cleanliness for the Lapps). Those who wear shirts change them often, but I can't claim they do it only for reasons of cleanliness—more likely they do it when the fleas or lice become too bothersome. In winter they put their spare clothes out to freeze, and in summer they boil them. I've also seen a sheepskin attached to a sled in a string of sleds to clean the wool. After several trips the inner coat grows clean and white from steady rubbing on the snow.

One day I rowed over to a small island in the lake with a pair of girls and some goat kids that were going to spend the summer there. We built a tent for them of large branches and turf where they could shelter from storms and mosquitoes. The weather was calm and warm, and on the way home Inga set her fishing net in the lake. The mountain Lapps don't fish very much; the settlers frown on that and want the fishing for themselves, and since the Lapps would rather live in peace and mutual understanding with other people, they don't fish significantly, even though they have a legal right to the lake. Nor do the mountain Lapps have much time for anything but attending to their reindeer herding.

The cows and goats owned by a number of Lapps go to the forest during the day, and in the evening they return on their own for milking, when the girls call them by singing out their names. A large smoking fire is left outside and the cows and goats stand in the smoke, chewing their cud, to be milked. In spite of the smoke, the cows can still be covered with a thick layer of mosquitoes, so that one girl milks while the other brushes off the mosquitoes. The smoke from the fire floats out over the lake and settles, like a large cloud, quite unmoving. Mosquitoes fill the quiet air with their sharp buzzing.

The milk that the Lapps get from the goats is prepared in the same way as reindeer milk, as far as it can be done: they make small cheeses, which are kept as *gáffesul* for more festive occasions, such as when they wish to treat guests by offering a small chunk of cheese to put in the coffee. The largest portion is saved for winter coffee. They don't prepare so much that they can use for porridge and other cheese dishes as in earlier times, when reindeer milking was carried out intensively. In those days a housewife could make six to ten large cheeses a day during milking season. The cheese whey is boiled down, and those who have a cow blend the whey with cows' milk. Into the brown whey cheese, which appears after many hours of cooking, is mixed a couple of handfuls of meal, and when it's cooled, it's poured into a *čalmmas*, the reindeer's second stomach, and preserved like the other cheese for *gáffesul* in winter. If sorrel (Rumex acetosa) is growing in the vicinity, it's picked and cooked in its own juices and mixed in the correct amount in that *cohkodat*, which makes it more "warming."

Sorrel doesn't grow in Laimo, but when Sara, together with some of the other Lapps, went to the Laestadian prayer week over in the Kaisepakte Lapp camp, she and many of the housewives came home with heavy sacks of sorrel on their backs, which they'd picked over there. It was quickly rinsed and cooked. Elle had gone along and she had a large bouquet for me, composed of ferns, rowan, and similar flowers that didn't grow near us. Lapps don't normally prize flowers—everything for them is *rasse* or grass—but the children saw that I liked flowers and sometimes picked them.

Goat milk was also used for coffee milk. It was heated each time and stirred into the coffee in very large amounts. When the coffee was strong and clear, it only heightened the taste. Cow milk was used to mix with cheese whey and for thickened milk. This last, with cream, was a great delicacy, of course, mostly consumed by children, as everyone had permission to "help themselves."

The children of the Lapps have for the most part many privileges and unlimited freedom and have practically no direct upbringing. They're not like children in our society, exposed to many sorts of influences. They see and hear only their own culture and learn it as naturally as eating and walking. The Lapps are therefore sorry to hand over their children to the influence of strangers in the prescribed school year. Both parents and children experience it as a great injustice and sorrow when they have to part because the school demands it. The children lead such delightful lives that you can understand it's difficult to leave. As soon as they're old enough to manage on their own, no one asks what they're up to or where they're going. Hunger will drive them back to the tent at nighttime. They can play for hours with small stones— their reindeer herd—that they find in the stream. Elle and Anne, the girl the same age from the neighboring tent, had most of their play area up on a flat boulder nearby, which was full of colorful pebbles laid out in a certain order. There they had their dolls, which they'd made from cloth; like other children, they sewed doll clothes in the same style as they themselves wore. They'd made small Lappish cradles and sleds for them and had even outfitted these dolls with lassos, reins, and food sacks. For hours the girls lay up there in the warm sunshine with their treasures. The idyll could be occasionally broken by playful boys, but the children always had to fight their battles themselves and figure out how to get along.

Sometimes they wandered widely around on their own, far from the tent, especially during berry-picking time. Yet their absence worried no one. It was important for them, after all, to learn to orient themselves in the forest and mountains. The boys' favorite occupation was naturally to cast the lasso, though the girls also practiced it. They cast the lasso, for lack of anything else, around the tree stumps and bushes, or around someone pretending to be a reindeer by holding up both hands to their head. If they had an antler close at hand, they held it up to their foreheads, and off they ran until the lasso whirred and the captured animal lay kicking in wild resistance.

In general, however, lassos were mainly cast around the dogs, if there were any among them so peaceable they'd allow themselves to be choked a score of times in the course of the day. Only one of our dogs was so sweet-tempered; that was Inga's Rill. He had been with Biettar in Norway herding reindeer, but it didn't suit him to toil away there under another master, so he returned home two weeks after the departure. One fine day a small skinny tired dog slipped into the tent and lay down; he was received with great joy by two of the dogs who'd stayed home. First, they looked surprised, then they licked him on the head and lay down before him, eagerly wagging their tails. Sara didn't have the heart to scold him, since the dog looked so miserable. She put food in front of him and was merely surprised that he was able to find his way home over big rivers and mountains when he'd been behind the reindeer herd for so many miles. It was also, of course, an extenuating factor that he'd wanted to return to his true owner, Inga.

If the children pester the dogs too badly and the adults see it, then they admonish the children not to be too hard on the dogs. The scolding helps, at least at that instant. Otherwise, obedience isn't a virtue the children possess. They only do what you ask if they feel like it. All the same, rudeness and disobedience are punished on occasion with corporal punishment, in the usual spot.

The children are put to work at an early age on everything connected with reindeer. That's something you don't need to ask them to do, because they always want to. Before a migration they go out to the herd if the animals aren't too far away, to hold the draft reindeer as they're gradually rounded up. Then they help lead the animals home to the tent. If there's an old tame pack reindeer, they're allowed to lasso it themselves. In this way a ten-year-old boy with a lasso and a large bundle of reins on his shoulder on his way to the reindeer herd is quite "big" enough; he's no less so when he marches home with a long line of reindeer after him and then helps with the harnessing and so on.

If school didn't come and break up this existence—for three, four, five years—then the children could be of use much earlier with the reindeer herding than is now the case. School interferes to no small degree. It's a great responsibility to undertake, tearing children away from their parents for such a long time. They're not only uneasy about their children not being well cared for physically by strangers. They're afraid that the children won't be the same when they return to life in the mountains. Quite often they come home with tuberculosis and don't survive long. This perhaps has much to do with the change from the Lapps' diet of mostly meat and fat to the farmers' plainer food, but even though in many cases it doesn't end so tragically, all the same it's not good for a mountain Lapp to get a farmer's child back instead of the child he sent away. Between the ages of ten and fourteen the mind is receptive to all influence—things are easily learned and easily forgotten. Three months of summer vacation home in the tent can't make up for nine months of farm life (all Swedish schools have three months of summer vacation), especially when spring and autumn are the time when the Lapp is most occupied. It's also the time when they need help most and when the children have the best opportunity of practicing everything to do with their future way of life. Most often the result is that the child is unfit for all his work after the school period. It's difficult for him to orient himself in the mountains. He doesn't recognize the reindeer's appearance to the high degree necessary, doesn't have "lasso-hands," and so forth.

But all that could probably be relearned if the passion for mountain life were only preserved, and here lies the heart of the matter: far too often, that's what is lost. The young have gotten a taste of the farmer's more comfortable and more respected life as opposed to the Lapps' more strenuous and disdained life. Many no longer return to the mountains, but stay down in the country-side living by casual labor. Then their parents sit up in the mountains mourning the children and their best labor force. Uneasily they see their old age approach. A Lapp calls himself "poor" when he loses his children. The most authentic of the young return, quite unchanged, and take up their old way of life. Yet the risk and the loss from so many years of schooling is too great for reindeer husbandry and Lapp culture to bear in the long run. The Lapp children could get the academic education they need through nomad schools in the mountains.[9] No one can worry that their Christian education will suffer. The Laestadian clergy takes care of that, as well as all the many missionaries who travel constantly among the Lapps.

V

I WAS SEWING MY LAPP-STYLE CLOTHES and on Saturday was going to try part of my dress on, but that couldn't happen in the tent, where you could be disturbed at any moment by visitors. So Inga decided we should go up to the forest. There, up on a flat boulder, the fitting took place with great hilarity. Inga, who didn't believe that the changing from "ladies' clothes" to Lapp dress worked to my advantage, sang, *Diibmá don ledjet dego geasseloddi, dál don leat dego boares dorka.* "Last year you were like a bird in summertime; this year you're like an old inner fur."

The evening was light and warm, and it was Saturday. Inga was finished with her wood chopping and me with my sewing. We weren't in a hurry, but strolled slowly and good-humoredly down through the forest. Suddenly Inga stopped, listened, and whispered quickly, "It's Jouna and Heikki, coming up for wood—now they've heard us."

We heard soft cajoling voices, and far off we saw two red tassels appear through the birches. (Young people in the mountains try to seize the chance to court when they meet outdoors. Since their play is very physical, a real wrestling match, the tent with its many onlookers is definitely not the most desirable place.)

Inga stood still a second, then she bounded noiselessly behind the nearest tree to hide. She looked slantwise up at me with a big smile. Her white teeth gleamed in the green darkness under the tree. Her wide eyes shone. Now the coaxing voices sounded closer. "Come on," Inga whispered, and with a couple of easy jumps she was hidden in the bushes. She ducked down and made herself small as a young rabbit that hides in tall grass. She held her breath and listened for her pursuers, but not a sound betrayed her hiding place. They lost her trail and gave up the search. When they were gone, Inga got up and tiptoed in her soft shoes between the birches. Soon we were at the edge of the forest, out in the sunlight, and a moment afterward home in the tent. Up in the forest Jouna and Heikki felled trees so that the axes rang. We smiled a small secret smile together and went into the tent with its fire and steaming stew pot.

As young as Inga was, she already had a wristwatch!—that is to say, a suitor. When a young man fancies a girl, he gives her little gifts—betrothal gifts or *gihli*—which consist mainly of scarves, often of silk; pretty aprons; a silver spoon (always in the old-fashioned Lappish style, with a short handle, which goldsmiths in towns nearby make especially for the Lapps); a silver ring with "leaves," that is, tiny bangles.

These days, however, the customary gold ring has quite displaced the former silver ring. An amorous lover or young husband can give the object of his affection three or four such rings (she only wears one of them, though). It's also become quite usual to give a watch as a betrothal gift. One often sees a young, manly Lapp wearing a small ladies' watch, which he uses himself until he gets the chance to give it as a *gilhi*. It's always a good idea to have a gift ready; a mountain Lapp can't go whenever he likes to a watchmaker and purchase a watch. But just because a girl accepts the gifts doesn't mean that anything is settled between them. She accepts gifts from all her suitors and is especially coy with some of them. As long as she hasn't chosen one in earnest, a *diehttelas irgi* (recognized lover), she has her complete freedom. Betrothal gifts are hidden very carefully in the girl's small colorfully painted chest with iron hardware. She only wears her watch, if she's lucky enough to have received such an expensive gift.

Later, when she's made her final decision and married her chosen one, all the other suitors get their gifts back. The rejected ones try again with the same gifts to other girls. Yet not every rejected suitor takes it so calmly. It's not uncommon to get revenge on a girl and her future husband by killing her reindeer—her dowry. Up to a hundred reindeer can lose their lives in this way. There's no surplus of young girls among the nomad Lapps; it's always considered, therefore, something of a success to find a wife.

Among the Lapps, a *boaresbárdni* (an old bachelor) is ignored. He doesn't have as much clout as a married man—*boaresbárdni borrá dihki* ("an old bachelor bites lice"). He's such a strange figure that he *baldá haesttaid* ("scares the horses"—the Lapps have a great deal of respect for a horse's size and strength).

It's very seldom that a girl remains unmarried among the nomads. I've known two, of whom one was crippled—the Lapps are very afraid of inherited disabilities—and the other epileptic. The latter was both pretty and clever, but it was said that she herself didn't want to marry. She wouldn't risk having delicate children or worrying her husband with her illness.

You can't imagine how snug and cozy a Lapp tent is on a Saturday evening. All the old birch branches are taken out and burned (they're never burned in the tent). If there are too many ashes in the hearth, the stones are lifted up and the ashes dug up and carried out, after which the stones are laid down in order again. Fresh birch twigs are fetched in large bundles from the forest, and when they are laid on the earth inside, the tent glows green and festive. Frequently juniper twigs are placed in the kitchen space underneath the cooking box, where they stay green the whole week. It's a pleasure to make your bed Saturday evening and lie down on all the foliage that smells of the forest and is cool to the touch. What does it matter, that small green caterpillars crawl through the leaves?

You'll have a Sunday feeling in the morning, in the bright, clean tent, when Sara wakes you with her friendly, *Lihke bajás, juga gáfe.* "Get up and have some coffee."

But the freshness quickly disappears from the tent if there should happen to be a prayer meeting. Then the Finnish settlers come from Kattuvuoma; they sit there most of Sunday and smoke pipes and spit in the birch twigs. And when they're gone, the Sunday glow has left the tent.[10]

One Sunday there was a Laestadian prayer meeting in a neighboring tent. They asked me to come along and I did, though I didn't understand a word of the long sermon in Finnish, which one of the settlers read aloud, while sitting on a small low chest. The sun shone in strongly through the smoke hole. On the leafy green floor sat the devout Lapps. The tent eventually grew packed. Children and dogs wandered in and out under the tent cloth wherever they wished, but finally the place grew so cramped that the children and dogs were kept outside.

The women were dressed up for Sunday in fine clothes, and the men as well. The young girls with their warm round cheeks, their dresses in yellows and reds, clustered together in twos and threes like ripe apples in the green foliage. The sun streamed in over their foreheads and high cheekbones, so that the downcast eyes and lower faces had warm shadows. They'd pulled their legs up under them, so only the small feet with their high insteps and narrow ankles in the smooth-soled soft leather shoes were visible. The supple fragility in the bent bodies was full of grace. A young wife sat with her baby at her breast, but when it began to cry, she left so as not to disturb the others' silent worship.

Ponderously and with great feeling, the serious Laestadian farmer read the Laestadian sermon from the book on his knee. At long last he was finished, closed the book, and sat unmoving for some minutes. Suddenly his face muscles began to work convulsively. He turned burning red, then tears began to fall down his cheeks. He started to sob and implore, "Jumala." The others sat silently, as if they were waiting, with downcast eyes. Then the old women began to sob in the same spasmodic way; they moaned and cried out to God. Gradually everyone was infected, both young and old, men and women. The peaceful, sun-filled tent was transformed in the space of a few minutes to a painful place, where human souls were whipped by remorse, fear, and guilt. Men and women sobbed and rocked their torsos back and forth. Then they got up on their knees and embraced each other by turns while crying imploringly.

Tightly embracing, with their hands on one another's shoulders, their shoulders swayed like trees in a storm. *Addá ándagassii Ipmal* ("God forgives!") sounded out, in all tones and rhythms. (That's to say everyone has his own peculiar rhythm and "melody." I've heard them literally practicing in a matter-of-fact way, and outsiders recognize the "melody"—who it is who sobs—even though there are a hundred people in ecstasy at a time.) In spite of barely understanding a word or grasping what was going on, I was infected by the general nervous excitement. I got the shivers and had to leave.

Outside lay the Sunday-still landscape, in peace and quiet, while the small gray dwelling shook, and wild shrieks inside cut through the stillness out over the mountains and wilderness. It was a long way to God in the high reaches of heaven. It took powerful means to be heard and to be forgiven from up there. That was why the horrific chorus grew in wildness and strength.

The ecstasy can last two to three hours, until they're completely exhausted. It can also happen that someone faints. But people gather their forces quickly through the heavy eating and drinking that follows immediately after. And soon, all outer traces of what has passed are wiped from their faces. The men light their pipes and the talk goes on as if nothing had happened. On Sunday afternoon you're especially grateful for a crumb of distraction, since nothing that resembles work must be undertaken. There are many strict rules for what you can and can't do on holy days. Preferably you should read from "the book," but not everyone can, or feels like giving their time to such an occupation; instead they chat and drink coffee. You mustn't sew or plait wool yarn or spin sinew thread. You mustn't use sharp tools, such as axes, knives, or scissors. But after six in the evening all prohibitions are dropped. The holy day is over.

Not until August did the reindeer and herders begin to return from Norway. The tent was often full of young people, who spent their free time joking around and entertaining themselves. Some talked of the herd and their summer experiences. Others sat cutting reindeer ear marks in birch bark. Some practiced the art of writing by whittling a wooden fire poker smooth on one side and writing on the white surface with a pencil stub. They also used the fine inner skin of birch bark instead of paper. On Sunday afternoon after the prayer service, they passed the time reading in books from their small stock. One read Finnish; another got hold of a small book of Bible stories in Lappish; another read hymns. Biettar ate and Nikki slept on the reindeer skins. A deep silence might have prevailed, if it weren't that they were all reading aloud—every one of them.

Toward evening a number of fellow believers from the neighboring camp came in to take their leave. The tent filled to bursting in an instant, as everyone began embracing and praying. Some stood with their heads right up in the halo of smoke and steam—the stew pot hanging over the fire boiled briskly. It took a long time before they got around the circle to each person.

Gradually they egged each other into absolute *liitkutuksia*, the Finnish word for their religious trance, with shouting and weeping.[11] The only one not caught up in this was Nikki, who was now finished napping and who sat zealously sliding a long ramrod into his Mauser rifle to clean it. The many embraces disturbed him not in the least; he reciprocated neither hugs nor words since he didn't share their piety. All his attention was on cleaning his weapon.

In the meantime the dogs took advantage of the general preoccupation to steal into the kitchen space, something they couldn't otherwise do when there were people in the tent. But naturally they didn't agree about the spoils and began to fight viciously. Since the fight took place at the edge of big fire, this would no doubt have ended with singed fur and burns, if I hadn't taken a firm hold with just my hands and a stick.

The scene was grotesque: the crying and shrieking of many people, the wild barking and fighting of the dogs, the steaming pot that boiled over, since no one was watching it. The tent itself shook from the loud noise and vigorous movements. Piety can manifest itself in many remarkable ways.

VI

THE LAPPS OFTEN HAD ERRANDS at the storehouses in Kattuvuoma, and when there was good weather, the young people gladly kept one another company. Once, returning home, we filled two boats. Things grew lively on the lake in the still, light evening. The long elegant boats left a frothing wake as they raced each other—one boat oared by girls, with a male coxswain; the other with two male rowers, while a girl took the steering oar. White furs, blue tunics, and many colors of red in caps and scarves, the happy brown faces and dark eyes gleaning in the evening sunlight, every movement and color shimmering in the mirror of the water.

Courting was in full swing; among the Lapps it was quite noticeable. The girls' coxswain was dragged away from them over to the second boat. They rowed so near to each other that only the outside pair of oars could be used. They wrestled over the gunwale, where they battled with oars and water, so the spray was high.

The dogs jumped, barking, back and forth from one boat to the other; the echoes rang between the mountains, the boats collided with a crunch, then swerved off. Then suddenly they darted far away from each other, and racing began again. A young housewife was also along; she had the cradle at her side, and while she gestured animatedly and lifted her voice to join in the merriment, she sat nursing her baby. After which the baby was held out over the water, its lower half quite naked.

Over at the small waterfall, where the lake was shallow but the current strong among the rocks, the boats didn't do so well—*vuoi, vuoi*—they hit the rocks with a crunch. But the last half hour, where you could possibly be seen from the tents, the hilarity grew more restrained. We glided nicely through the small stone islands, back to the gray tents with smoke rising from them, under the mountains. The sun had long been succeeded by the moon; across the lake lay a broad golden band in the black water, and behind Ripanen a gleam flickered up over the sky, the faint northern lights. The evening began to darken. Autumn wasn't far off.

But now, with the herd nearby, the *siida* was full of life, busy with work. One day Nilsa came running, flung the door open, and cried, *Eallu boahtá, čana beatnagiid gitta!* "The herd is coming, tie up the dogs!"

The whole camp sprang to life. You heard the tent doors continuously flapping open, then falling back against the tent as the children and adults hurried off. In the neighbor tent they were sitting and eating, but when they heard the call, everyone ran out and away. The oldest of the children, a seven-year-old boy, snatched up his lasso and said, "Food is good, but the herd is better," after which he shot like an arrow through the forest.

It was only a smaller separating of the herd, which was being gathered in an open field in the forest for a couple of hours. Still, the usual tasks would be carried out: milking, castrating, and butchering.

The corral itself lay half a dozen kilometers away.[12] For several days the women went up in vain with their milk pails. The herders hadn't succeeded in getting the reindeer down to the corral, but finally the herd came down inside it for some days in a row. We started off from the tents at seven in the morning, but when we got up there, we couldn't hear either people or reindeer. A campfire was started in the thin edge of the forest where the leaves were already gold with frost, even though we were in the middle of August. We passed the time in coffee drinking and merriment. Then we heard from afar dogs baying loudly and the hollow thunder that always heralds the coming of the large herd.

Everyone jumped up and began to scan the mountains in the direction of the sound. Up there the herd looked like turbulent gray dots. It came rapidly nearer, and at furious speed the living mass rushed down over the mountain side like a hailstorm. The women practically sparkled with delight and excitement. Everyone hurried to take up a guard position, so the reindeer had to go through a funnel of people and were chased into the corral through a relatively narrow opening. This was quickly closed off with chopped-down birch trees, which lay ready. Everyone slipped in; only the dogs were kept out. The reindeer stood for a while with tongues hanging out, trembling with eagerness and strain after their swift downward rush.

The reindeer inside the corral galloped at full speed with their little white tails in the air and their heads thrown back. They ran round and round like horses in a circus—counterclockwise, as is their habit. Gradually, they grew much quieter.

Now the lassoes whistled; an *áldu* or reindeer cow was caught, the noose was loosened and placed like a halter around her head. If the *áldu* is particularly wild and unruly, she's tied to a tree or tree stump. If she's tamer and used to being milked, the husband stands holding her with his lasso while the wife milks. Men and boys creep around to sneak up on the animals, and the women are ready with the milking cup or *náhppi*.

The sun shone, the high snowfield glittered, and the golden leaves made a splendid background for the colorful lives in the corral, where everything was in motion. The Lapps were in their true element here. This was pure entertainment for them and working hard the happiest kind of play. There was milking and ear marking; calves were slaughtered and bulls castrated. But in spite of all the grappling with the half-wild animals, not a single coarse or hard word could be heard, and there was no sign of violence. These were tasks they'd mastered, and they were carried out deftly and powerfully, without unnecessary flailing about.

Many of the small, dark three- or four-month-old calves had to lose their lives. August and September is the right time to take the skin for fine furs. The Lapps, like other people, show their prosperity by wearing beautiful clothes; such a single-colored dark fur garment of *borgenáhkki*, or freshly prepared skin, is quite elegant. The poor don't have enough calves to be able to pick and choose between colors; they must take light and dark together, whatever they have, and that naturally makes the fur less attractive.

At the end of the afternoon the reindeer were released from the corral. They took immediately to the mountains, except for the cows that had lost their calves; they ran looking and calling inside and outside the corral. Sometimes they stopped, listened intently, and looked to every side; then they began running again, grunting and searching. In that manner they grieve for three days, the Lapps say, and they stay at the site where they last saw their calves. After that they seek out the rest of the herd.

The slaughtered calves were flayed and their guts removed, both of which tasks took place outside the corral. All the meat and other parts of the reindeer were wrapped in fresh birch twigs and loaded on draft reindeer that had just been rounded up. The women wrapped the dried jerky in scarves and, for the same purpose, brought out the *čalmmas* holding fresh reindeer milk and carried it on their backs. The pack train set off homeward. A Lapp had taken a young bull on a lead to slaughter him at home by the tent. The bull was untamed and in a complete rage; it took both skill and strength to tow the wild animal forward between the trees and rocky outcroppings for seven or eight kilometers. The path of the Lapp and the bull was very irregular; ultimately, they disappeared far ahead of us. The reindeer caravan stepped sedately behind, with people and dogs. Now came the reaction to an exhausting day; everyone was rather silent and tired. Little by little, it grew dark and the stars came out. It was late when we finally glimpsed the glowing tents far below. Inside sat those who'd stayed home, longing for news of the herd and for fresh reindeer meat.

VII

In August the Lapps have quite an important task; they collect "shoe-hay" to use during the year. For stuffing their shoes they use very long sedge grass that grows in certain places. Whole small expeditions are equipped for this purpose, which for the most part consist of girls. They carry a sack of food and some bedclothes, so they can be away for a few days. The grass is cut off near the root with a sharp knife. The straw must not become tangled; later, when the day's yield is sorted out, the grass is gathered into small bundles that are tied together at the top. The roots are knocked hard against a stone, so all the loose, coarse bits of straw fall off. The bundles of hay are hung up to dry, two by two, over a pole. When they're thoroughly dry, they're twisted together in a long strand, which is further twisted into a thick ring. One can use this *suoidnefierra,* or hay-ring, all year.

In Västerbotten and the southern areas of Lapmark the women do more with the hay. There, they run a comb with very sharp steel teeth through it until it grows quite fine and soft. The fine-combed hay naturally feels warmer and is comfortable for the foot at first, but it clumps together faster and grows damp more easily than the coarser hay used in the North.

Already in August we had heavy snow squalls, but the approach of winter wasn't seriously apparent until September, when the snow could linger several days, and the ice on the lakes and marshes was quite thick. Of course that alternated with splendid days of sunshine, and the mountain forests were a marvel of color. The birch's shiny gold coins fell down on the reddest of red ground. The lower slopes of the mountains were golden; further up, violet.

On top lay new snow and above that a high radiant blue September sky. When it grew dark, the northern lights fanned out and waved under the stars. One evening there was a golden gateway to the south, and to the north sharp bright rays shot like bundles of rockets up under all the stars, as if from the top of Ripanen. The tents glowed like small volcanoes; out of the open cone poured a column of fire—red smoke and sparks, which climbed and died out in the darkness above.

One evening it snowed, so there were five centimeters on the ground, and long after it was dark, the children ran around outside. Even for Lapp children the first snow has something festive about it. They also amused themselves with wading through ice water in the brook, where it was deepest and stoniest. The game began with jumping over the brook with the help of a vaulting pole, but since the jump ended badly in the water, the game turned into who could get over the worst section. That they were wading in water practically up to their waists didn't bother them; after all, they had on leather trousers, although it wasn't clear if, after drying out all summer, these were watertight. The children merely hardened themselves to the difficult life that awaited them as herders.

The time for moving on grew near. Like the other men, Nikki went off for a few days to look over the sleds and winter belongings that had been left behind in the mountains last spring when they had to shift from sleds to pack reindeer. They were mainly worried about damage from mice and rats (thefts of such possessions happen very seldom). During a lemming year, which we'd just had, rodents swarmed everywhere. The lemmings themselves don't do any damage to furs or other things, but they're accompanied by all sorts of rats and mice that spare nothing they encounter. If a mouse gets inside the tent, in a single night it can destroy very valuable property by gnawing holes in furs, sacks of flour, shoes, and so on. Therefore, if someone discovers a mouse in the tent, the whole tent is cleaned out, no matter how cold a winter day it is. They won't stop until the animal is captured and killed. On the other hand, they don't pay much attention to a lemming if it gets into the tent. It's taken, too, as an unlucky sign if one's clothing is attacked by mice; but if they make a nest in the fur without chewing on anything, that means good fortune for the owner of the fur. However, Nikki returned to say that their belongings were in good condition.

The summer living quarters began to lose their beauty. Snow and rain and wind were our daily weather. It was hard to get the wet kindling to catch in the morning. So Inga and the children rowed quite a distance one day to look

for dry wood, wizened willow branches, to make lighting the morning fire easier during this wet time of autumn. They came home toward evening with the
boat fully packed. The children had picked armfuls of angelica, which didn't
grow in this vicinity. In the spring, the fleshy young stems are much loved by
the Lapps. They eat them raw or grilled on the coals; additionally they use the
one-year-old angelica plant, *fadnú*, to mix with reindeer milk for winter use.

Now, however, the stalks were tough and wooden and quite inedible. Yet
they made more aesthetic use of them. A young Lapp came into the tent at twilight, while I was alone with the children. He chose a suitable stalk, trimmed
it to a kind of flute with many holes, and blew through it, monotonously but
expressively. Before long, the music absorbed him so that he noticed nothing
else around him.

The big chunks of wood on the fire fell inward. The firelight glowed up into
his brown face and on the long black hair that fell over the high red collar of
his tunic. The fire was reflected in his dark eyes like moonlight on the water.
What he dreamed of, I don't know, but the melancholy notes sounded like a
farewell to the sun and to summer. Wulle was so taken up by his reveries that
he paid no attention to Sara's displeasure over the "hideous noise." She'd come
into the tent and scolded both him and the children for their impiety—for
the children were also sitting trimming flutes and attempting to blow them.
The monotonous notes reminded me of Lappish singing, or joiking.[13] It was
a long time before Wulle was finished with playing and making new flutes;
when at length he tossed down the last one, he immediately got up with the
same distant expression on his face and left without saying a word.

By the end of September we waited daily for migration weather. Now
the happy summer was past and the strenuous, frequent moves were about to
begin. Yet it stormed, rained, and snowed as if it would never stop. Finally, on
September 27, we could finally say farewell to Laimolahti. The day broke with
quiet sunshine and a clear frost. The women were busy from early morning
with packing everything up and taking the tent down; afterward, everything
had to be hauled to the boats.

Almost all the men were away with the reindeer, so the women had to
manage alone. The big children were given the job of taking care of the small
ones, while the women and girls put things in order. The children thoroughly
searched the tent site, when the birch floor was removed, to find small lost
objects, sewing needles and the like, which they carefully collected up. Here
and there burned huge bonfires made of the birch flooring. Old discarded
woolen trousers and such things were cast on the fire. Not a scrap must be left

behind; however, nothing at all of the reindeer was burned; not the least little fragment of leather or tuft of hair.

The boats were loaded to the brim and, in the middle of the afternoon, as many as were ready rowed over to Kattuvuoma. Now the summer living quarters stood deserted and the abandoned fire pits smoked at the tent sites as we glided away from the deep little bay. The lake's water level was low. In a couple of places it wasn't easy trying to get the heavily laden boat across and we had to "out and walk" and take part of the baggage on our backs. There was laughter and crying children, dogs baying and water splashing. After we'd gone some way along the shore, while the boats were poled over the stony patches, we got onboard again. They settled me on top of the baggage together with the dogs; and a woman from a neighboring tent placed a cradle with a baby in it on my knees so that she could take the steering oar astern. It was, by the way, high time we left, for the ice was already causing problems. Even though it had only frozen overnight, it had to be broken up with the oar before we could get to land.

Most of the Lapps were staying with Finnish people, and only a couple of families had put their tents up, since we were only going to be here a few days. Besides, the friendship with the settlers wasn't quite as warm as it had been in summer when they were one another's guests at the prayer meetings. The reindeer divide them; now that the herd had come down from the mountains, the settlers feared for their hay and suddenly the Lapps and reindeer were pests, which they'd prefer to exterminate. It never occurs to them that it's the Lapps who are the rightful owners here and the settlers who are merely intrusive strangers. The Lapps are almost irritatingly peaceful and compliant; they allow themselves to be downright bullied by the tougher Finns.

In Kattuvuoma almost all of us caught influenza; it was hardest on the reindeer herders who suddenly became ill outside while working. Up at the large corral in the mountains where the thorough separating of the reindeer was taking place each day, many were ill. It didn't help to lie there during the frosty nights with a fever, without nursing care, and with a minimum of bedclothes.

The stay in Kattuvuoma grew to be a bit longer than estimated. For over a week it was said, "Tomorrow we'll move out," but it still didn't happen. There's something called Lappish "unreliability and not keeping your word," regarding times and dates. Yet we shouldn't reproach them for that too strongly. The fact is, they're not the only ones making decisions when it applies to time; the reindeer are the masters. It can take longer than predicted to gather the herd. Some reindeer may have strayed and must be found, and the task can be delayed by fog, storms, and other mishaps. In addition to this, the Lapp isn't fastidious about time or punctual at all. His existence isn't chopped into pieces or decided by any timetable. One day or the next—it doesn't matter much, if it doesn't have to do with the reindeer herd.

I wasn't able to set out with Sara and Nikki because of influenza, but several days after their departure I followed with a young married pair, who also belonged to our *siida*. They'd been busy in the storehouse with putting away the summer things and taking out the winter gear. Everything had to be organized in *gisas*, or saddlebags, of the exact same weight, one on each side of the reindeer. The pair sat on the ground outside the storehouse and occupied themselves with the packing. Out of the storehouse came a mixed smell of leather, fish, dried meat, and much else. On poles under the roof hung a couple of fine fur parkas and tunics, and a silver belt gleamed. There were goatskin sacks packed full of meal, grain for porridge, and coffee. In a corner lay big bundles of reins, cleaning materials, and split wood. There were utensils for milking and making goat cheese; dried reindeer meat lay on the floor next to winter shoes and mittens made from reindeer hide, ready to be used along with many other things. The wife lovingly stroked her fine flowing dark fur and said proudly, *Dat lea mu beaska.* "This is my fur parka." It contrasted with my own recently acquired one, which, like a poor Lapp fur, had many shades of color and for the most part consisted of coarser skin from a calf that had grown too old.[14]

VIII

On a clear and sunny October day we left Kattuvuoma in a caravan of sixteen heavily laden reindeer in three separate strings. The path that others had traveled before us went over moors and marshes eastward toward the mountains. The reindeer plodded heavily but steadily; their burdens were a little too much for them. The lead reindeer in Sanne's string carried the white skin-covered cradle where little Nilaš slept. The slightly bigger Ingaš was also tucked into a cradle draped over a reindeer. The two older boys ran alongside, and like the dogs they made their way twice as long, even though Sanne asked them to save their strength, since we had a long way to go. In a forest of slender birch trees the gray reindeer blended together with the silver gray trunks. The red forest floor was in harmony with the colors in the Lapps' clothes. Splashes of sun and long stripes of shadow made everything shimmer with a surreal light. But the day slipped away—we walked and walked. Whenever I dropped down on a hillock or stone for a moment, Sanne laughed at me: "We have far to go and we're going to sleep outside. We won't arrive until after dark."

I had flashes before my eyes. I didn't have a thought in my head, only an unpleasant sense of powerlessness. Anything that might be called a trail had long since disappeared. We often waded through spongy marshlands where you could sink up to your knees and where, into the bargain, willow branches could twist themselves around the curled-up toe of your shoes, so it was hard to pull your foot out.

A mist came up toward evening. I trudged back behind the last reindeer, which was hauling the tent poles. In front of me the thin sharp poles glided perpetually onward, like black snakes that wound over and around every obstacle. I saw them everywhere I looked, and now and again a ball of light exploded in front of my eyes, along with the other fireworks that came from exhaustion.

The reindeer were also tired and walked with their tongues hanging out of their mouths. Eventually one fell to the ground and neither pushing nor shouting could get it on its feet again. For that reason, we had to stop and spend the night there. All the animals were unhitched and were allowed to graze and rest. We did the same after we'd lit a big bonfire. We drank coffee from Sanne's largest coffee pot, which quickly came to the boil. Each of us sat with a fat rib from a large sun-dried side of reindeer that had been pulled from the food sack. The fire drew people and dogs together, as the fog walled us in; we had a home as far as the glow of the fire reached. It cast a reddish light on Jonna—on the men—with their blue-black hair and brown faces with white teeth; it shone on the dogs and on Sanne, who sat with the smallest at her breast, laughing and glowing. Next to her on the moss was the cradle in its white winter covering (a case sewed from the white skin of the reindeer's lower leg). Sparks from the fire flew into the air like little red stars and were put out by the mist.

By bedtime the shoe-hay was dry and shoes slipped on again. Some bedclothes were pulled out, and under a pair of tent poles with a piece of canvas over them, we lay down and slept. Jonna and Sanne lay whispering with the children and laughing. The dogs settled themselves around us and on us, wherever they found it most comfortable. The sky was dark and the earth was dark; only the fire sent, for a short while, a bit of smoke and flame up into all that darkness. Then the fire was extinguished and we were one with the dark.

At five in the morning, people and dogs crawled out from the bedclothes, and the bonfire was lit in the gray light. Gradually it grew red in the south and the sun rose. It cast a pale golden light out over the godforsaken bog, where a stunted birch or two caught a little light on a bent white trunk. The morning fog drifted between the mountains and over the small lakes out on the endless marsh.

The reindeer were rounded up so they could be loaded again. They stood steaming with a halo around them from the night's dampness on their fur. It was Sunday and the Lapps don't believe in working on Sundays, yet everything to do with reindeer and herding is excused from the severe religious prohibitions.

We continued our march when the reindeer were loaded up. The one that had fallen the evening before was still too weak to carry anything. It walked freely behind the caravan and tried to keep up, but it could barely stay on its feet and sometime later was found dead, ripped apart by wolves. When a single reindeer or small group happens to walk alone, away from the herd, it's quite vulnerable to attack by wolves.

We brightened up later in the morning, when Sanne pointed ahead and called, *Gea, suovva!* "Look, smoke!" I think we were all a bit exhausted when we came to a halt on the hill where tents had been set up by those who'd arrived before us. The reindeer were unharnessed and Jonna led them to the herd, while we settled around a fire already lit by another Lapp family that had recently arrived and now, like us, wanted to enjoy some rest and food before they tackled putting up their tents.

Later in the afternoon I went to look for Sara and Nikki's tent, but no one was home. They showed this in the usual way by propping a piece of wood against the outer door flap. They'd gone to the reindeer corral. We went inside anyway and touched the ashes, which were cold. They must have left early in the day. Next morning Jonna and Sanne went to the corral, a few kilometers off. Sanne had longed to go up there, for it was now "like a fair," and Lapps from several *siidas* were gathered there to separate their herds and to milk. Everyone had taken food, along with a little bedding, and they camped out in the open for more than a week. Those who were living closer, for instance, our *siida*, came home every evening—except for the herders of course. They had to be on their feet all the time or be prepared to relieve each other. It wasn't easy for them now, since a number of people were ill with influenza up there.

Biettar, who was convalescing, couldn't participate in reindeer herding. He helped only with the work in the corral. Since dogs are firmly forbidden inside the corral, Cæppe was ordered to stay home with me in the tent. But he was a miserable companion; he sat the whole day on a hilltop next to the tent and whined. From there he had a view across the large bog and could just make out, far away, the many bonfires and could hear now and again the sound of reindeer and dogs. Every muscle was tensed; his gaze was fixed, and his ears pricked up like the cocked hammer of a rifle. When any great noise came from that direction, he dug his claws into the sand as if to jump up and gave a small anguished bark. But such a dog is trained; he followed orders and stayed home. When I went up to console him, he leaped up, wagging his tail, but immediately sat down again like a stone statue, his eyes boring into a far-off point of activity.

When the communal tasks in the corral were finished and when everyone, as far as possible, had found his own reindeer, the herd sometimes came down to the *siida* and we gathered on a hill nearby. The women went up and milked energetically. If there weren't enough boys, then every girl or woman had someone cast a lasso to capture and to hold the cow while she was being milked. The women worked in pairs; one used the lasso and the other the milking cup.

During that time so much milking was done that we were able to have fresh reindeer milk in our coffee and could even take a slurp from a spoon. The milk from August and September, procured before we'd begun our trek, had rennet added to it. It had been hung in a *čalmmas* or a reindeer stomach. What was being milked now, except for what we drank fresh or used for coffee, was kept in a *čalmmas* or a wooden cup to freeze. Later, in the course of the winter, when we needed milk for coffee, the correct amount was chopped off and thawed in a frying pan over the fire, then added with a spoon to the coffee.

At Abrantjåkko where we had our tents now, several *siidas* had come together, but the tents lay quite a distance from each other, and it was a major journey to make a visit.

One morning at dawn, Sara was called to a birth in one of the tents farthest away. Up there, where no other help is available, they aid each other. Sara was one of the oldest and most experienced in the district, which is why women readily sought her assistance. For that matter, it's not uncommon among the Lapps for some men to help their wives in such circumstances—even to the extent of being called to other women giving birth. The Lapps have their own methods and household remedies, and it's very seldom anyone dies in labor. The Lappish women give birth standing; only when the child has been delivered is she allowed to lie down. Both mother and child receive careful nursing. In most cases mothers stay abed for a week or so, though naturally there are women, among the Lapps as well, who can get up the same day or within the course of a few days' time. I even heard of one case (in Härjedalen) of a birthmother who, a couple of hours after the birth, had made coffee for her helper, her mother-in-law, despite vehement protests. Sometimes a woman gives birth during the migration. After the baby is born she puts it inside her fur parka at the breast and continues onward until she reaches the camping place and can get some rest and nursing.

Right after the birth the baby is bathed in warm water. Altogether, bathing plays a large role in Lapp child care, but perhaps the most important part of caring for an infant, at least some years ago, was making sure the head was attractively formed. The Lapps value, to an unusual degree, a round head, and already during the first bath they begin to *deakčut oaivvi* (press the head). Not everyone can do it correctly and well, but Sara still knew the art, and her mother had been particularly skillful at head-shaping. It's done gently; whoever bathes the child for the first time evenly presses the forehead and sides of the head, trying to shape the head to be as round as possible. After that, the head is wrapped rather tightly with cloth to maintain the impression and shape. Later, the child receives a small, tight-fitting smooth leather cap (nowadays the cap is cloth).

Bathing the child takes place even when it's very cold, but the little one enjoys, with evident delight, the warm water and soaping. When the child has become so big that his whole body up to the neck can't be under water— bathing is done in a copper pot—his back, or some other part turned away from the fire, is covered with a woolen scarf. The mother settles herself in such a way that the child is protected from drafts. While the child is bathed, the cradle sits clean and ready in front of the fire, so that it will be warm for the child. The Lappish cradle is made of hollowed-out spruce (spruce is the lightest kind of wood up here), a log about a meter long. Narrow lathes of birch are bent and attached like a bonnet over the end where the child's head rests. The whole cradle is covered in smooth, tanned reindeer skin. In winter the cradle is often provided with an extra outer cover, sewn from the white sock of the reindeer's lower leg. For the cradle's inner lining, in this Lapp district they use sphagnum moss, which is collected in summer and tanned with birch bark, then carried along in a sack. The befouled moss is burned and replaced with fresh moss.

Over the inner lining, a few clean cloths are placed. If it's extremely cold, the cradle is kept warm with a hot stone while the child is bathed. When the child is washed and dried off, he's dressed in a small soft fur of newborn reindeer skin with the fur side toward the body and placed in a cradle with the fur turned up so he won't get wet. Around the feet a small piece of leather is tucked, and under the head the child has a small down pillow with an embroidered case and over that a slip of white rabbit skin, so the head can lie soft and warm. The little one is placed very carefully in the cradle with arms along the side of his body. The outside of the fur is well packed in a soft wool shawl, after which the cradle is laced up, its leather covering stretched from two sides like flaps that envelop the child. With the help of leather loops and a woven band, the whole thing is laced up with suitable firmness, so the child is wrapped up to his chin. A braided band goes from the bonnet to the bottom of the cradle. The last section of the band is wide and unbraided; it fastens to the cradle with a silver button, so it can be undone when the child is taken out. There's another silver button where the three-ply band shifts to a single width, and in the middle, right in front of the child's face, is a necklace of large Italian glass pearls; on this necklace are also silver buttons with "leaves"—small dangling trinkets, like delicate rings or leaves, and so on. All that silver in the cradle is meant to be protection against the "Uldas" (underground beings).[15] When the baby wears sterling silver with a hallmark, he can't be exchanged for an Ulda child. In earlier times, other amulets were placed in the cradles.

The cradle is hung up in the tent or outside, with the help of a leather strap attached to the upper end and with a loop fastened to the bottom end. The child is carried on the back when traveling (sometimes the man carries it for his wife). Inside the tent, when the child is to sleep, the cradle is generally hung from the *doaresmuorra* (a cross branch that connects the two braces). The mother, or whoever is taking care of the child, gets him to sleep by rocking the cradle back and forth and jiggling it while she often half-joiks and half-sings Lappish cradle songs almost without words.

In the good old days, and probably still today on occasion, a Lapp child was soon given his own *luohti* or joik song. This can come from the parents or one relative or another. He can even be given several such melodies, which are his own and which he keeps his whole life. One of my acquaintances, an older Lapp girl in Västerbotten, had four such *vuolli* (as they're called there). They can have flattering words but they can also be a sort of slandering song. Even so, it's always an honor to have many of them; and yet, those who sing their own song are considered conceited and boastful.

These person-songs are known among one's own circle and perhaps outside it, if there's something special that makes them worth of notice. When such a tune is sung or hummed, those within earshot know right away who is referred to. Even quite small children practice joiking; yet joiking grows less and less common since it's attacked and condemned by Laestadian pastors as something quite sinful. It's going out of style among the Lapps themselves now that the schoolchildren learn Swedish songs and never hear a word of acknowledgment about their own musical heritage. Even though it's not always beautiful, it is original and well worth saving from oblivion. It gives expression to true Lappish moods and emotions.

The infant that Sara helped into the world that gray dawn at Abrantjåkko had only a short lifespan; by Saint Andrew's Day, November 30, it was buried in Jukkasjärvi. The mother, however, took it quietly. She'd been prepared by a dream before its birth for the baby's death. In the dream she'd dressed the child in white, and from that she knew the outcome. Generally speaking, the Lapps believe strongly in dreams. If you've dreamed something dreadful, you should relate the dream right away in the morning, in order to take power away from its evil. In dreams the underground beings come and talk with you.

Some years ago Sara and Nikki lived for a time in a turf hut by a lake in order to fish. Each night an old woman came to Sara in her dreams and asked them to move their dwelling place, for it stood just on top of their settlement. Since it was the habit of the Uldas to sleep during the day and be up all night, it disturbed them greatly to have people moving around above them during their sleep. In the beginning Sara didn't think much about the message, but then one night the old Ulda mother came again and asked her seriously but in a friendly manner to move their hut. Otherwise, they would not prosper. She well knew it was a lot of work to move a turf hut, but they must do it. So Sara and Nikki moved their dwelling and found peace.

Some Lapps are quite the interpreters of dreams. Just as they themselves speak often in parables, so are dreams also symbolic for them. The Lapps' inclination to express themselves in parables can make understanding the conversations they have among themselves difficult, even when the language doesn't present an obstacle. For example, they can sit talking about the reindeer, and suddenly you realize that it's actually certain people that they mean. They can discuss the *siida's* affairs and people down to the smallest detail and still only be talking about the herd, so an outsider believes it really has to do with reindeer.

Their ordinary speech is larded with comparisons both humorous and apt, often very beautiful and quite inexhaustible. About a pretty young girl, for example, they'll say, *Son lea čáppis dego láttat.* "She is pretty as a cloudberry." And to denote her youth: *Son lea nuorra dego rássi.* "She's as young as a flower."

Their sense of beauty is well developed; their feeling for form and color fine and certain. The men are born artists as far as form and ornamentation are concerned when they work in reindeer antler and in wood, and the women's taste is just as sure when they sew their caps, belts and other things. The children have an aesthetic sense from birth. Once, when I walked together with Elle, she remarked as we passed by a new sled a Finn had made, "Fy, how ugly that sled is!" At a fleeting glance the sled was like all other Lapp sleds, but when you looked more closely it wasn't elegantly shaped and the parts didn't fit together well. The child saw this immediately and was offended by its ugliness.

IX

NOW THAT AUTUMN HAD BEGUN IN EARNEST and all summer pastimes eliminated, conversations and the whole of life turned solely on the reindeer. The subject can never be exhausted; it's the only thing that totally interests the Lapps. A visitor they'd been in contact with—even if he were the king himself—pales in memory and is paltry compared to any event related to the herd. The tourists with their frivolous questions, even their presence, are erased from the Lapps' minds as soon as they depart the summer settlement, even well before. They're barely mentioned when they go out of the tent. Fortunately for themselves, the Lapps are generally single-minded and healthily egotistical. The reindeer herd and their family relationships, the religious and the mystical are what fill their lives.

The Lapp feels at home with these things and can display his skills. Out in the wilderness he copes with life and situations. There he is superior and self-esteem increases. Other people become insignificant—he scorns them. And why should he feel kindly toward strangers from the other race, who for thousands of years have only been his enemies and done everything to destroy him and his property? How should he suddenly come to trust those individuals who now sincerely wish him well? He has never before met *genuine* goodwill and true friendship on an equal footing. The Lapp often encounters a certain friendliness, but in most cases it's so superficial and condescending that he, with his fine instinct for people, doesn't allow himself to be blinded by it.

Meanwhile, the Lapp has always understood that to be oppressed is to develop a great deal of sharpness and flexibility that, along with his intelligence, makes it easy for him to adjust how he responds to whatever he faces. Lively as he is, it's easy for him to pretend to be more interested and obliging than was his intention when all's said and done. He believes in little besides his own people, and why should he? From ancient times down to quite recently he's been an object of taxation; no one was his friend, no one advised or helped when he was squeezed. The priests wiped out his old religion in a hard and unsympathetic manner. The authorities pressed him for taxes; the government made laws and regulations that restricted his freedom. The farmers fleeced him and killed him and his reindeer. And yet people reproach the Lapp for his distrustfulness. Why should he have so much more of Christ in him than the people around him, who boast about their old Christianity and culture?

In more recent times there are those who work to improve the circumstances of the Lapps and to understand them and their way of living. The Swedish state has seen the significance of the Lapps as a people and the claims of nomadism to the wild regions of the high mountains where farming can't flourish (but hopefully they also understand that the Lapps can only get their income from the barren high mountains when they have access in summer to grass for the reindeer and in winter, during the hardest time, have access to the pine forests). The time is past when one "squeezed taxes" from the Lapps. Now, on the contrary, they're quite favored in that respect. Yet that situation hasn't lasted long enough that it's really sunk in, in such a way that it could wipe out centuries of old mistrust for everything called government, the authorities, and "the gentry." The Lapps still have difficulties grasping and believing the fact they now have sincere friends in Sweden, people who completely understand them and who do great and effective work to preserve and promote their occupations and their survival as a people. You must not blame them for being slow to embrace confidence and warm feelings for these new friends. Wild game that has been tracked and hunted from all sides for many years will also have difficulty believing in friendly overtures.

The daily life of the Lapps is far from "poverty-stricken." The exterior setting is magnificent enough: mountains, sun, dark, storms, the huge sky, stars, northern lights, and a vast countryside. Who in our society has such a backdrop for his work? Add to this the variety and excitement of reindeer herding, profit and loss, the battle with nature, the endless moving around, the coziness of domestic life in the tent with family and the connection with relatives. There's not much time to be bored in a Lapp tent in the high mountains for one who lives there. They are, of course, other diversions, other comforts, and other kinds of variety than those we're used to, but they're no less worthy—nor hard to lose for those born to this life.

That the mountain Lapps' existence is difficult can't be denied, yet the hardships are divided equally among the adult family members. The men take on the heaviest part of the workload, perhaps nowadays especially when the women are more often spared the reindeer herding, at least the married women, who never participate in ordinary herding. It's the job of the men and unmarried women to herd the reindeer and manage everything connected with it. And with the migrations the work is divided so that the men round up the herd or bring them to the vicinity of the tent, whereupon they choose draft reindeer, and the women take care of packing up everything while the reindeer stand there.

If it is a pack reindeer to be used, they get all the chests ready and set them two by two, of equal weight, next to each other with the harnesses and coverings that go with them, so that the loading can happen quickly. The reindeer must never wait. On the other hand, you yourself have to wait. We had everything ready for our move from Abrantjåkko. The sleds were laced up (from here we were to move out in a caravan of sleds, and what we didn't need until next spring was left behind at the same spot where the sleds had been previously, well covered with birch bark and turf, over which was laid tree branches; that's how the Lapps hide their things here and there in the mountains, freely accessible, though theft from these storage sites is quite infrequent). The tent was completely empty. Yet only in the evening did they gather the reindeer, so we couldn't travel on that day. So the sleds had to be opened and the bedding taken out, along with the most essential kitchen utensils. But an empty tent like that, without twigs on the ground, is a cold place to be.

Even before it was light, the men went out to fetch the reindeer, and we left very early. A frosty violet winter sun had just managed to peek over the mountains and to throw a soft sheen over the beautiful long caravan, which wound around the mountainside in colorful stripes. The earth was white and the full arc of the sky very clear, but the snow cover was thin and the sleds were roughly treated. They bumped over rocks and uneven terrain, rolled completely over, and had to be continually righted, which wasn't an easy job at all. It fell to my willing lot to keep an eye on the strings, since I didn't have a string to lead myself.[16] No one is allowed to be idle, and the help you can give during the move is gratefully accepted. There's always some anxiety during a Lapp migration, a certain hurriedness, which stems in part from the reindeer's strength being quite limited. They can only go without food and rest for a certain amount of time and don't have the tough stamina of horses. If one gets tired, it lies down, and it can't handle being forced up to continue very many times before it drops in earnest and can no longer do anything more. Both the reindeer and the Lapps walk steadily and fast. They set their pacing from the start and keep to that speed hour after hour.

"Yes, the Lapp walks quickly," said Sara. "He knows that the darkness and snow will come."

Behind the last sled in the caravan they tow a very resin-filled piece of firewood, from which they hew chips to make an easy fire during the early days of winter when the Lapps live in the high mountains and in the topmost edge of the birch forest. Sara pointed at this piece of wood and said, "This is as valuable as wheat bread."

We walked and walked many hours over the bogs and hills. Both people and animals were tired, but it wasn't until afternoon, after the light was judged to be evening, that the sweet pause for coffee arrived. The burdens were taken off the reindeer, and they scraped the snow away from the ground and ate lichen while they rested.[17] We gathered all the wood for the fire. The fuel was mainly old brittle tree stumps left behind here and there and that were dry and easily ignited. They were much sought after during these halts along the migration path, when it came to making a fire quickly. It was cold up here on the slope above the actual tree line, and not everyone could enjoy the fire fully. On the windy side sat the housewife, who boiled coffee and saw to the small children. They were warm without being bothered by the smoke. On the other side of the fire, you were almost scorched and choked by fire and smoke. And if you had been sitting in the snow a little ways from the fire, the warmth you'd acquired during the trekking soon evaporated; your clothes froze fast to the snow. Yet the coffee restored our spirits, and with renewed strength we kept walking. While Sara stood ready with her caravan and waited for something or other that needed sorting out, her big tame reindeer Leksu began to chew eagerly on Sara's old fur parka, which was hairless in front and shone with wear and grease.

Once more we walked a couple of hours. Nikki gave me his string to lead, since he had something else to do. It was my first real trek with Sara and Nikki, and I was quite reassured at his comment, *Don leat sávri vázzit.* "You have a lot of staying power as a walker." They had been very hesitant to take me along and had tried to frighten me off by vividly describing the cold, storms, and all sorts of difficulties. It definitely would have been inconvenient for them if I'd grown tired during the trekking and couldn't keep up. They would have had to take extra measures on my behalf. Therefore I was happy at his encouragement and that, without more ado, he trusted me with the string. There were many new things for me to learn, now that the autumn migration had begun—literally, a mass of new vocabulary to grasp. Because of that Biettar said, "Yes, you can speak the summer language. Now you'll learn the language of winter."

It was evening when we arrived in Pirtimis-ætno. Snow lay thin on the ground; only willows and juniper bushes gave the earth a little dark color. Everything was frozen, and the wide, smooth river was iced over, an enormous zigzag that reflected the quiet yellow sky and the tall, withered vegetation at its edges. The ice had only appeared overnight, and higher up the waterfall roared. Large flocks of white ptarmigans ran around like pearls in the landscape. The untied reindeer spread out and moved in small groups and singly to graze, and, little by little, as they satisfied the worst of their hunger and thirst, they approached the main herd up on the mountain. Our tent was erected on a small rise near a willow thicket. Since Nikki was already migrating using sleds in his reindeer strings, we couldn't, like the others with pack reindeer, set up on the other side of the river, but had to wait to cross until the ice could bear the heavy sleds.

Shattered fragments of ice clinked when people and reindeer stepped out into the river and waded through the deep strong current. The smaller children rode on the reindeer; the older children were carried over. In the middle of the river I saw a young woman with her cradle on her back in water up to her waist, carefully wading across, pulling the string of reindeer after her. It was early in November and it froze hard that evening. The men stayed partly dry in crossing; their reindeer-skin leggings go up to their thighs and their well-greased shoes are completely watertight when the ankle bands are wound firmly around them. But the women's trousers are of wool, and their leather leggings go only a bit above their knees. Naturally, it didn't take long before smoke and sparks appeared above the tents across the way.

It didn't get dark that evening, for the moon was yellow and enormous over Raggisvare in the clear frost air. We walked a few steps in between the willows and cut twigs with the "big knife" for the layer under the sleeping area. Twigs and firewood were sparse here—you couldn't sleep on anything soft or get warm. Here and there in the mountains stood birch trees of course, but they were scrublike, less than a meter tall, with a small, thick gnarled trunk about fifteen centimeters long, which almost crept toward the earth, stunted by wind and frost. While Elle and I walked and cut twigs and the moon hung there as if very close across the low mountain, Elle pointed to it and asked if I knew what you could see in it up there—well, it was a Lapp, who one evening went out to steal reindeer and in the midst of it, the moon came up and illuminated everything. The Lapp was angry at the interruption; he ran home to his tent and fetched his tar cake and tar whisk and began to tar the moon black. "But the moon sucked him up and there he still stands, with the whisk in his raised right hand and the cake in the left. You can easily see that it is a Lapp." *Sápmelaš lea dego gotka.* "The Lapp is like an ant, skinny in the middle—belted." Above and below his fur bulges and balloons out.

When after some days the ice was strong enough, we moved again. The draft reindeer weren't brought over to this side of the river, but the sleds were pulled down from the tents and over the ice. They were heavy to drag through twigs and over frozen tussocks, and this was women's work when the men were out after the reindeer. Later in the afternoon all the caravans were organized for the departure on a slope between the tents. The sun shone low, far out on the horizon. The long blue shadows shifted perpetually in the shining rays of the sun in this tumult of reindeer, people, dogs, and loaded sleds. The animals snorted, the Lapps laughed or cursed, depending on whether things were going well or not for them in their work. The tents were taken down and packed up; only the fire pits flared up and smoked a little. Some families were completely finished with tying everything up and now emptied the contents of the coffee pots in haste. A cup of coffee just before you loaded up was customary. The cups were quickly packed in a small round wooden basket; this, along with the bag of sugar and the valuable reindeer milk in a bladder, together with the coffeepot, were carefully wrapped and placed in an easily accessible spot in one of the reindeer packs.

The strings now set off from the hillside in a long colorful caravan out into the snow-bright landscape.

When the mountain people migrate, it's always rather silently. You almost never hear loud shouting or lively conversation. Besides, sounds vanish in the enormous space. After some difficult travel among stones and willow shrubs, and a strenuous but short climb, we reached the mountain plateau of Puollamåive around sunset, where all vegetation ceased and the snow pack was thick. Up here was a snowy owl on a big boulder right beside the path. It didn't fly off but turned its head calmly and looked at the long strange caravan that striped the plateau. Low in the south, far off, was the sun at the edge of the earth, heavy and glowing red. In front of it stretched a marsh eight kilometers wide, full of lakes of fire; in the middle of the marsh low mountain ridges rose up behind each other. Their crests were red and the clouds dark violet. Down below, the earth lay wild and hot in the sun's fire, but up here on the mountain the snow glimmered in the pure light of paradise and the long gilt-edged clouds moved steadily along with the caravan, as if we wandered right into the heavens. The reindeer stepped lightly and lifted their antler crowns up to the evening sky, which glowed in the very oriental colors of the Lapps. It was a sacred procession traveling away from ordinary death and darkness. Everyone was silent; only one of the women sang softly, a pair of verses from a hymn. In front of the caravan, up toward the next mountain, the herd of several thousand animals was being driven. Nikki was at the tip with the lead reindeer; after them came all the reindeer in a broad wedge, held together by herders and dogs.

When we'd crossed the mountain plateau and the sun had gone down, the profound feeling from earlier dissolved almost into playfulness. We began to chat among ourselves when two strings came so near each other that conversation was possible. Or we talked among ourselves or with the children or to the reindeer. Down the mountain slope people and animals paraded in merry confusion. There were no difficulties that day either, only the disturbance made by an untamed reindeer tied behind the last sled in Inga's string. It carried on wildly from time to time, leaped to the side, struggled, fell, and rolled around; in short, it wore itself out with anger and fear, so that its blue tongue hung out. However, little by little it grew meeker, and it wouldn't be long before you could harness it to a sled and link it to the string behind a very tame and sedate reindeer.

The moon was high when we swarmed down into the frost-white birch forest to set up camp. The caravan stopped and the whole herd came like a storm pell-mell down on us from the mountain. In an instant the quiet white forest was alive with sound, color, and movement. There were enough people to raise the tent since the herders had left the reindeer herd, which would soon lie down to rest after grazing, so Inga and I went off immediately to fell trees for wood (it's infrequent that the Lapps chop down trees very near their tents. Trees nearby are needed to hang things on, when you don't intend to stay long enough to set up a proper storehouse). Remarkably enough, you don't pity the trees felled by a Lapp's ax. When you're in the high mountains you soon learn the birch is invaluable for those who travel there. It's as if the birch grows in the mountains, up there where nothing else can make itself useful, only to make possible the existence of the Lapps.

X

Here on the south side of Puollamåive, at the edge of the birch forest, we came to stay quite a long time, longer than the reindeer liked. The old corral we found was repaired; and almost every day the reindeer were inside the enclosure, in part so they could continue to be separated and in part so they could be milked. Around the middle of November the milking would as good as cease altogether.

A neighboring *siida* half a dozen kilometers off also used our corral when they wanted to gather the herd for separation. They had their tents completely above the forest, actually on the bare mountain, and had to content themselves with twigs for fuel. The corral there was in use almost every day, and many guests came to visit from other *siidas*. Some brought reindeer to be separated out, and others came to get the reindeer that had been separated out. The whole autumn until Christmas, almost the whole winter, the men traveled from *siida* to *siida* to fetch reindeer and gradually bring the herd to its full count.

For a couple of days no reindeer had been in the corral; a heavy frost fog hampered the reindeer herding for a quite a while. The trees had short frost spikes on every little twig, and the faintest puff of wind set the forest to tinkling. In the morning the sky was the same color as an old-fashioned Provence rose, and the frosted trees resembled smooth, dark squirrel skin in the reddish-gray light. The tent with its striped wool covering stood in the middle of this fairytale magnificence and looked warm and safe. Light shone from all its chinks, and the spark-filled smoke slipped up through the trees.

It was so quiet. All the reindeer herders and dogs were away, but later on in the day came the sound of the herd on the frozen snow and the dogs' loud sharp baying. Soon afterward, the reindeer marched past, down the hill. Everyone in the *siida* had heard the noise and everyone hurried up to the corral. The man with the lead reindeer had already reached the entrance of the corral and continued to coax them, calling, *cus, cus*.[18] Behind the herd and alongside it, the Lapps jumped up and down and swung sticks and caps, while the dogs hunted down the fugitives. Rapidly the animals rushed into the corral, and the Lapps were already poised to close the opening with logs they had ready, when the ground shook almost like an earthquake, the branches snapped, part of the corral was trampled down; the whole herd "turned" at lightning speed. You would be severely damaged if a couple of thousand reindeer galloped over you. Sara fell like that once without being able to get up;

her face was plunged into the snow. She was nearly suffocated and trampled to death before she was rescued. This time the herd didn't trample anyone, but the reindeer headed for the mountains and didn't return to the corral that day. The Lapps were tired and sweaty; many of them had been out longer than usual because of the fog. In such weather you could easily lose too many reindeer if you didn't watch out.

A couple of the young men had been away two days. They must have lost their way, and since they had no food with them we began to worry about them. Biettar went looking for them with a sack of provisions, but came home without finding them. The next day, however, they returned, and we were able to hear of their adventure. They'd traveled quite far to the south to gather reindeer—which always move south during autumn—but they found no reindeer, and they lost their way in the dense fog that prevailed day and night. They walked and walked for two days and nights; they had nothing to eat and didn't dare rest, since it was freezing hard. The younger man threw himself down to sleep over and over, but the older forced him up again. Finally, they were lucky enough to come to a turf hut where some Finns stayed now and again when they were out trapping ptarmigans. It was unoccupied, but they discovered a small store of food left behind: flour, coffee, and a bottle of spirits. While the oldest began to build up the fire, bake bread, and brew coffee, the youngest tasted the spirits and immediately was overcome. When they'd eaten and rested, they set out once more and were immediately lucky enough to find a group of reindeer, and with help from their tracks they found the right direction. But they couldn't go home that night either. They had to protect the herd they'd come across. Not until the morning of the third day did they arrive at the corral, where they worked many hours. It was evening before they came into the tent and were able to eat and rest. But there wasn't time to stay long in the tent—already the next day they had to go out again. This story wasn't taken with any great seriousness. The youngest was teased and mocked for having tasted spirits, and not much more was said of such a trifling matter, which can happen to any reindeer herder.

The daily use of alcohol by the Lapps is quite minimal, and that applies to the southern part of Lapland as much as in the North, where I've been able to observe it. It's both said and written that the Lapps drink stoutly. That anyone believes this is probably due to people seeing them drunk at the annual fairs and the few times they come to the city; however, it doesn't justify labeling a whole people as drunkards. The use of spirits at home in the tent is almost zero. I've only once seen a Lapp take a little cognac as medicine, and the man was really ill. Merely that he could have a bottle of cognac in the tent for many months and just use it as medicine speaks clearly enough of true abstinence. This example is far from unique. In the almost sixteen months I was among the Jukkasjärvi and Karasuando Lapps, I never saw anything to suggest that the Lapps were especially inclined to lust after alcohol—far from it. Of course, I know that you can encounter some who get intoxicated when they come to Tromsø in the summer, but you can find drunken men in every country. This moderation in alcohol consumption is much more admirable and remarkable, since we know that in former times Lapps were heavily into drinking. In those days the farmers sold them spirits and took payment in reindeer. This is how many Lapps became impoverished and sank down to become reindeer herders for the farmers.

Since then the farmers have had to give up their private distilleries, and almost everywhere they're not allowed to own reindeer, so this traffic is over. But these circumstances, along with current difficulties in Sweden obtaining spirits, can't be the only reason for the Lapps' moderating their use of alcohol. The reason lies deeper. The Lapps are a vigorous people, good at surviving, who've seen the harmful effects of alcohol, seen where it leads. They have, quite simply, turned away little by little from alcohol—without temperance agitation and big words. It's like the way a powerful constitution gets over an illness without a doctor. (They did have a temperance agitator, in the north of Lappmark—the pastor Lars Levi Laestadius, whose work was great and full of importance in this area as in so many others.)

In any case it's remarkable that the Lapps could have preserved themselves as a people and preserved their racial characteristics to such a high degree in spite of strong influences and pressure from all sides. It testifies to a surprising health at bottom and an ability to survive—to the degree that it would be a moral crime to restrict and undermine it. Yet this can be done comparatively easily—the modern "humane" culture is a worse enemy for the Lapps than the spirits of the old days, the taxes, and many sorts of persecution. All those things the Lapps have survived and conquered with flying colors, whereas schools, residences for children, and the settlers break down their strength day by day. The strangely mistaken view that a settler, no matter where he makes his home in the old Lapp areas, is a more valuable element than a prosperous nomad, that's what takes the ground from under the Lapps' feet. It's a common perception that agriculture is more worthwhile than nomadism, but the "agriculture" of the settlers is, in the vast majority of cases, not agriculture at all. They live—often enough very miserably—from harvesting hay in the Lapps' old countryside or in some wretched bog somewhere.

If settlement is continually favored at the expense of nomadism, reindeer culture will very likely be suppressed or in any case limited to a meaningless minimum. Then it will turn out—unfortunately too late—that instead of prosperous Lapps you'll get poor "agriculturists" who can do nothing with the land in the high mountains and who need support. When you deprive a person of the possibility of a livelihood, the strongest constitution has to succumb.

On the other hand, the Lapps won't go under because they're a primitive people with an innate lack of vigor. All things considered, it appears that the theory of primitive people dying out doesn't hold up. There are large numbers of primitive people who to this very day steadily live on, even though for a hundred years they've been sentenced to death.

The young people, always out with the reindeer, don't lead a life wholly to be envied, especially when the pasturage is bad in the high mountains, as it is now, and the reindeer move steadily down to graze. The Lapps maintain that the reindeer know for certain where to find food and that's where they go. When the grazing isn't good where the herd is, it's almost as difficult to keep reindeer from going down to the pine forests in autumn as it is to keep them from moving into the grassy areas in the spring. The reindeer, who otherwise always travel counter to the wind, don't obey this instinct in the autumn, when they crave the forest and in spring when they crave the grass. If the pasturage is fine and other conditions good, the Lapps can control the migrations and direct the herd. At the moment the pasturage wasn't good, however, and the reindeer moved farther and farther from the camp. Still, the herders brought them home in the evening, or in any case close to the tents. When those who remained home heard the barking of the dogs and the sound of the herd, they knew the different dogs by their voices and therefore knew which herders were nearby.

The atmosphere turned festive when the reindeer spread out among the tents, their bells jingling as they eagerly kicked and dug around for urine. When it was bright out, either from the moon or stars, the family went around inspecting their property. They pulled their arms in toward the body, if they were cold, so the fur arms hung empty. Carefully and unobtrusively they stole around taking a look at the reindeer, according to their markings and the like. The dogs also prowled quietly around; they knew well enough that the reindeer were sacred and untouchable when they were walking among the tents. The children couldn't withstand the temptation to throw the lasso at one or another very tame old reindeer, which merely shook its head at the disturbance. They were certainly not all so good-natured, for when I attempted to touch one of the tame draft reindeer up around its antlers, it kicked my hand away with its foreleg, so that it hurt for a long time afterward.

The adults soon went into the tents again; they could quickly get an overview of the herd, see which animals were missing and which were unfamiliar; but the children stayed outside a long time. They were carefully practicing the art of recognizing reindeer. They noted the countless variations of antler shapes and their names, the various colors of their hides, and the characteristics of the reindeer's build and whole appearance, including the different sounds of the bells. Given so much regular time together with the herd, the children acquire, in an easy and natural way, the knowledge so necessary to become a skilled herder. If all that isn't practiced from childhood, almost in play, it's extremely difficult, even quite impossible to learn as an adult. Certainly the desire and natural interest will be lacking, and without true desire and interest in the herd, existence is only an intolerable succession of overwork and danger. If, on the other hand, the child is equipped with knowledge of the country and district, of the herd and its character, of the training of dogs and their talents and, along with all that, with a knowledge of what he can take on and can tolerate, then he can handle his work and can find meaning and joy in it.

The story of the two young men from the *siida* who got lost inspired Sara to tell of something similar when we sat in one of the tents with our work. The Lapps have an extremely developed sense of place, and it's very seldom that anyone gets lost, but in dense fog and in snowstorms it can certainly happen (the Lapps themselves say that in the darkness they can easily orient themselves, but in fog they can get lost, something they can neither understand nor explain). A young girl from a neighboring *siida* had been with the reindeer in the dense fog, and when she wanted to return home in the evening it was completely impossible to find the tent. She walked many hours, but finally lay down to sleep. When she woke the next morning, she saw to her great astonishment that she was lying in the vicinity of the tent.

If the Lapps get lost in a snowstorm it's very common that they let themselves "snow down." It's not nearly as dangerous to allow yourself to be buried in a snowdrift when you're wearing warm clothes as to get to the point of exhaustion and then fall down in the snow—that is certain death. Jonna, the

man from Kattuvuoma I trekked with during the migration, was once surprised by a violent snowstorm in the mountains at night. Immediately, as
soon as he noticed that he couldn't get through it, he lay down in the snow
and allowed the snow to drift over him, while he calmly slept through the
night until dawn and he could orient himself. The single precaution that the
Lapps make in such cases is to place one of their skis or ski poles up by the
side of their head so they can dig themselves out again should lots of snow fall
in the night.

Sara also told me that the year before a Lapp girl from another *siida* went
out in the evening to gather the reindeer, but when a terrible snowstorm came,
she didn't dare stay out in the wilderness at night, but tried to reach home.
On the way home she got completely lost; they didn't find her until the following spring. Sara believed it was the girl's own fault that she "went missing."
When such fearful weather comes over a reindeer herder in the wilderness, he
should merely follow the herd, going after the "big bell" (the largest of the
untamed bulls has the biggest bell around his neck; he is the herd's leader and
the other reindeer follow him). It can be difficult enough to keep up with the
reindeer, since they're very restless in storms and run to find shelter, but if you
can follow them you're sure to save your life. When the weather has calmed
down, fresh herders always go out to gather the reindeer, and it's customary to
always look for the big bell first, the lead reindeer of the main herd. Those
who have been out are rescued. Sara spent stormy nights out like this many
times when young. Of course it doesn't always save your life to follow the herd.
If you can't manage because of hunger and cold, it doesn't matter if you're near
the herd. If, in autumn, you're quite thinly clad and can't manage to build a fire
either for lack of fuel or because of the weather, the situation grows critical. In
most cases it's more cold than hunger that kills a Lapp who's gotten lost. They
actually have a great deal of practice in being hungry.

When a reindeer herder gets ready to go out in the morning, as a rule
he enjoys only a couple of cups of coffee. "If I eat, I'll be too heavy to ski." But
he stuffs the hay painstakingly into his shoes, wraps the ankle bands so they
don't ride up, takes his lasso around his shoulder, and puts on a cap, or *luhkka*.
Nothing on his back, no food, only the ski pole in his right hand. Often the
herders from various tents gather and conduct a short deliberation before
they head out. After that, feet in the skis, off they go in one another's tracks,
until farther along they separate and each goes in his own direction to find
and gather the herd. If there have been herders with the reindeer during the
night, the arriving relief finds out from them where the animals are and other

necessary information. If they themselves herded the day before and allowed the herd to be alone during the night hours, which is very common in the winter, when there aren't wolves in the vicinity, they know the reindeer's habits and territory so well that they understand more or less where they should search for the animals. If the pasturage is good, these animals don't go far between resting periods, but wander slowly, grazing up toward the wind. In deep snow it's hard for the reindeer to get around; they tread as far as possible in one another's hoof prints when they're going a greater distance. The lead reindeer goes at the head and treads the path for the others. When one grows tired, it falls out and another takes over the lead. Yet not all the reindeer can and wish to find the way and tread the path, the Lapps say. It's clear that in this fashion a reindeer herd can't move faster during one night than a herder on his long smooth skis can quickly catch up with them in the morning, especially when he has the tracks and the wind to guide him. If those things fail, he can, with his sharp practiced hearing, listen for where they might be found.

The reindeer herder's objective is to go around the herd and "ring it in." If the animals are to be gathered and brought to another place elsewhere, the dogs are used. If the dogs haven't been given working orders, they follow right on the heels of the herder. A smart dog closely observes every movement of the herd, and as long as it moves steadily forward, he doesn't do anything in particular; however, he's ready as soon as any little irregularity occurs. If it's as straightforward as fetching a reindeer that's bolted from the main herd, the herder merely needs to make a hand gesture. The dog races off and brings the reindeer back, however far he has to pursue it. During the deep snow of winter neither reindeer nor dog can move quickly. If, on the other hand, the whole herd changes direction, the dog is given a particular order, after which he runs ahead and meets the reindeer, so that they turn and go in the desired direction.

If a reindeer herder happens to have a poor dog, the herder must do the dog's work himself. He can do it, however hard that is to believe. He can catch up with the fleeing reindeer, and "turn" the herd himself; in short, everything a dog is otherwise used for. In this way he can manage to ski many miles a day without a single energizing bite of food or any ordinary rest. And if, for any reason, he can't leave the herd at night, he has to content himself with the rest he can get between the times the reindeer are feeding. He can lean against a rock for an hour or two, until the animals again begin to move, or he can make a bed out of twigs, if he can find them, and rest with his outer fur pulled over his head if it's so cold that he has to protect his face from frost. If his feet are freezing, he can bury himself halfway in the snow, if it's the snow season, and in that way keep himself warm while he rests. He can also be fortunate enough to have a faithful comrade in his dog. If the herder sits down to rest, many dogs have the habit, much appreciated, of lying on top of the feet. If the herder has the time and opportunity to make himself a fire, of course he does that, but sometimes for various reasons he can't have a fire. Perhaps there's nothing to burn nearby or the weather makes impossible to tend a fire. Nor has he very often time to collect as much fuel as could maintain a fire. In this way, a night without fire in solitary darkness can last a long time. You never hear, however, the Lapp talk about it or complain, or about cold or hunger either.

But when he's finally come home to the tent after half or a whole day's fasting if not longer, he satisfies himself with food and coffee in very large quantities. Yet a Lapp never greedily grabs at the food, even if he's been without food for a long time. He preserves his calm balance, eats slowly and in silence, and while he eats he is holy and inviolate (*Bora ráfis*, "Eat in peace," is the housewife's friendly admonition when someone bothers you with questions during a meal). Silence during meals is demanded and offered. While he eats, he's free not to share any news; he's not pestered with questions or conversation of any kind, even though he's sitting there with information that couldn't be more interesting and though those around him are tortured by curiosity. When the herder is finally finished with eating and coffee drinking, he begins to see to his shoes, changing the hay if it's wet or laying it out to dry by the fire, putting other boots on and turning over the damp ones he's just taken off. Before they're hung up to dry, they're carefully pulled into shape and stuffed with hay to hold their form. A Lapp is more than a little vain when it concerns feet and footwear. Then he changes from his heavy herding fur parka to a thinner fur. He hangs his gloves up to dry, and while all that is going on he can, very likely reluctantly, give a few pieces of news about the herd. Gradually the most necessary of what he has to share comes out. But afterward he lies down to sleep, deeply and completely lost to the world around for several hours. In almost all the Lapp tents you can see sleeping menfolk during the day, tired returned herders. Strangers who come to the Lapp settlement and see the men sleeping during the day often draw the mistaken conclusion that the Lapps are lazy and have nothing to do.

When we, by reason of the foreman's being away, couldn't begin the migration, the herders had to follow the herd on their way down. They gradually got so far away from the tents that they couldn't get home to the *siida* every

day to eat and drink. They equipped themselves to be away for longer periods and took with them bread, butter, sugar, coffee, and tobacco. Fresh meat
they could get on their own by slaughtering a reindeer, if that was necessary.
Besides provisions for themselves and their dogs, they took with them half an
old tent cloth and as bedding only an old, almost hairless reindeer skin, along
with a very large coil of hay for shoes, twisted willows to use for ski bindings, a pair of extra shoes, a coffee kettle and a small pot to cook meat in, an
ax, binoculars, and a gun ready to fire. Now there would be camping out.

The other herders from the same herd had similar equipment, and they
naturally stayed together. When they were out in the vicinity of the herd and
had chosen a fairly good central place in the mountains, they set up their little
lávvu, as such a small temporary tent is called. It consisted of some birch
trunks, thin at the crowns, straight and crooked, which were the best they
could find now up there at tree line. Over the round tree frame made by the
trunks they spread the half tent cloth they'd brought along. It couldn't reach
all the way around, but the opening served as a door.

Yet this small airy dwelling, which was really only a shelter against the
wind, furnished a welcome haven for all the young herders of both sexes. They
had fire, food, and good humor, were surrounded by reindeer and felt at home.
That they often worked devilishly hard and had to do without all the usual
conveniences never occurred to them. There's naturally not much time for
socializing; the reindeer take up all the attention of the herders, who have
to take their rest when they can. Yet all the same, the jokes fly quickly and
playfully in the evening when a group is at home to eat and rest. Everyone
picks up wood for the fire on the way back to the *lávvu*, takes a branch, a tree,
or a lapful of twigs along. In this way each brings along fuel to cook his food
and coffee. When the stew pot steams and the fire warms, fatigue disappears;
they talk over the day's experiences, the position of the herd, and everything
that goes along with that. They tease, flirt, think up pranks. The dogs sit
sleepy and hungry in front of the fire and wait their turn to get food. Around
this lovely little bright spot the darkness is thick, which gives the place a cheerful, pleasant air.

When the meat is eaten and the shoes are filled with dry grass, everyone lies
down to sleep, fully dressed. There is, in fact, no other bedding than the worn-
out reindeer hide on a thick layer of twigs. Some might have a tattered rug
over themselves (you only take old shabby things along to the *lávvu*, because
for the most part things are unattended and exposed to wind and weather and
sparks from the fire). As a pillow they use one another or a bundle at hand. If

there are many people, they can lie down in a ring around the fire to have room. In the course of a short time, it grows quiet, the fire collapses, the darkness advances, and the little bright spot from earlier is swallowed up by the wilderness.

But a night's sleep in the *lávvu* can be easily disturbed if one of the herders returns and immediately starts the fire going again, breaking branches and putting them in the fire. He lifts a couple of legs away that have come too close. He shoves a dog aside and moves one of the sleepers just enough so that he can squeeze out a place to sit and heat his food. When he's eaten and drunk, he shoves his way into a spot between the others and falls asleep. The night's rest can also be disturbed in other ways. Biettar told me that one night when he was alone in the *lávvu*, the "big bell" came right up there, restless and clanking his bell around. Of course Biettar immediately awoke, jumped up, picked up his gun and put on his skis. A wolf must be on the prowl when even the lead reindeer, the wildest bull in the whole herd, ventured forth to ask for help.

Sure enough, he found the herd milling wildly about, in total confusion. He didn't get the offender, though; it had fled without having done any harm when it noticed Biettar nearby. Biettar gathered some of the herd in his care and skied around it. Of course he spent the rest of the night with the reindeer.

Life in the *lávvu* and with the reindeer has so little to do with the normal reckoning of time that one who's been out a long time can easily mix up the sequence of days. Once, when Biettar came home and his sister, in the course of a story, came to mention that something had happened last Saturday, he asked, in all seriousness, "When was it Saturday?"

He could also be excused for making mistakes about the days, for in the eight months I lived with his parents, Biettar wasn't at home in the tent a whole week running at any time, but always with the reindeer. Biettar was a zealous and skilled herder, something he was aware of himself. He wasn't alone in being self-confident. Čæppe was too, to the same high degree as his master. He was the most skillful dog around, sparkling with energy and intelligence. Along with that he was a good dog; he never harmed a little reindeer calf, a virtue not all Lapp dogs possessed. If Čæppe came upon such a newborn calf in spring, defenselessly toddling around on long legs, he merely jumped in front of it to play. This had been noticed often. He could therefore be used even during calving season, when the Lapps see if they can manage without dogs, since the dogs frequently harm the calves or drive the pregnant cows too hard. Biettar said that even if someone offered a thousand crowns for Čæppe, he would never sell him.

Čæppe unfortunately didn't get a chance to live out his life (the Lapps calculate a dog's life to be no more than six or seven years; then he's worn out and is killed). Čæppe was in fact a fighter who resorted to using his teeth on rivals when he grew hungry for the opposite sex. It was his fate to die for the sake of his hot blood. One autumn day, while the reindeer were in the corral and everyone was very busy there, a dog fight arose among the pack of dogs outside. Čæppe was vanquished. When two dogs fight and the others see which one is weaker, they attack the weak one together. Čæppe didn't have the strength to fight off his bigger opponents. No Lapp saw what was happening. Otherwise, they tend to break up fighting dogs. When later they let the reindeer out of the corral, there lay Čæppe, dead and pitifully mauled.

XI

WHILE WE WERE CAMPED ON PUOLLAMÅIVE's south side, the *isit*, or the *siida*'s foreman, together with a couple of others, skied to Kattuvuoma to pick up some sleds that were needed. No *siida* moves before the *siida*'s foreman decides it should happen. He also decides where to set up camp and attends to the *siida*'s interests, both internal and external. Now, however, our foreman had left for Kattuvuoma and the trip stretched out a long time for various unforeseen reasons. We couldn't begin our move. There was much grumbling about this long absence—"the sled-fetching trip makes folk herdless." That is to say, the herders couldn't hold back the reindeer. They contained the main herd well enough, but large and small clusters snuck away and went south in search of better grazing. Among them, Sara's tame old Leksu had disappeared. And it wasn't a good thing for reindeer to be descending alone now in the big forest during slaughtering time, for that's where the farmers lived, and when the Lapps were up in the highest edge of the birch forest, they couldn't control what happened to their animals so far away. Along with that, such unguarded reindeer could result in having to pay compensation for damage to the hay.

The eternal hay compensation that makes the relationship so tense between farmers and Lapps could be prevented rather easily, if the farmers were ordered to take their hay home within a reasonable time. If the hay wasn't taken home by a more definite, fixed date, then the farmer himself would have to bear the blame for what happened. Currently these miserable haystacks in the reindeer's way act as bait that makes for a not-inconsiderable extra income.

Hay compensation in Sweden and grass compensation in Norway are in many cases nothing more than pure extortion from the Lapps. Both countries should make it a point of honor to abolish this unjust relationship. Certainly, there are Lapps who are careless about watching the reindeer, but it's far from as bad as complaints make it sound. The Talma Lapps, with whom I traveled in the autumn and winter, were skilled and conscientious herders. Still, they couldn't prevent some groups of reindeer leaving the herd and going off by themselves; such a group is particularly impossible to watch. There's no over-abundance of manpower among the Lapps.

Finally, around November 17, we started moving away from Puollamâive toward the mountain of Tavanjunje. It was the first time I would attempt to drive a sled pulled by a reindeer. Before we left, Sara ordered me to wear a heavy fur parka. Nikki said when he saw me, "Now you look like other people." The dogs obviously felt the same; they no longer squinted distrustfully at me, and I didn't need to do what I had before—arm myself with a stick before going to the other tents. Lapp dogs have, like other dogs, a sharp eye for clothes, and as long as I wore woolen clothes (summer clothes—the fur parka was so heavy that for the longest time I tried to avoid it) here in wintertime, I was suspect.

We had to walk the first part of the route away from the tents. Only twenty-five centimeters of snow had fallen, and tussocks and rocks sixty cen-timeters high stuck out everywhere. It was enormous work to plod forward in the snow and bumpy terrain with the physical weight of the fur on me. I felt my body inside this tremendous envelope like a thin pole that's been loaded too heavily.

In Sara's string were two driving sleds, one for her and one for me, and when we came to more or less smooth sledding conditions, I was given per-mission to seat myself in the sled, if I couldn't make progress any other way. This had to happen while the caravan was moving, and the heavy parka didn't allow me to be quick or graceful. I got myself placed in the little vehicle, but the smooth conditions soon ceased and the ride went in uneven jerks between knolls and stones and dense willow thickets, where I felt like a cat whose fur is being stroked the wrong way. To make things even merrier, I had a barrel of salted fish in the tip of the sled to struggle with. It rolled around and pinched my legs while I, with my hands outside, had to hold the boatlike sled on a straight keel. Every once in a while the sled rolled over, and Sara laughed when, after a short involuntary stroll, I tried to recover my place inside it with the fish barrel. She consoled me with the fact it could be much worse; once little Nilsa had gotten the sled on top of him, like a lid, and was pulled along under it. Such misfortunes are naturally common and always a subject for hilarity.

In the meantime, I was having constant bad luck the first part of the trip. The reindeer behind me had conducted itself in a friendly way; it had often almost rested its muzzle on my shoulder. It walked peacefully and blew its strong hot breath onto my neck or into one of my ears. I'd become used to seeing its large antlers in the immediate vicinity of my head, without needing to worry that they'd stab or dig into me. But, suddenly, our friendship was over. It began to tap me on the neck, until it was knocking me quite emphatically on the shoulders and head. At first I thought this was happening inadvertently and didn't say anything, but when it continued, even more forcefully, and I turned to give it a smack, I saw the reason for its changed behavior. The harness was in disarray; the poles connected to the sled had loosened. When it was adjusted, we continued our journey with the same good understanding as before. When we came through the birch forest, the reindeer paid careful attention so as not to bump its antlers against the trees or get them tangled up in the branches. It paid better attention to its antlers than to the sled it was towing. It could give a little swerve to avoid a branch, but with that, the sled rotated so the traces attached to its tip ended up on either side of the tree trunk.

It's always very dangerous when it isn't the lead reindeer that does this, but one following: the reindeer in front continue marching freely along, while the one with the sled is, quite simply, strangled because the others tug at the traces—if help doesn't come in time. He who leads a string through a forest, whether in light or darkness, must therefore be extremely attentive and must constantly look backward and feel the least little tug in the string. If a sled is caught fast, he has to run quickly and tug the reindeer ahead back enough so that the one behind doesn't get strangled. At the same time, he must, often with great difficulty, get the sled free of the tree. If it's his bad luck to reach the sled so late that he can't save the reindeer any other way, he has to take his knife and quickly cut the traces so that the animal can breathe (the traces are attached to the reindeer's forehead and around the neck under the chin). A reindeer can't tolerate overloading; it chokes easily and falls easily if you give it burdens too heavy to carry or pull. A reindeer grows emaciated in a few days if it doesn't get enough to eat, and it dies rapidly of hunger. On the other hand, a thin reindeer fattens up rapidly in good times if it's otherwise healthy.

We didn't have mishaps of any kind on this leg of the migration, except the usual small impediments that can be hard to avoid when you travel with a lot of baggage in the dark through rocky, pathless wilderness. Later in the evening, we stopped, the intention being only to spend the night and then continue on the next day. Sara insisted on putting up the tent, but some of the other families contented themselves with lighting a large campfire and sleeping around it. Here was abundant firewood. The flames blazed, the blackened coffee pot sat at the edge of the fire while the light shone on all these fairytale figures with furs and red-tasseled peaked caps. Lights and shadows flew to and fro, and high up under the stars, the flames of the northern lights dashed around like celestial elfin girls in a soundless dance. There's a singular festivity about the Lapps when so many of them gather together to rest around a large bonfire, and they don't skimp on jokes and wisecracks.

The next morning the other families had to erect their tents. The reindeer had spread out so much in the night that it took almost three days to gather them again. The herd was then brought almost up to the tents for a couple of hours, while the draft reindeer were captured and harnessed. The children played to their heart's content, ordering dogs around, throwing lassos and romping with the animals. But when they caused too much commotion in the herd, they were told sharply to tone down their zeal to work a little. One of the children ran around with a bell that had, for one reason or another, fallen off a reindeer cow. A grunting calf ran up, searching, but when it saw the child instead of its mother, it stopped in fright. All the same, it continued in its perplexity to follow the child ringing the bell instead of listening for its mother's call. Just as the Lapps recognize each individual bell by its sound, so do the reindeer.

When we left, we had the whole herd around our ears, but they were quickly out of sight, and the strings followed sedately after them.

We traveled now in rather short intervals. The reindeer longed to move steadily south for better grazing. But to be certain of finding good grazing in the area that these Lapps had been reduced to, our foreman went on skis down to investigate the conditions before they'd allow the reindeer to go down. The reindeer themselves knew well where they could find lichen, but it could be covered by a crust of ice or other snow conditions that could make for difficult or completely impossible grazing. That was what the *siida's* foreman now went to check on.

When a Lapp goes out in winter like that to investigate grazing conditions, he takes along, instead of his usual ski pole, the "pole shovel." This is a stick that ends in a narrow wooden blade with which he can dig away snow and see if the ground is clean—that is to say, without ice or a hard snow crust. The weather in autumn very much controls how the winter grazing conditions will be. The autumn is best if snow comes late and immediately freezes. If the snow comes early, thaws to water, and freezes, then the dangerous and feared ice crust forms. The reindeer can't break through it, even with their hooves. But even if the autumn is good and the snow lies directly on the lichen, without ice in between, there can still be perilous times later. If, for example, such strong thaw weather comes in winter that the top layer of snow melts, which can happen easily, then what the Lapps call *ceavvi* happens. In a *ceavvi* winter they lose many reindeer in different ways.

There are many kinds of weather and many kinds of conditions that make life difficult for the nomads. These were the sorts of conditions that the *siida*'s foreman went out to investigate before the herd could descend. If there were unfavorable grazing conditions southward, they had to keep the reindeer up in the high mountains and in the birch forests until the grazing conditions improved with a change in the weather. However, it was always risky, partly because a large number of the reindeer would steal away on their own down to the pine forests, partly because it was preferable to save the grazing areas for spring, when absolutely no other grazing area could be used because of snow crust.[19]

The Lapps' present territory is so reduced that as soon as there are difficult feeding conditions, an enormous number of reindeer starve. The herds can in one year be decimated quite considerably, with hundreds lost; when it's particularly bad, thousands of reindeer die of hunger. Yet a reindeer herd can increase quickly again if there are better times.

It's very painful for the nomads when their animals die of hunger, even though they, in individual cases, can bear the loss without being completely ruined. It's not pleasant, in a Lapp tent, when the herd is faring badly and can't be helped. In the year 1906, when thousands of reindeer died of hunger because of miserable grazing conditions over a large area, few cheerful words were heard. The women sat at home with the children and cried, the herders were silent and depressed, and everyone who could get outside worked in fear and sadness to save at least a part of the herd.

The Lapps had gotten permission to chop down branches with beard lichen and took these to the animals, which stood around in the deep snow, too exhausted to walk anymore. The dying and the dead lay everywhere. It could only be a question of saving a fraction of the herd with beard lichen; in other words, the Lapps tried to keep the tame draft reindeer alive. If they died, it made the migrations impossible and all was lost. Of course, the usual herding stopped under these circumstances; the strongest animals tried to get to places where they thought they might find food, and only the very strongest bulls could scrape down through snow and ice, just barely escaping death. There, where the bulls had scraped a hole in the snow, the weaker animals looked further, trying to find the last bits of lichen, but all the calves and young animals died irretrievably. It often happened that you took beard lichen branches to a fallen exhausted reindeer that barely managed to turn its head, look at the food, and then sink back and die.

The Lapps are heartsick over such things; they dream about them at night and think about them during the day. They suffer not only because their economic position is threatened. It's almost worse that their pride and joy, the reindeer, suffer so horribly.

All the same, it didn't go quite as badly as it seemed it would during the worst of it. A number of reindeer had saved themselves in time by moving to better pasturage. They were believed dead; no one had time to keep tabs on individual animals. The Lapps couldn't trouble themselves with rounding up the herd in the normal way. Later, when conditions improved and they had time to search and gather, they found some strays scattered about, so that those who'd thought they were ruined found a little to begin with again. Some *siidas*, who had people and energy enough, kept large herds alive by summoning all their energy to procure beard lichen in large enough quantities and early enough that the animals could be saved. A poor widow, for example, was out continually with her ax and went from reindeer to reindeer with food. She wore the skin off her hands and sweat and tears flowed. She got only a little sleep and rest while the hardest times lasted.

Sweden's government managed with great difficulty to obtain permission for the Lapps to go to the good grazing ground in Finland, but the Lapps whose herds were far from Finnish territory couldn't imagine moving with their weak and dying animals.

The winter of 1907–8 was a good one though. The Lapps didn't complain, but only spoke in general about how difficult it was for them to manage in the restricted regions—you marveled at them.

After some time away, the *siida* foreman returned with the news that there were good "reindeer conditions" to the south. It wasn't dangerous to allow the herd to go down there. Along with that, he let Sara know, to her joy, that Leksu was in the best of health. Leksu had gone with some other intelligent reindeer to the winter grazing ground, following their own almanac.

Sara (Siri Turi) and Emilie Demant Hatt, Laimolahti, 1907 (Nordiska Museet Archives)

Elle (*left*, Anne Turi) with a friend, Laimolahti, 1907

Inga (Ristina Turi) in the tent at Laimolahti, 1907

Elle and Nilsa (Anne and Andaras Turi) reading on Sunday, Laimolahti, 1907

Sara (Siri Turi), Laimolahti, 1907

"The *siida* foreman" (unidentified) and his dog, Laimolahti, 1907

Biettar (Per Turi), Laimolahti, 1907

Sara (Siri Turi) packing up the sled, with her tame reindeer Leksu, 1907–8

Sara and Nilsa (Siri Turi and her son Andaras) with the reindeer Leksu, winter
migration, 1907–8

Rauna (*left*, Margreta Rasti) with a puppy on the spring migration, 1908

Johan Turi in
winter dress.
Borg Mesch

Putting up the tent en route to Tromsdalen. Gate, Heikka, and their daughter
Rauna (Anne, Jouna, and Margreta Rasti), 1908

Children tobogganing, spring migration, 1908

Reindeer unharnessed to rest, spring migration, 1908

Ingaš (*center*, Ellis Omma), her sister, and her father, the *siida*'s foreman (Anders Omma), Tromsdalen, 1908

XII

For us, home in the tent, life went on as usual. Comforts grew fewer, as the darkness and cold increased. The moon shone in the middle of the day, the northern lights flickered, and everything froze between your fingers. The knife at your belt froze fast in its sheath, and if you wanted to eat with a knife or spoon, it had to be warmed next to the fire so it wouldn't stick to your lips. You couldn't take hold of any iron objects, like the handle of a kettle, without gloves. When you washed your hair and brushed it in front of the fire, it froze stiff and the water fell from the comb in the form of snow. (The Lapps, both men and women, often wash their hair; they never brush it when it's dry, only after they wash it. It's not so much for the sake of cleanliness as to comb the lice out of the wet hair.) All the food was frozen—meat, bread, butter, fish, and milk. The bread was warmed by the fire and the frozen lump of butter smeared out with a warm thumb. Frozen meat goes into the stew pot; the reindeer milk for coffee is chopped up with an ax. The water kettle froze solid during the night, so it woke you with its crack. It snowed steadily. In calm weather the snow drifted thick and fine down through the tent poles and melted on the fire. If the snow drifted like that, it could soon form smaller piles, and in the morning you could lie, nice and cozy, with a beautiful solid fifteen centimeters of snow over your legs or along the sleeping place, as if the wind had been there. If it blew in the night, the door was open like as not, and the sky's wind and wet weather entered freely. If it was really snowing hard, it could be very uncomfortable in the tent.

Sara told the story of how once it snowed so intensely for a couple of days that they continuously had to shovel snow out of the tent, and when she woke in the morning there was a large, thick pillar of snow from the fire circle up to the smoke pole. She couldn't get a fire lit. Since it had snowed quietly, the sleeping places were snow free. However, Sara used her hands to chip away at the "thick man" and tipped the snow over to the opposite side, where her son-in-law and Biettar lay soundly sleeping. The first one jumped up, confused and groggy with sleep, shouting *Vuoi neavri, mii dát lea!* "What the devil is this!"

They had to wait a long time for their coffee that morning. It took a long time before the snow was gone, since almost the whole tent was snowed-up and the door was impossible to get open. One of the other tents was so completely drifted over that neighbors had to dig them out.

But when the snow and cold isn't quite so intense, nothing prevents daily work. The Lapps seem to almost ignore the weather. The women sew, do band-weaving, patch old skin clothing, and so on. Patching is continual work, and when Sara tackled the repair of her everyday fur one day, it needed it badly. "I'm so tattered I could fly," she said. Sara had an excellent disposition; her favorite expression was *Ii daga maidege.* "It doesn't matter." With that she got the better of hardships and troubles, when they weren't of a serious nature, that is.

Now it was "the dark time." When Sara woke in the morning, around five or six, and woke up Inga with her oft-repeated *Daga dola*, "Start the fire," it was blackest night. To get the coffee kettle boiling quickly and the tent warmed up, the morning fire was always a big one. The many twigs crackled hard and blazed. Long thin fire-snakes traveled in sinuous lines from the fire up into the dark sky through the tent pole opening. The first cup of coffee Inga drank herself—whoever makes the coffee always drinks the first cup—after which Sara and Nikki drank. Then whoever got out of their sleeping sacks first had a cup. We used only two cups in wintertime, and they went from mouth to mouth without being washed. We drank coffee from the saucer and usually had to go without milk, but the stars were reflected in the dark liquid, as if we were going to drink them.

When we were warmed by the fire and cheered up by the coffee, we took our stiff-frozen shoes from the head of the bed, drying and warming them, as well as the hay. We put on our shoes, belts, and aprons, while tugging our clothes into order, and the morning toilette was finished. Later in the day we could always wash up a little, if we felt like it. We rarely did.

If you wanted it to be pleasant in the tent, you had to learn to make the best use of the fire and at the same time be wary of it. That is, you had to be careful not come too close to the fire, when you were wearing fur or skin clothes. Even if you didn't literally burn them, the hair could turn brittle from too much warmth, and if you were wearing a piece of clothing with the fur or hair on the inside, you could easily damage the outer, skin side. They always said to me and the children when the cold was intense and the fire was large, *Váruhehket beaskka ja gábmagiid.* "Be careful of your fur and shoes." However, there's something you can't always guard against, and that's the sparks that jump from the fire. In certain ways they're quite harmless since they almost never cause a greater conflagration, at least not during the day. But they can burn holes in your clothes and can singe your hair quite badly. If you yourself don't discover them in time, the cry always goes up, *Šaddá civna.* "There's

smoke." Then everyone zealously begins to look for where the smell is coming from. If a spark flies out into a man's thick hair when he has his cap off
during a meal, the danger is rarely discovered before a fine strong spiral of
smoke climbs up from the crown of his head and one of the bystanders calmly
announces, *Oaivi buollá*. "Your head's burning."

If a birch branch is on the fire, you don't need to be afraid of sparks. It's
"quiet" wood. But if you burn *gaskkas*, juniper, which is a very popular fuel in
the high mountains because it is highly combustible and gives off a great deal
of heat, your clothes inevitably become as perforated as a reindeer's back in
spring (from the warble fly larvae, which burrow into the reindeer's skin and
hatch out). You simply cannot guard against juniper sparks. They often spew
forth like a rainstorm. Coming down into the pine region, it gets even worse.
Spruce and pine downright salute with complete explosions that are dangerous for bedclothes, tent covers, and everything else inside. You can't lie down
to sleep in the evening before the fire has calmed down, if you don't want to
risk serious misfortune. It happens not infrequently that a tent goes up in
flames. It almost always happens when the fire hasn't been well tamped down
in the evening or when you leave the tent and the fire blows up again, a tree
trunk turns over, and one of the burning logs rolls down and lights the floor
twigs. From there it catches the bedclothes and you wake in smoke and fire.
Or if it's during the day, the Lapp comes home and finds a pile of ashes where
a tent once stood. It's comparatively easy to save your life if you're surprised
by a fire during the night. All you have to do is lift the tent cover next to
where you're lying and then you're outside. But if there's anyone else to save—
sleeping children or belongings—it's far from safe. Few escape without burn
wounds. Along with that, the whole tent and its contents are in most cases
gone; that's no small loss, there being no insurance, of course.

The true dark period of November and December isn't as heavy and sad as
is generally imagined. If the air is clear, the dawn appears quite early and the
soft sunrise cloud shapes continue for several hours before they, later in the
afternoon, turn into sunset light. Then, the moon and stairs also shine, and
quite often the sky is brightened by the most varied northern lights in mar-
velous curves. The snow itself glows quite a bit. From little Nilsa we always
knew when the daylight was approaching. When he, as the last, had drunk his
morning coffee and had shaken off the cold and sleepiness, he usually began a
confused search for his cap. He needed to go out, and to go outside without a
cap is, for a Lapp, inconceivable. To walk with bare feet in the cold and snow
a few minutes, that doesn't bother anyone. But minus a cap—impossible for

both men and women. The reason isn't that your head freezes; it's that you're simply not properly dressed with a bare head. The Lapps also sleep with a cap on at night. It's mostly for warmth's sake, but usually it rolls off during sleep and you have to hunt for it in the morning. It was particularly difficult for Nilsa to find his cap. Often he was almost at the point of tears from rage, knocking dogs out of his way, overturning all the bedclothes, shoving pokers around to get more light. Kidding and good advice rained down him: *Čana gitta go gávnnat.* "Hold it tight when you find it." Or *Leagos dus gáhpir oppanassii?* "Do you even have a cap?"

When, finally, the red tassel finally popped up and the cap sat on the thick long hair, the lad disappeared out the door. The chilly morning air soon blew his anger away and we were regularly invited to share his meteorological observations: *Dat lea juo dál čuovgame.* "It's already getting to be light."

Gradually the stars paled over the smoke hole, and around nine the mountains rose up red against the milk-blue sky and the morning glow shone over the dark tents. Even though the sun didn't appear, you could see enough until two p.m. to work at whatever you liked. Inside the tent it grew dark sooner, of course. If you were to stop work when the daylight disappeared, you wouldn't get much done. The rest of the day we worked by firelight.

It often happened in the evening that I was alone in the tent with the children for an hour, when Inga and Sara went for a visit to another tent with their handiwork—band-weaving, or sinew-thread sewing. We passed the time in the best way. Elle loved to draw, and in a notebook I'd given her, she depicted with her pencil, in childlike fashion, the *siida*'s daily life, while Nilsa whittled at a stick. The children amused themselves also with striking matches, holding the flame up to see how it burned out. That was how they predicted the next day's weather.

Once I had a bundle of newspapers sent from Denmark, and when the children got one of the large sheets, they first carefully studied all the pictures. After that they burned the paper bit by bit. The game consisted of watching the glowing flags climb and disappear up in the dark sky through the tent opening. Drachmann's and Bjørnson's portraits, printed in large format in the paper, disappeared in the same way.[20] When Nilsa had looked a moment at Bjørnson's gruff expression, he pulled a hideous grimace of disgust and horror and shuddered. *Vuoi, vuoi lea fasttes olmmoš, son galgá buollit!* "Uha, this is an ugly man; he's going to burn!" And so Bjørnson, red with sparks, fluttered up into the black sky, soon followed by Drachmann. Neither answered to Nilsa's Lappish idea of an attractive person.

Elle appeared one evening with one of her baby teeth, around which she'd twisted hair from her head and which she then laid under a hearthstone. I didn't hear her say the usual formula that here, as in the rest of Lapmark, sounds like this: *Dolla, dolla, dát lea dutnje silbabátni, atte munnje baikabáni.* "Fire, fire, here's a silver tooth for you, give me an ugly tooth." (They also say to the fire, when they've burned themselves, *Dolla, dolla, dát lea dutnje gollenáhkki, atte munnje mu baika-náhki ruoktot.* "Fire, fire, here's a skin of gold for you, give me my ugly skin back.")

On Sundays, the most fitting occupation was to read a book, and one Sunday Sara had encouraged her children to read instead of "other useless play." Elle crossly took up the Bible stories and sat near Nilsa. After paging back and forth a little she said brightly, "Let's read the story about Samson, that's the most fun." (In the northern Lapmarks, school is taught in Finnish and schoolbooks are in that language.)

The two big children should have been chopping wood, but most often they didn't do that. They really had many other things to take care of that, in their opinion, were more important and much more fun. Among these things were making snares to catch ptarmigans. The first thing the children did the morning after a move was to find the ptarmigans' hiding places and there they set out the snares. This was, moreover, a sport that all the housewives engaged in too. If they were lucky and had the time, there could be quite good takings from the nooses during the course of winter.

The children inspected their snares first thing in the morning. Most of the light hours of the day went in that way. The ptarmigan snares were often quite far off and the children never hurried. You could come back early enough to chop wood, and if you were fortunate enough to return with three or four ptarmigans, sometimes with even more, you were a person who deserved respect and could then had the right to use your time however you liked. (The ptarmigans were kept in a closed sled, so the dogs couldn't get at them. In frozen conditions they could be kept fresh almost until spring if necessary, but before that they could be sold to a passing buyer or at the market in Jukkasjärvi in December.)

When the children came home from their expeditions, their legs and feet were usually soaked. They weren't very particular about their shoes if they were in one piece—sometimes in the mornings, when Nilsa held his shoe up to the light, he informed us that it was *dego nástedáivvas,* "as full of holes as the starry night"—or if the ankle bands were neatly wrapped. When that wasn't the case, the bands were loosened and filled with snow that was quickly melted by the warmth of the foot. Then the hay was dripping wet when it was taken out for drying, even though it was minus twenty. For the girls it was even worse. Besides getting snow in their shoes, they could also get their *bittut*, skin leggings, filled with snow if they did them up carelessly, so that they hung loose around the legs quite down to the knee instead of clinging tight high above the knee. When they went skiing between the trees, the fine loose snow, which was like sugar, could easily penetrate everywhere. The children ignored such things of course. When they returned home to the tent, they allowed the snow to melt and they dried out the best they could. One morning I'd gone out in the forest with Elle to collect *njižus* (a kind of resin that is chewed to a tough reddish lump). Both children and adults consider resin chewing a pleasure. The salivary glands work hard and spitting is frequent and diverting.

She had forgotten her ski pole and said, *Čuoiggaheaddji soappi haga lea dego seaibbehis beana.* "A skier without a pole is like a dog without a tail." When we'd gone a ways into the forest—we'd now migrated so far down that there was spruce—Elle passed such a large old tree that she threw one arm around it, greeting the tree and saying, *Bures, bures, beahci, dearvvuođaid dutnje duottarsoagis.* "Good-day, good-day, mountain spruce, I bring greetings from the birch of the high mountains."

It's a beautiful old custom that some of the Lapps up there still have that they greet the trees as they come down to the forest from the high mountains.

The children's morning outings usually resulted in Inga having to tackle wood chopping as it was getting dark. Thus, she put her band-weaving or sewing aside, stuck her ax in her belt, and went to the forest on skis. Shortly afterward we heard powerful ax strokes, and she returned with a birch trunk on her shoulders and with its crown dragging after her in the snow. When the Lapps have descended into the pine forest, felled pine trees are also very much in demand for fuel. They heat well and have a great deal of resin, so they light easily. However, those who have a tent covered in woolen cloth don't usually use it, because pine heavily blackens the tent. The woodpile grew rapidly in front of Inga. The white trunks were chopped into logs about a meter long. Next to them, the twigs lay neatly; you only needed to bend down, take a lapful, and chuck them in through the tent door.

Now enough wood was placed on the fire. The whole afternoon we'd sat next to a pair of smoldering coals, because we didn't want to waste precious light hours by going out to chop wood. The fire flamed wildly in the air. The twigs and birch bark burned first, but slowed quickly. The twigs burned up, and the bark on the inner side of the logs burned off, and the tent sank again into darkness. Such a twig or bark fire looks dangerous, but means neither light nor warmth in the long term. It's also one of the Lapps' many sayings about what looks enormous and all the same doesn't turn out to be anything: *Dat lea dego beassedolla.* "It's like a bark fire."

Sara was especially quick to put more wood on when she wanted to have the tent cozily warm and light, but the big fire, with its blazing bark and twigs, sometimes set the sooty smoke pole alight. One day it burned up, so that Nikki had to hurry to replace it with a new one. Luckily it didn't happen while a big kettle of meat was cooking. In such case a serious misfortune could have occurred. When someone came in afterward to the tent for a visit, they saw the new smoke pole right off and smilingly teased us a little about needing so much warmth that we'd burned our smoke pole. But Sara, laughing, turned the taunts aside.

The twig and bark fire did help to dry the new wood, and little by little the logs began to burn steadily, so you could be near to the fire and see to do your work. It was all the same both tiring and uncomfortable for the eyes, to sew or do detailed work in the flickering flames, without a *dollacoggi* (a fire tender). When the fire was allowed to die down, it didn't illuminate sufficiently. If you wanted therefore to see well for anything, one of the children had to be the fire tender. Still, you had to continually repeat, *Dasa dola.* "Keep the fire going." Wood had to be placed steadily on the fire, the logs turned and placed on top of one another, so that there would be continual fresh surfaces for burning that could blaze up in flames. It's a hot, not much coveted occupation to be a *dollacoggi*. Nor is it widely appreciated. More and better light is usually demanded than the fire tender can create. *Dasa dola* isn't always said in a mild voice.

During the dark time, all the same, work is done deftly by firelight. The men tar skis and twist willow branches for ski bindings and other uses. Skis are tightened into shape. Some people repair harnesses, work with wood carvings, or stake out a reindeer hide. The women sew shoes and gloves or repair their own or the men's furs, watch the children, spin sinew thread or similar tasks.

Later, when by clock time it's evening, the big stewpot is put on the fire and thus it's no good anymore to see by firelight. The stewpot is supposed to cook steadily, and it doesn't tolerate too hot a fire. The fat mustn't boil; to avoid that you secure the stewpot handle with a hook, which, with a cord, is fastened to one of the tent poles farthest away. With this you can haul the pot over toward the kitchen space so it avoids the strongest heat. If the stewpot begins to boil too violently, the order is given to he who sits nearest, to lift the pot up by the hook: *Bija báðe faggái.*

When the meat is almost done, the fat for dipping is removed with a small wooden scoop. In order to see this through the steam and smoke, you must use a light with a *beassespáiddar*. This occupation usually fell to Nilsa. He took a rather large piece of birch bark, stuck it on the poker, and lit it on fire. This torch he held high over the stewpot while Sara bent her face, reflected in the red light, with the loose black hair around it, over the steam and removed the fat in the spoon. The artistic position of the boy, with the outstretched torch, cast a fantastic shadow on the tent walls. The black sky above the smoke hole was pierced by the flame-tinted, spearlike spikes of the tent poles. The whole scene resembled a theatrical setting for witches.

When the meat was cooked, the stewpot was lifted by the chain and set on the hearth to cool. It took strength and deftness to take down the full pot and place it well without spilling it. You could scald or burn yourself if you were a touch clumsy or not strong enough. The pot held twenty-eight liters of water—you could read that out on the outside, written in iron letters. When the men were around, they always lifted the pot down, but they were relatively seldom at home. Then Sara and Inga did it without too much effort.

The Lapps never eat their food hot. It stands a while before it's served. It's also impossible to touch the red-hot pieces of meat with bare fingers. Forks would be quite useless when you don't have plates at the same time. No one can reasonably suggest that nomad Lapps should be traveling around with those sorts of unnecessary goods, which would get broken on the first trek. All the same, they have aesthetic standards that could very well resemble our own in some ways. You must not chew noisily, nor eat with dirty hands. Nor it is respectable to stuff yourself. Of he who overeats, it's said scornfully, "He eats till he sleeps." You're not supposed to eat in a careless posture or with your cap on, in the case of the men, nor lick your fingers. It's not allowed to move in front of someone who's eating.

In the tent two or more eat from one bowl—"only Stallo eats alone." And if two people eat by themselves, neither one is supposed to place the food bowl on one of their outstretched legs or knees, because then you eat the good fortune away from he who sits with the bowl. It's not easy to maintain decorum in a Lapp tent, as many might believe at first glance.

When the meat has been eaten and the bones carefully scraped clean, they're placed on the hearth, from where they'll later be removed. You never put the shoulder blade away without first having made a hole in the actual blade with a knife. A half-forgotten or, more correctly, completely forgotten, old superstition is connected with this practice. Only the custom lingers on.

Some bones are of course given to a begging dog; they make sure there's one bone the dog can gnaw on and get something off of. Along with the bone the dog is admonished to take it outside: *Guođe olggos.* Obediently he disappears out the door with his spoils.

Marrowbones are a little snack of their own before the true meal. The marrowbones are placed end-up in the boiling stewpot. After a short time they're turned. The men are well practiced in cooking the marrow to just the right degree so they don't become oily or liquid or red and raw. Better the marrowbone be boiled too little than too much. Everyone gets his allotted marrowbone; you rarely get more than one. First you scrape and pick the bone clean of meat and membrane, which you eat. Afterward it's split with the big knife or a common knife, on a hearthstone. The Lapps are practiced in splitting it elegantly the length through. To crush it with the blunt side of an ax or smash it to pieces is considered tasteless. It's also only children who, in their eagerness, can think of using a *meres* to help (*meres* is a dull ax, which is used in the tent for various things—for instance to chop up ice in winter or to loosen a stone from the earth and so on). The marrow is sucked out directly from the split bone or with the assistance of a knife tip. It's eaten without bread or salt. The rest of the bone is thrown back into the pot to be cooked fully.

The fat marrowbone is the Lapps' greatest delicacy. Other delicacies include reindeer tongues, but these are mainly sold, so you get them more seldom. Liver must be added to these dainty dishes. It's cooked very lightly, so it keeps its juicy succulence and fine taste. It's eaten exclusively by the men and always as a little hors d'oeuvre before the real meal of meat.

The head of the reindeer is also a fine dish, especially the fatty eyes. These are used to frighten the children from taking it, with jokes about them getting an eye in the middle of the forehead. In the reindeer's jawbone there's also a smidgen of marrow that's taken out and eaten. Yet ancient beliefs say you should always give the dog the marrow of one jawbone. That way you can make sure of his help in danger. After the evening meal you drink a few mouthfuls of soup. Sometimes you can get coffee on top of that, if you're very thirsty. The Lapps always put in a couple of grains of salt, but it's rare that the coffee tastes salty. The salt is partly to "clarify" it and partly so that the coffee won't taste "insipid."

When the meat is eaten and the coffee drunk, everyone begins to straighten his sleeping place (the wife straightens the couple's bedding; aside from that, everyone takes care of himself). This should be done carefully and well during this cold time. You can take some sacks or something to plug up and seal the bottom edge of the tent wall. If not, you can hope that a dog lies down in a convenient spot during the night. Otherwise, it can be hard to keep your back or one side warm, the one turned in the direction of the tent wall. As a rule, in winter many degrees below zero, you only have a reindeer hide under you. Sometimes you can also feel the cold from below, especially the first night of a move, when the layer of twigs is thin. The snow doesn't melt under the twigs on the sleeping places, even if you're in one place a long time. In those cases, it can melt about twenty-five centimeters in a circle around the fire. When you move around during the night you can feel the snow creak under you. But it doesn't matter, when otherwise you're lying there warm.

The tent is pure chaos in the evening, when everyone all at once begins to straighten up the camp. The young ones grow sleepy, shudder, and say crossly, *Daga saji*. "Straighten the bed." Actually, "Tidy the space." The bedding that's been lying rolled up by the tent walls is so cold that you can only handle it with gloves. It's often frozen stiff, rimed with frost, so it has to be banged on with a stick and warmed in front of the fire before you can creep inside. But the thick sheep or reindeer pelt, covered with a wool blanket, is toasty. The cover is so long that it's pulled up over the head. Without it, you wouldn't be protected enough against the nighttime cold. But for those not used to it, it's difficult to breathe inside all that thick wool. Down at the bottom end, the cover is sewed together about fifteen centimeters up into a small case for the feet. The Lapps don't use actual sleeping bags.

There's wild confusion in the tent until everyone has gotten his respective bed in order. Inga and the children sleep together, and there's always a bit of wrangling about both the sleeping positions and the bedding.

"I was freezing last night; you pulled the covers off me. I want the calfskin because my feet were frozen."

"No, I want it, because last night only my backside was warm," Nilsa says.

Then there are the positions: *Mana soggái*, "Lie over by the wall," but there are few people who like that. Naturally, the good-natured Inga yields. She's strong and hardy and rather indifferent to where she sleeps. When the bedding is finally ready, everyone takes his shoes off. Some of the older people put on a pair of knitted socks, if it's not so cold that you need to keep your shoes on during the night.

There's a short comfortable time in a Lapp tent, when everyone sits by the fire and warms their feet for the night and chats about whatever comes up. Older and married folk like to tie up the mosquito tent, even in winter, where it creates quite a bit of warmth. The light linen canvas glowing by the fire was a fitting backdrop for Sara's pretty figure when she sat in front of the first in the evening. In spite of her age, near sixty, she was straight-backed and graceful, as almost all Lapp women are. She was especially beautiful in her golden *dorka* (inner fur) with white leather gloves, and a tall, white stand-up collar that attractively framed her intelligent brown face with the lively eyes and the loose black hair under the red cap.

One evening when she sat like that, with her legs pulled up under her and her well-shaped hands in her lap, erect and stately, with her gaze far off in thought, I broke out with a few admiring words, quickly echoed by Inga. She looked at her mother and said with pride, *Raisduoddara fávru, su birra leat juoigan dološ áigge.* "Beautiful Rais Mountain, we joiked about her in former times."

Sara grew seriously angry and shushed her. It was sinful to think that way and talk like that. Inga was immediately ordered to go out and fetch wood for the morning fire and to make sure there was bark to light the fire for the next day. She did this obediently. A smooth *čoska* (a birch trunk chopped up for burning) was laid on the fire and rotated around until it was easy to loosen the bark with knives and to tear it off in large pieces. These pieces were further dried by the fire, after which they were placed on the hearth for use the next day. Only after that was taken care of was there quiet in the tent as everyone found his bed. If the flames were strong, they were damped down with water, or the burning wood spread out so much that it couldn't burn. This happened no matter how cold it was. The embers smoldered and soon went out. The dogs prowled around as usual to sniff out any leftovers, but if they touched anything on the hearth by mistake, or it sounded like they were in some forbidden place, someone would say, sharply, *Ce rise, boaššust, suolabeana.* "You're going to get a licking, get out of the kitchen, you thief of a dog."

The offender, who hadn't meant any harm at all, crept quietly outside, perhaps taking with him one of the bones from the evening meal. You heard him lying there a long time, gnawing at it energetically. When the dog was done and wanted to sleep, he shoved his way in through the door, which was only fastened at the top. The bottom part remained hanging half open, and that brought the cold in.

The peace of the night is quite often disturbed in a Lapp tent, between the dogs and late arriving herders, who make a fire and heat up food before they lie down to sleep. The most frequent disturbances come from the dogs, however. When you've gone to bed, they wander freely around you and lie down wherever they decide to—even if it's right across your face. If only they'd lie quietly after deciding on a place, but after a short time they move on. And when they—if it's very cold—creep completely under the covers, soon they're too hot and have to get up again. Until they freeze. Then they repeat the maneuver. These kinds of disturbances you can get used to enough to sleep through. But when they suddenly rush out of the tent, barking wildly in the middle of the nighttime quiet, you have to wake up and listen. In an instant the whole *siida* can turn into a single dog baying, so you'd believe all the armies of the dead are marching. Most often, of course, it's a false alarm. The vigilant animals start baying at any strange noise they hear, and the wilderness has so many sounds. Fortunately, the dogs are strongly trained not to bark inside the tent. If one of them offends, he gets a sharp reprimand: "Don't make a racket inside the tent!"

Our dogs were not particularly alert. Sara said about them, half-scornfully, "They wouldn't bark even if they saw their own ghost."

For those who aren't used to sleeping outside, the weather can disturb your sleep quite a bit. In winter, when the tent is in the forest and there's a hard freeze, you continually hear crash after crash in the big trees. In the same way, the water kettle, which has frozen by sitting on the hearth, cracks loudly. But the weather that most persistently disturbs sleep is a storm. The door flaps unceasingly, its wooden pins hitting the doorway poles, until finally the door is thrown up onto the tent, where it stays until the next gust of wind blows it back down. If you get up and fasten the door, it grows quite unbearable to hear the wind tear at it. So it's better to have the tent door open so the hard wind can whip freely through the opening. Of course it's not only the door that makes noise; no, the whole tent creaks and groans, like a vessel in a storm, and the tent cover thrashes up and down on the wood frame around your ears, so it's impossible to even think of sleep. Sometimes the cords that hold the covering fast can loosen here and there or snap; suddenly there's a crack in the air—one of the tent coverings is torn off, and the storm breaks brazenly into the tent.

Now sleep is completely gone, and what you've been lying there expecting has happened. You might get off lightly if just one half of the tent cover flies off. It's relatively easy to throw it over the pole structure again and tie it fast, even though it's uncomfortable to go out into the stormy darkness and maneuver around outside the tent with the heavy sodden covering. It's worse when the storm rips the whole tent up, so it simply splits apart, which can happen in the high mountains when bad weather suddenly breaks out.

If you can predict the storm or feel that the wind is increasing to a disturbing degree, you can protect yourself in time by various means. A two-branched tree trunk, or *bieggacaggi*, can be set up against the place where the interior crossbeam joins the tent poles, as a support on the side facing the wind. When there's a really bad storm, you can also bring two such wind braces inside the tent, where they cross each other and take up a great deal of room. To make the structure properly sturdy, you can further wrap a rein around a suitably large stone and hang it up in the smoke pole. Likewise, it may be necessary to cover the outer edge of the tent to hold the cloth down. In such weather it's impossible, all the same, to have a fire on the hearth. The storm scatters both fire and ashes; you can't protect either your eyes or clothes. But if the storm comes in the night and you haven't had time to prepare yourself, that's when you risk the worst of all—the whole tent being torn up.

XIII

IT'S NOT VERY COMFORTABLE TO TREK in stark cold or other bad weather. The Lapps avoid it as much as possible, but ten or fifteen degrees below zero isn't reckoned as much, and when the reindeer herd has grazed up a place, the Lapps must move on. Regarding "grazing up," that doesn't mean all the lichen is eaten up, only that the reindeer can no longer dig new holes in the snow in the same area, because all the scraped up and trampled snow has frozen so hard that the reindeer can't dig new holes. They need new territory, and so the Lapps have to depart. Early in the morning the herders go out, even before it's light, to gather the herd and capture the draft animals. (The whole herd never travels south in one trek; the necessary baggage-carrying reindeer remain behind, and their number steadily grows, in part by rounding up reindeer left behind on the migration route, in part by separating out of reindeer from other herds. This also has the advantage that the whole herd isn't gathered in one place, which protects the grazing area a little, but also demands much more work.)

It's not until afternoon that they come home with long trains of draft reindeer. While the men are away, the women are fully employed with packing everything in the sleds. When a sled is completely packed, it's covered with a reindeer skin and tightened fast and secure with rope that is drawn crosswise through the loops of reindeer sinews, made taut along the sides of the sleds. The hind legs of the reindeer are always used for the loops. Because the sinews there, the Achilles tendon, are thicker in the middle, they're not suitable for spinning.

It makes for cold hands to pack and lace up twelve or fifteen sleds, and there's not much time or opportunity to thaw out your fingers and get a bit of warmth and food inside the tent. Besides, the tent is quite stripped of its coziness when all of its contents lie in the sleds and even the twig floor has been taken up. If the twigs aren't too battered, the best are placed at the bottom of the sleds, so that the small chests and other hard objects can be stored more securely. The twigs are used to plug gaps wherever there's empty space, and at the end they're laid on top of the skin that covers the contents. They stiffen it and hold the objects when the sled is laced up. Finally, you also have some twigs to start with when you come to a new place in the dead of night. The few twigs left behind at the tent site are burned, according to ancient tradition, "so we always have our draft reindeer gathered."

If the string isn't too heavily laden and you have strong reindeer, sometimes you take a pair of the best hearthstones along. It's difficult when arriving to find stones under the snow, and it's difficult to maintain a fire without hearthstones. In such a case the fire must be laid on two other pieces of wood that are placed at an angle to raise the fire a little from the earth. But they quickly burn through and the fire needs a draft from below. All the same, you have a slightly bad conscience when you "trek with stones," and can easily be exposed to teasing from the others. There is certainly no lack of stones in Lapland, and the reindeer have enough to carry already.

When there was time for it, we often got a good warm meal, just before we left, that consisted of small, finely chopped bits of meat and fat cooked with water into a strong meat soup and thickened with a couple of handfuls of meal to a tasty porridge. There was always a piece of frozen reindeer shoulder that was thinly carved with a sharp knife and therefore cooked quickly. You could withstand the cold well after such a hearty, warm meal. Some of the children sniffed the meal and mumbled, *beatnaga čuogus* ("dog food"—the gruel the dogs got was also thickened with meal).

It's an unpleasant moment when the tent comes down around your ears. The sooty cord is untied around the smoke opening at the top. Also unloosed are the ties around the hearth, where the two tent coverings cross over each other, and the ties on either side of the door, where the tent cloth is tightly fastened. Thus the tent's walls slip down and you sit there in the open air and feel so strangely exposed. The newly acquired small puppy, who'd never experienced a trek, so unlike anything he'd come to understand, became quite panic-stricken when the tent was taken down. He howled and ran around in confusion, and only quieted down when I took him under my capacious fur parka. The puppy remembered this, because during the later migrations he came straight to me and tried to get inside my fur as soon as the tent coverings fell.

When the tent structure is brought down and disassembled, it's tied to the last sled in the caravan of strings. In that same sled are placed the cooking pots and kettle chains that beforehand were burned clean after being thrown in the fire, along with a food sack that contains the most essential things for the first meal. Everything is then covered with the tent cloths. The same reindeer is always harnessed for the tent-sled; you can count on it to be sedate and dependable and to understand how to maneuver around obstacles without difficulty. The long, stiff tent poles dragging behind it can easily cause trouble. Once when the string of reindeer swung quite sharply around a tree, I saw the tent-reindeer make the swing as wide as it could, given the length of the traces. Afterward it turned its head to look and see if the poles had come clear of the tree. Sara smiled and said, "Yes, the reindeer is always careful. It's used to pulling the tent-sled."

It's lively in the *siida* when all the tents are packed and the reindeer are harnessed together. For some the process is steady and easy. They have tame reindeer to drive. Others aren't so fortunate; they have gotten or purposefully taken one of the not quite broken-in reindeer to tame it further. There can be an energetic battle of the wills. Both man and reindeer tumble around in the snow. It always ends with the reindeer giving in. When it is harnessed behind a sensible tame reindeer and has a heavy sled to pull, it soon learns to walk properly. If anyone wishes to punish an all-too-unruly draft reindeer and subdue it, they cut off one or both of the front points of the antler with a big knife. That's a great humiliation for the animal, which is very proud of its antlers.

When the caravan is almost ready, the little child, if there is one, is painstakingly packed into the cradle and placed in the front end of the mother's own sled and carefully covered, so that neither the draft nor the cold can touch the child. The mother also sits in the sled and drives her own pretty, tame reindeer. The housewife's driving cow is characteristically a stately animal with elegant antlers and special colors, and it has a more beautiful harness than the others.

The older children aren't as carefully attended to—they're used to the trip and are only ordered to put on a warm fur parka and stuff their shoes well with hay. Sara looked after them readily so they did it the right way, and when

Elle or Nilsa placed their hay *dego rievssatbeassi* ("like a ptarmigan nest"), she took the shoe and taught them correctly. When that was done, they had to manage for themselves during the treks, if nothing went wrong. If they grew tired and there was no room in a driving sled for them, they were allowed to throw themselves for a while on top of a sled that wasn't too heavily loaded— either the tent-sled or the sledge (the Lapps often have a low sledge where they transport lighter things that can't so easily be packed—skis, the ladder, the snow shovel, reindeer antlers, and the like). When the children have rested a little they take to their skis again and follow the string, but they, like the dogs, must take care not to come alongside the reindeer. That can cause nasty problems in the string if the draft reindeer are frightened.

The dogs and reindeer aren't good friends, and a silent hatred and great distrust prevails on both sides. If a dog, out of thoughtlessness or because he absolutely must have company, comes too close to the string and a reindeer therefore jumps, frightened, to the side, the dog is bombarded with the most horrible oaths and threats, so he swerves away in a wide arc and keeps his distance. Often the reindeer itself contrives to keep the dog away from its vicinity by giving him a well-aimed blow to the ribs with its antlers or a powerful kick with its front leg. However, it's mainly the young, less experienced dogs that act so badly. The older dogs attempted to see enough to be on their guard, at least around the strings. They recognized each reindeer and knew from which ones they could expect difficulties. But the dogs have a hard time keeping themselves away. They're often quite tired from previous work and would love to steal onto the beaten track created by the strings. It's tiring for them to run through the deep snow when it doesn't hold them up. It wears the skin off their legs.

If the caravan makes a short stop to correct something or other, the dogs immediately lie down to sleep. They turn into a circle and hide their noses in their bushy tails. The Lapps believe that if a dog can just keep his nose warm, he won't otherwise be cold. Sometimes a tired dog falls so deeply asleep that he remains lying there long after the caravan is gone, but as the Lapps say, "We don't take our tracks with us."

It was twilight when the caravan glided out of the low birch forest. As far as possible, we followed unforested stretches so as to avoid trekking through the trees. In the south the evening glow still burned, but the colors were cooling off and soft clouds spread out. It grew dark, but it was a strange white darkness; the earth and air were one, without horizon, without division. In this white darkness the long caravan moved slowly forward, as slowly as a burial procession. There was no other sound than the sleds gliding over the snow and the continuous clicking of the reindeer's tendons. The Lapps themselves felt the mournful tone of the march, for I suddenly heard Sara ask Nikki to go a little faster: "You're leading the caravan as if it was a funeral procession."

Finally we arrived at the camping place; that is to say we stopped in the middle of the snow and were going to inhabit a deserted spot for a short time, perhaps only overnight. The reindeer were unharnessed; people and animals splashed around in the deep snow. In the dark we continually tripped over dogs, tackle, sleds, and tent poles, while everyone sought to go about his tasks and sort out the confused state of things. Nikki dug out a snow shovel from the sledge and began, almost at random, to shovel snow away in a circle, where the tent was going to be raised. It was impossible to select a flat area when the snow covered everything. The ground also appeared to be very rocky, but it didn't help to be too picky. For now, the spaces between the rocks were filled in, since the snow could never be shoveled clean away; only the loose top layer could be removed.

Sara and Nikki set the tent up, while Inga and I chopped spruce branches for the underlayer. If you're near spruce trees, their branches are preferable for the first layer when it's far too much work and quite impossible in the dark to collect enough fine birch twigs.

The small children and puppies cried and whimpered from impatience over in the sleds in their narrow casings, but they had to wait until the tent was ready and the fire lit.

It's quite troublesome for the Lapps to have small puppies along during the migrations. They need a lot of care. The puppies are taken very early from their mothers, so early that they must be fed and cared for in every way. The mother is given no time to nurse the puppies; she's supposed to take up working with the herd as soon as possible. During the treks in winter the puppy is tucked into a sack of hay, and there, without a fur, the little living bundle is tied gently in the forward part of the sled, most often in the housewife's own sled. Sometimes the puppy is taken out suffocated. Sometimes too it has frozen to death, but in the best circumstances, it has survived. The Lapps criticize themselves if a puppy is badly treated; they literally have a saying that she who can't raise a puppy won't make a housewife.

When the tent is up and the fire burning, the mother goes to fetch the child in the sled. At the same time she releases the puppy by dropping him in the snow. And while she carries the cradle inside, the little furry lump wades almost up to his ears in the snow over to the black tent, where each chink shines redly and where human shadows move against the woolen walls and from whose top sparks fly upward in a cloud of smoke. He bores his way in under the door, and places himself right in front of the fire, begging for food (his food consists—though there's not much of it—of a little chewed meat and bread that's been heated in bit of soup.).

The child is taken out of the cradle and attended to, while the husband or one of the others sees to the food and coffee.

After the work is completed, everyone gathers in the tent. As soon as the reindeer are unharnessed, the tackle needs to be put in order, the traces wound, and everything untangled and put in its place. The sleds can't be left any which way after they've been disconnected. They must be arranged nicely, side by side, and dragged over to a suitable spot near the tent. If the wind's cold, you can place one of the empty driving sleds, with its vaulted side, along the sleeping area, on the outer side of the tent where the strongest drafts get in. Only when all that has been accomplished can you go into the tent for light and food.

A large kettle of snow is hung over the fire to make drinking water and water for coffee. The Lapps never use the topmost loose layer of snow, which makes little—and bad—water. They dig that away and take the firm, absolutely pure snow that lies underneath. This gives more water; all the same, it's a slow method of creating water. As soon as the snow begins to melt, we slake our immediate thirst, reaching with a ladle for lukewarm water that we cool with a little snow. Those who sit nearest the water kettle are duty-bound to offer water to everyone who asks for it. Those who sit farther away in the tent can't go over to the kitchen in front of those sitting closer. That wouldn't be considered proper. Goives' *munnje čazi,* "Draw me some water," is never ignored, no matter how busy with work the housewife or the ones sitting closest are.

The big coffee pot is also filled with snow and placed on the fire. As soon as the snow inside the pot melts and sinks down, the pot is filled from the water kettle. To get the coffee boiling quickly it's often placed directly on the fire, but—oh, horror—it happened to us once that, when the coffee was almost ready and everyone waited longingly, a piece of wood slipped and the coffee pot overturned its contents, simultaneously putting out the laboriously lit fire. In spite of the disappointment, everyone burst into laughter and patiently began to light another fire from scratch, to melt snow and boil coffee. And when you've put away your three or four cups of coffee and had some food, a benevolent contentment spreads through the senses. Later, when the reindeer herders come home, it's their turn to drink coffee and eat.

In a Lapp tent you don't have any other entertainment than what you create yourself. The puppy clearly thought the same way. One evening he diverted himself by running, barking wildly, around the tent, near the fire area. No one hindered his joy; on the contrary, everyone looked pleased at the little furry chap's playfulness. But when he wanted to jump over the pot of gruel on the hearth, which was half-full after mealtime, he turned the lid over and Tji-Tji disappeared into the gruel. Then, oh dear, he was hastily fished out and put in front of the fire, dripping with soup and rice grains. Reproachfully, pitifully shabby, he looked up at us, while the laughter rained down over his small, pathetic figure. Sara brushed moisture and grain from his wet fur and tucked him in under her covers—the night bedding was made up. "Now he can dry off with me tonight."

There's nothing more to add to this story than that the children and I ate the living gruel the day after with good appetite. Sara came in just as we were breakfasting. "No, ugh, are you eating the gruel the puppy was in! Let it be, the dogs can have it." She shuddered with disgust and scolded us sharply.

Sara was in fact an excellent housewife. She took good care of us, both people and dogs, and she was hospitable to quite a few others. If someone came from a neighboring tent while we sat and ate, she treated them with food if there was anything especially good she had to offer. When you've arrived by chance like that and are invited to eat something tasty, you have what the Lapps call *čoavjelihkku* ("belly luck"). And no one could eat enough at Sara's. *Bora vai ealát nohkkat,* "Eat, so you can live to sleep," she called out in the evenings.

XIV

Toward December, when we had the tents in the vicinity of Tavanjunje, there began to be much talk of Ándenbeaivi (Saint Andrew's Day) and *meassoáige* (market time) in Čohkkerasas (Jukkasjärvi). The Lapps were accustomed to travel there to carry out their annual spiritual and worldly business, there being a Lapp market at the same time. The subject was discussed so often that, in tent conversations, the reindeer quite often had to yield place. The children counted their ptarmigans—here was an opportunity to sell them. Elle wished for a mirror box for her ptarmigan money (a small brass snuffbox with a mirror in it and two compartments the Lapps use for toothpicks). Nilsa wanted a new rope for a lasso. (Nowadays the old-fashioned lassos, which the Lapps themselves once made of twined reindeer tendons or of fine tree roots, are seldom used.)

Infected by all this talk of the fair, I tackled sewing a new dress I had material for, so I could accompany them to Jukkasjärvi. Sara cut it out for me. A reindeer hide was spread out on the twigs with the hair-side downward; on this comparatively even surface, the cutting out took place. The Lapps don't take true measurements. They employ finger widths and so on, which as a rule work capitally.

There were many long seams to sew (the sewing machine, however, is now beginning to be widely used. It's carried in a solid case, which also serves as a table when the machine is used in the tent). Sara inserted a multitude of gussets in the back width, since it's considered attractive to have flowing clothes that "fold like fingers." In all the topmost hems, around the neck opening and as a border below, narrow strips of fine red and yellow cloth are inserted, which are decorated with silk stitching.

Unfortunately, snow fell constantly during those days, which made the few hours of daylight quite dark and the tent fill with smoke.

When it snows and is so still that the snow remains lying on the tent cover, the smoke is intolerable inside. Already, as soon as the morning fire is lit, someone has to go out and with a strong birch branch knock the snow off the tent, so the air can filter through and carry the smoke up through the smoke hole. If the snowfall continues, the process must be repeated several times a day, but still the snow plugs up the tent cover's many pores, and the smoke can't escape in the heavy air. During such days the smoke in the tent is un-bearable; your eyes run and breathing is quite restricted. You can't stay out in the snow, much less when you have sewing to do. You have to settle for now and then filling your lungs with smoke-free, clean air by lifting the tent cover and sticking your head out under the bottom. Likewise you can, in order to drive the smoke away a little from your immediate vicinity, make yourself a *heaggaráigi*, an air-hole. That is to say, you lift the tent cover about fifteen centimeters out into the air and keep the opening wide open with a stick or something similar, so the air can rush in. But it's cold. You can't tolerate the draft and once again, you have to be tormented by the smoke and coughing. Your eyes smart in the evening, when the fire is put out. You can't go to sleep for several hours because of the pain in your eyes. The Lapps suffer in exactly the same way.

It was a rush to get the dress done in the few dim hours in the middle of the day, but you learn to be unaffected by surroundings and conditions. I had to sew my fine needlework by firelight, even if someone sat next to me and tarred skis—brandishing them over the fire lengthwise and crosswise in the tent. One day when we were going to set off on trek, and all was in order, the tent taken down, the sleds packed, and we were just sitting outside waiting for the pack reindeer, Sara said, "You must take out your needlework, you don't have time to sit idle if the dress is going to get done." That was true enough and you could just as well, if you didn't freeze, sit outside and sew under the open sky in winter as well as summer. I hauled out my sewing bag and got far with the hemming before the reindeer came.

For the Lapps, the wilderness, forest, and mountains are their ordinary living room. Their home is where they happen to find themselves. They don't need four walls to feel secure or to work at household tasks.

The dress was finished and departure day dawned with dark clouds—in the tent. Nikki had refused to allow Sara to come to Jukkasjärvi. That had completely upset her mood. She was silent and stiff the whole morning. Nikki himself had to sew the harnesses that needed a little repairing. She didn't participate in anything, and when Nikki suggested to her that we might have pancakes and or something else warm before the departure, she didn't answer at all but took her skis and went to check the ptarmigan snares. We didn't get any pancakes that day and had to travel on buttered bread and coffee.

The reindeer stood tied to a tree. The sleds were ready. The small bundle with clothes for church and food was tightly tucked into the tip of the sled. Otherwise the sled was empty. The Lapps have no pelts or rugs in the sled to pack themselves in. You sit in it with the same clothes you would otherwise be wearing.

In all, we were seven from the same *siida* going to market, four men and three women, but we neither traveled together nor managed to glimpse one another's departure. The reindeer saw to that. The wolves had scattered the herd that night, and when Nikki went out to fetch the draft reindeer, he had to take the best ones he could get. There wasn't time to look for those that were particularly tame—it would be up to the herders to round up the whole group. The two he returned with were far from used to being driven. The one who was harnessed to my sled could only have been driven one time before. Nikki himself took the one that was a little tamer, to better lead the way for us both.

My sled was tied behind his, and I had no need of the driving skills that Sara had impressed upon me in the tent when she'd taken a rein and demonstrated how you managed. The first advice was, "Never let go of the rein, whatever happens. If the reindeer get away from you, you're left helpless in the wilderness." But there could be no talk of steering the wild animal that now stood ready in front of me. I barely got a hurried request from Nikki to seat myself in the sled and to obey the order immediately. With the rein wound firmly around his hand and arm, he jumped into the sled, and with a violent jerk we sped like bullets through the air.

On that trip we traveled to a large extent more in the higher spheres than on earth. The sleds flew from hillock to hillock in large arcs, and their contents were flung out in the snow, but one, two, three, like lightening we went after our sleds and were back onboard while they were moving. The trouble was that it had snowed far too little, and when we were a couple of kilometers away from the *siida*, the stones and tussocks weren't covered. We dashed between them, over them, and on them, like a dinghy in the most frightening sea. We would have needed to be fitted with the strongest suction cups to stay in the sleds. To stop the reindeer, especially when the wild animals had gotten their speed up, was impossible. If we wanted to stay with them, we had to hang on.

We managed to hang on, but there was always some part of the body outside the sled. The furry skin gloves I had to tear off, the better to cling fast, and when the sled was half-turned on its side, the top half of my body ploughed through the snow, which pushed into my sleeves and around my neck where there was just the slightest opening. Often we were dragged behind the sled with just one hand hanging onto its edge. I believe my hair was stiff with fear. I only had one thought: to get through this.

When, in the course of a dozen minutes, we'd been overturned countless times, Nikki finally got hold of the reindeer and stopped in a small stand of birch. He looked exceedingly thoughtful as he said, *Dat gal ii mana bures,* "This isn't going very well."

I didn't feel called upon to contradict him, but when he suggested that I should attempt to steer by keeping my legs outside, I said, no thank you; I was too fond of my legs. So he cut a long solid birch stick, to give support and balance to either side when the dinghy again began its wild dance behind the reindeer. It plainly helped to have something to steer with. Now the excursions from the sled weren't so frequent. But my efforts to remain in the instrument of torture were desperate and not always crowned with success. It was most dangerous when we came down to the forest and the hills were steep—there I had to be on guard for when trees sharply braked our ride. The half-wild reindeer grew quite desperate with fear when the sled rammed its back legs.

There were hours of this, filled with adversity and tension, and I wondered if we would really reach Jukkasjärvi with all our limbs. Yet there was something comic about the whole journey, so that I had to choke back laughter each moment in order not to completely lose control over my hard-tensed muscles.

We came to a rest hut en route; we saw smoke from the chimney and Nikki went in, but he didn't think we should stay. The company inside consisted of some Finns, who were transporting a coffin down to a churchyard, and the coffin-sled lay nearby. Therefore, we continued the journey in the dark, after this extra little cheering up.

Later in the evening we saw firelight in the midst of the forest. Some of our fellow travelers were resting; we drove nearer, and not long after we were all gathered together. Things hadn't gone any better for them, and if they'd suspected how awful the driving conditions were, none of them would have set out on this trip to the market. The Lapps said they'd never experienced anything like it and also hoped to avoid repeating it ever again.

The reindeer were quickly unharnessed and tied together with a long rein here and there by the trees, wherever you'd first made sure there was lichen where they were tied up. It's immediately apparent if the reindeer find food or not; they don't make the slightest attempt to remove the snow if there's no lichen underneath.

An immense fire had been lit from the roots of a big wind-fallen pine tree. The food and coffee kettle came out, the latter filled with snow that was soon transformed into strong coffee.

The powerful fire roared; the flames flared up and lit the huge root of the overturned pine tree. With its knotted, twining arms, it formed a background for the fire, and the small cluster of skin-clad people gathered in the midst of the snow-laden forest. It was cold and our warm breath turned our hair, furs, eyebrows, and eyelashes frost white. Our skin was red and frostbitten, but in front of the fire everything melted and our spirits returned. Naturally, the horrible driving conditions were the subject of conversation, and everyone inquired kindly after one another's health. The women crowed just the slightest bit over the men being just as worn-out as they were. It was all taken in good humor, however uncomfortable, even dangerous the reality was.

When we'd eaten and drunk coffee, the reindeer were moved to other trees to graze further while we rested, some in the sleds, others around the fire. The Lapps thought briefly of spending the night here but gave that up.

I fell asleep almost immediately. When I woke a little while later, reality was like a continuing dream: the night-dark silent forest, snow that fell softly from heavy branches, the sleeping fur-clad figures in the firelight, which didn't resemble real people, but were like childhood's fairytale characters come to life. Yes, they looked so much like them that they gave even their surroundings the same gleam of fairytale and remoteness that made life with them and among them so rich and beautiful. After a couple of hours rest we left the campfire in the forest and began again the difficult trip to market. The reindeer had now rested and once more dashed heatedly forward. It was dangerous to drive a sled in the forest; in the dark it's easy to be flung against a tree and crush your head or break your back and limbs, a manner of death not unknown among the Lapps. Fortunately, I didn't hear these stories until later.

As we emerged from the forest, again there were stones and frozen tussocks, and the wild flight continued, but now I'd gotten more practice in keeping myself inside, which surprised Nikki so much that he exclaimed, once we came to a halt, *Dat lea gummá, don bisut gerresis.* "What a surprise that you can stay in the sled." All the same, I was once thrown so hard out of the sled that I got back to it too late, only to see the sleds disappearing like a black streak on the snow. Finally, Nikki picked up my shouts and stopped.

But when we reached Suutusjärvi our troubles ended. The snow lay evenly on the ice, and tired nerves and muscles relaxed deliciously. The reindeer probably felt the same. Here there was nothing to be afraid of; besides that, it grew a little brighter. The moon came up and hung red over the mountains. Finally, it was a pleasure to sit in the sled and feel it glide smoothly over the snow. We were followed now by everyone, all of us in market-going spirits, but there wasn't much said. Only Gaiso sat and hummed, alternating with little calls to the magnificent reindeer with many-pointed antlers that pulled her sled. Around the lake the forest was dark against the snow. The moon rose higher and shone so that its greenish shadows followed us.

Suddenly, far off up in the mountains, a number of small points of light appeared. Was it the traveling Lapps who'd started a fire? No, there were far too many campfires. I called to Nikki, *Mii dope lea?* He answered back in his gentle language: *Girona* (the town of Kiruna). Electric lamps up in the iron ore mines were visible out here in the wilderness.

Toward midnight it grew cold. Frost sang in the ice, and clouds crossed the moon. Both people and reindeer were tired. I wondered what my bed for the night might be—probably a reindeer skin on a hard floor in the main room of someone's house. It was very dark when Nikki searched out a tiny little house where a pair of older Lapps who'd given up the nomad life lived. Nikki kept their few reindeer in his herd and therefore was accustomed to live with them when he was in Jukkasjärvi.

He banged on the door and soon a frail little Lapp woman came and let us in. All three of us were received warmly—Nikki's son-in-law had come with us.

Soon the open hearth was blazing. Lapps are never impatient at being disturbed in the night; they're used to it from tent life. Inside the small room it was shining clean. The whole house consisted of this single room.

The man of the house, a gnome of an old fellow, sat up in bed chatting and asking for news about his reindeer. The grown son lay on his sleeping bench with open eyes. On the floor lay a visitor to the market who'd arrived before us the same evening. After an hour we all slept in spite of the strong coffee we'd just been treated to. The son gave up his sleeping bench to me. He lay down on the floor with the three others; there were sufficient reindeer skins and bedding.

When I woke the next morning it was still completely dark. The woman stood small and thin in front of the hearth and made coffee. The fire shone over the wrinkled brown face and made her pretty old Lapp clothing sparkle. The room was a paradise of comfort. With a sense of well-being I fell asleep again and only wakened completely when Gate stood in front of my bed with a cup of coffee and a friendly, "Good morning, how are you?"

It was reasonable to ask about my state of health, I understood, for on the floor sat Nikki stripped to his waist, looking pitiful, while someone enthusiastically rubbed his back with grease. He was that exhausted from the journey. By the way, all the Lapps became more or less ill a couple of days after that trip.

It was strange to wake inside a room after almost six months of tent life. One of the oddest things was to look out the windows, after so long having seen the sky through the tent hole. On a large old water pump outside sat a magpie with his long metallic tail and fine white breast. Other magpies strolled in the snow. There lay the old gray Finnish farms, and behind them you could see the mountains far off. It was Sunday, and an elderly Finnish housewife came wandering along the path, enjoying her morning pipe with relish. From the wide chimneys of the farms, smoke rose up in the gray-red morning air. It froze hard; footsteps in the snow squeaked and creaked so much they could be heard in the room.

When it was time for the service, the Lapps gathered in and around the church. The small gray Finnish village took on a lively appearance with their arrival. They glowed like flowers on the paths and in doorways and windows.

The church was soon full, partly with Lapps and Finns, partly with townsfolk who'd traveled out from Kiruna to feast their eyes on the mountain peoples' colorful clothing and unfamiliar appearance. Inside the church before the service, it wasn't such a solemn affair as when farmers and other people gathered there. The Lapps chatted among themselves, strolled freely around, looking at everything. Children of all ages had come along, and here and there, a dog that had snuck away from home went around sniffing at everything.

When the priest came, however, it was quiet, as far as dogs and small children could keep silent. The sermon was in Finnish, and after it several Lapp children were baptized; then Communion was held, during which a couple of women got *liikutuksia* and began, as in a Laestadian prayer meeting, to sob aloud and cry out to God. They were women who were grieving. Afterward there was a burial. When the priest had read some words over the corpse, it was carried through the church and out to the waiting corpse-sled to be driven a long ways over the lake to the small island where the graveyard lay. While the priest spoke, a woman sobbed without ceasing. This mother was burying her second grown son. He had died during the summer up in the mountains and was now brought, on winter roads, to the churchyard. Finally she sank, fainting, in the snow.

As the weak daylight disappeared and the darkness and stars came on, the funeral procession moved out over the ice in a long, multicolored line. The Lapps have no mourning clothes; they don't walk in solemn procession; mothers carry their small children in cradles on their backs and dogs come along, just as they do wherever the Lapps travel. It is as if these people were completely unprepared to grieve, and thus grief goes deep into their hearts. Often they can be deeply unsettled for several years if death takes those they're most attached to.

The Lapps stayed several days in Jukkasjärvi. It wasn't just the spiritual business that needed taking care of. They also needed to shop. This wasn't a true market such as we know: no performances or booths of any kind, no drinking or festivity, such as in times past. Only a few merchants from the nearest town had set themselves up with their wares in a farmhouse. A baker showed up outdoors, for just one day; he sold bread from his wagon. But he was soon sold out and vanished again.

The only bright spots for the visitors to the market were the many Laestadian prayer meetings that could last far into the night. Otherwise, the days passed silently in the darkness; when you went to have coffee with people, it could be difficult enough to find your way around the farmyards and to get yourself safely home. By early afternoon it was completely dark, and through the darkness you could hear the stately booms of the ore blasting in Kiruna. The flashing, lit-up mountain admonished, with its self-important voice, not to forget reality during the dark months, when dreams could so easily get out of hand.

When the children had been baptized, the dead buried, the buying and selling ended, and the traveling preachers gone, we too set out on our journey home.

The reindeer had, during these days, been together in a group in the vicinity of Jukkasjärvi. The Lapps had worked in shifts to guard them day and night, but since there were wolves in the neighborhood, the reindeer had been very restless, and in spite of the herding they'd moved so far off that it took a couple of additional days to get hold of them so we could depart.

The homeward journey was quite without adventure and adversity. The trip here had somewhat tamed the reindeer, and besides, the snow had grown heavier in the interval so that the driving conditions were excellent. Everyone stayed together all the way home. Nikki's son-in-law drove last. He had a string of three or four baggage-sleds, with his own and several others' goods from the market, but when we arrived at the rest hut, misfortune overtook him. He'd lost a sled without noticing it. That can happen easily, if the sled knocks hard against something and gets stuck, so that the towing rope is loosened or breaks. In the pitch dark it's not easy to keep an eye on the string. Still, he had to be glad that the reindeer hadn't come to any harm. Now the poor man had to backtrack a few kilometers to fetch the sled and pull it forward himself, while we drank coffee and ate in blessed comfort. Those sorts of events are laughed at, when you're not the unlucky one.

The air was downy and mouse gray; a fine snow fell. In the forest the big freestanding spruce rose up like Chinese pagodas. When we came out of the forest it was very wild, without road or path; no horizon, no shadows, only an empty gray nothingness.

The reindeer drawing my sled had quite changed its nature. It walked slowly and allowed itself to be pulled by the reindeer in front, which therefore soon grew tired. Moreover, Nikki drove first, and his reindeer trod a track for all those who followed afterward. It was tough work in quite deep, loose snow, and thus the reindeer lay down frequently. Finally, Nikki sat down in the snow alongside the reindeer and told us he couldn't find the trail any longer. Now we could stay here until it got light, then we could orient ourselves. But the son-in-law wouldn't hear of it; he knew where we were and wanted to go home. So he took over the lead position and we followed behind. It wasn't more than a couple of hours before we smelled smoke from the tents and heard the dogs, who had recognized us from far off.

In between the trees, the sparks of the fire rose up in the dark air; there was the *siida*. When we drove in between the tents, several door flaps were lifted up; a figure showed itself against a fire-lit background to see who the arrivals were.

Never had the tent seemed to me so large and cozy as that evening. Fresh spruce branches had been laid on the floor. Sara sat in front of the fire with her friendliest expression, the coffee ready in front of her. The children looked expectant, and the dogs were near to eating us up with delight.

XV

THE TIME BEFORE CHRISTMAS WENT QUICKLY; dark and cold, the days slipped by, without an hour's worth of boredom. The cold sharply intensified and reached its lowest degree on Christmas Eve. The herd was closely watched, since wolves had come quite near. The part of the herd we had here consisted largely of the valuable tame driving reindeer that we still had use for during the migrations. The remaining part of the herd were reindeer left behind and those that later were separated out of others' herds.

Nikki and Inga took turns guarding the herd, night and day, like the others in the camp. It was mostly the men and girls who had to stay out; all the other herders were with the main herd in southern districts in the true winter grazing lands.

To watch for wolves is hard work. The herder needs to be on skis the whole time, can't rest at all, and what's worse, he has to hoot and holler without interruption to frighten the brute. But he can't shout in the direction where the wolf is said to live; for the wolf is versed in magic and can strike him dumb.

In spite of close watching, more than a few reindeer went to the wolves. If some individual reindeer leave the main group and "the enemy" is nearby, the wolf can get in to do damage before people and dogs can stop it.

A couple of evenings before Christmas, when we had gone to bed and the fire was out, the door was quietly lifted and Turi appeared in the opening, weather beaten and frost white. At his *Bures, bures*, "Hello, hello," Sara stuck her head out of her mosquito netting, and a little afterward, everyone was awake. The fire was stoked up. The guest was offered food and coffee.

Turi had come to inform me that he couldn't keep his earlier promise to take me to Karesuando and Kautokeino, because such a trip surely would cost him the driving reindeer we'd need to use. The wolves were far too numerous that winter, and on such a long trip he couldn't guard them every night. In this way, a couple of solitary reindeer would therefore inevitably go missing. It was a great disappointment to me that the trip wasn't going to happen, but on the other hand, I was happily surprised that Turi brought a great deal of Christmas mail, many letters and packages. The latter contained mostly cakes and sweets, which were particularly welcome to me and those around me.

Turi stayed with us for a week. He wanted, after the holidays, to set his traps nearby, in case he could get rid of a wolf or two.

Christmas Eve dawned with a temperature of minus forty degrees. Inside the tent we couldn't see each other for a fog of frost, and the tent was white with frost on the inner walls despite the huge fire. When the thermometer sinks to such a low temperature this fog appears—hot steam from the fire mixes with the ice-cold air coming down from the smoke hole above and pouring in under the bottom edge of the tent.

Outside, the sky was completely clear, quite unearthly clear in the half light of the middle of the day. I went out into all that silent white and followed a single ski track that turned north, away from the tents. After an hour's time, the tents, the forest, and all sound from there was gone. Everything was white—not cold chalk white, but glittering, like pale hyacinths. The colors of the air sank over the earth. In the west, Tavanjunje Mountain climbed sheer and solitary; the steep slope in the north lay in lilac shadow, while the south side sparkled faintly like mother-of-pearl.

The ski track ended in a little scrub-covered rise in the terrain; ah yes, it was here that the children had their ptarmigan snares. Fortunately, no ptarmigans were trapped. If a white bird had been flapping in the snow I would have let it go with a clear conscience.

I went farther through the stillness. It seemed almost unpleasant, hearing the skis gliding over the snow, and I stopped. All sound ended immediately. Only in my head did the blood ring faintly. Then from far off came the sound of a reindeer bell. The herd was going up around Tavanjunje. Immediately I believed, in my Christmas mood, that it was the sound of a church bell, which wouldn't have been a good thing. The Lapps say that he who hears a church bell in the wilderness will die the same year.

No, the sound of holiness doesn't reach into the wilderness, where the underground beings live. The church and its believers leave us alone here. And just as I stood there, I heard a weak but clear half-humming song deep under the snow. I listened for a long time, and the silence made it possible for me to make out plainly where the sound came from. There must have been a reasonable explanation—probably a spring had frozen not far below. I stuck my ski pole to the bottom; it was completely dry when it came up, but the sound stilled at the same moment and I continued on after having waited a little.

When I returned to the spot, I heard the faint singing again. Afterward I told Sara about it and she said, "You've heard the underground beings, the Uldas. That's unusual during the winter."

Now the forest with the tents became visible again. The smoke twined throughout the trees like the finest elven web. The sound of axes rang out everywhere; all were busy chopping wood, which needed to last over the holidays in great cold. Soon the stacks would be high enough and everything ready. The twilight had already set in, even though it was only a little past one.

However, the abundant wood-cutting was the only thing that indicated a major holiday approaching. The children were given repeated admonitions not to make noise or run around the tent: no loud voices or wild play. You need to be very careful and quiet when "the evil one" is out and is looking for sinners as a big holiday approaches, particularly *ruohttaeahket*, Christmas Eve.

Turi and Inga chopped wood, and I joined in to keep warm. It was so cold that every little downy hair on your face stood up like a quill, and if you blinked, your lashes froze together in a split second. The evening by the fire could feel long; you had to sit there idle for many hours. The holiday and cold brought all activity to a halt.

Where there was enough wood, the white pieces of birch were arranged in a nice-looking pile. The twigs were placed in the same way so that no branch stuck out, and the camp was cleared of tree litter. Turi instructed us and helped out. Before he went inside, he set up a very long birch branch next to the chopping block. Later I realized the branch was for Stallo, who could tie up his string here when he went inside on Christmas Eve, after his custom, to see whether all was in order in the manner it should be. He's thirsty after his travels and drinks water; that's why the kettle needs to be full the night before Christmas. If it's not, he sucks out the brains of the youngest child in the tent with an iron pipe (it's usually the task of the children to fetch water).

As the day darkened, the camp fell into deep silence, as if all sound had frozen. The chopping of the axes had ceased. No human voices, no dogs barking. The only living thing was a thick, spark-filled smoke that billowed out the smoke holes from the large fires in the tents.

When Nikki came home in the afternoon from the herd, he brought with him a dead reindeer that he'd found just after a wolf had killed it.

"The *návdi* [wolf] wanted to have himself a *ruohttamális* [Christmas dinner]," said Inga, but she was shushed by Sara. It was better not to speak of dangerous things at the most dangerous time of the year. Gray-legs had been particularly evil that day; many in the community had to provide reindeer for his Christmas meal. Little Oula, a nine-year-old neighbor boy with overflowing spirits, had been especially loud during the day's play, hooting and hollering, so that Sara had often scolded him. Now he was the subject of her harsh reproaches. The dead reindeer proved how dangerous it was to make noise so close to the holiday. The boy looked skeptical but accepted his talking-to with equanimity. But Sara was in a bad mood; one of her best reindeer cows now lay bloody and torn apart.

Nikki pulled it outside the tent, behind the kitchen space, where all the butchering took place; a little later he came in with the steaming entrails in a large bowl. Afterward, against all usual custom, he dragged the dead reindeer inside, under the tent cloth, to skin it and cut it into pieces. Outdoors everything would have frozen between his fingers.

The Christmas tent wasn't cozy. First: there was the dense, clammy fog of frost, which almost prevented any feeling of being indoors; Nikki, with his bloody work; the dead reindeer, whose large, dulled eyes created such a dismal mood; and Sara, silent and cross, she who was always good-humored. The children weren't to be seen; they were probably in another tent, where the mood was livelier. They only returned home in the evening.

The stewpot was hung over the fire, but it didn't lift our spirits to see that Nikki had filled it with meat from the reindeer killed by the wolf. This sort of meat is quite bad, in part because the animal is hunted to its death and in part because the actual bite of the wolf has a sharp taste, the Lapps maintain. Additionally, this reindeer cow was skinny, and lean reindeer meat is never a delicacy.

I asked Sara's permission to bring inside a small spruce tree and to set it in the kitchen and light it with the Christmas candles I'd gotten in one of my packages. The children were quite excited about the idea but Sara sternly rebuffed our pleas: "People shouldn't have those sorts of amusements on Christmas Eve."

We had to be satisfied with the Christmas lights provided by the fire, the moon, and the stars. It was so cold that many particles of ice in the air were visible as a rainbow-colored ring around everything that shone. Such a large, colored ring was around the moon, the large stars, and around some of the flames in the fire. Even if you struck a match, the same colored ring appeared around the flame. I placed a candle on a little spruce in the snow outside the tent. It stood there with its halo, burning fine and quiet in the large forest, but it was so cold I couldn't hold out long enough to see it melt down.

In this paralyzing cold and the endless dark, it was like standing apart from earth, exposed to the icy rays of the universe, surrounded by a dead nothingness that spread its terror over a poor night-black globe, where here and there a small clump of skin-clad people gathered around a fire in the deep snow.

But even though it was Christmas Eve and far below freezing, the herders had to go out to the herd if they didn't want to risk being without reindeer the next day, the way the wolves were hunting. Nikki had been out during the day. Now it was Inga's turn to take the night watch. She got up, snatching her fur-lined leather gloves, called to the dog, and as she went out she tied her cap under the chin. These were her only preparations for the long night.

It was cold for the two who left, but it was no warmer or more comfortable for those who sat at home.

Shortly before the meal was served, Turi disappeared to his sister's tent, where they probably weren't having "wolf meat" for supper on Christmas Eve. We gathered, meanwhile, around the food and served ourselves from the dishes, but the meal was passed in deep silence, and when we were finished, everyone took off their gloves and began to straighten the bedding.

Sara, occupied with something in the kitchen, suddenly exclaimed, "No, I've never seen anything like it before—long icicles hanging off the end of the log burning on the fire!" It was hot steam pouring out of the new wood that had momentarily frozen.

Christmas night was a cold one to get through; in spite of the fur-lined boots and dry hay, your feet felt like blocks of ice. The water kettle was solidly frozen and made creaking noises; the trees outside groaned with the cold. Little Nilsa walked in his sleep and sat down by the door, but Sara woke and got the boy tucked under the covers again.

"I thought it was the Christmas-Stallo who'd come into the tent, when I saw you sitting over there by the door," said Sara in the morning, when she told us about it.

I couldn't sleep well with my face under the covers, and so I used to wrap my head in a woolen shawl. It was quite uncomfortable to wake in the morning with this garment covered in ice over my face; the shawl always froze stiff from my breath, so it had to be pried apart. If you pulled the mosquito tent around you, for warmth's sake, you lay there in a small snow house in the morning, where everything inside was white with thick frost crystals. The dogs too were white with frost; their breath frozen. Our little puppy had now grown up to such an extent that he decided on his own where he wanted to sleep, and he'd chosen a spot under my chin. There he lay with his head near my face so that my breath could keep him warm. Often when the temperature dropped, I was awakened by the puppy sticking his ice-cold little snout completely against my nose under the shawl. Even after the puppy grew up to be large and strong, he kept his spot.

It was eight in the morning when Inga and her dog Rill came home, chalk white with frost and snow and with long icicles in their hair. No one wished her "Merry Christmas." No one said anything at all. The mountain folk aren't troubled by sentimentality; no one uttered a word about it having been a difficult Christmas night for the young girl. She knocked the snow and frost off her clothes at the door, hung up her gloves, and sat down silently to wait for morning coffee, while Rill lay down in front of the fire, zealously picking the lumps of ice from his coat and licking his exhausted legs.

XVI

As soon as the first holidays were over, we migrated. The aim was to escape from the wolves as quickly as possible; for that reason, we were only a short time in each place.

On New Year's Day the children came in to report that the sun was visible—this was only a false alarm, but it was true that you could hardly stand to look at the brilliant southern sky. The sun couldn't be far away.

The extreme cold lasted over Christmas and kept everyone except the reindeer herders partially idle. All there was during these days was work with the migrations, wood chopping, daily cooking, and, for those who had small children, careful child-minding. No one could keep up with any sort of handiwork. Besides, we unpacked the sleds reluctantly, when we had to move on again. Only the most important household utensils and bedding were taken into the tent. During the rapid migrations two families could also merge together in one tent for the sake of convenience. That's always rather uncomfortable, however; the tent grows crammed with people and dogs. Five or six big dogs take up a lot of room and warmth; they naturally place themselves in front of the fire when they're home, and you have to continually thrash them away if you want to get any heat. The dogs are also severely infested with tapeworms, which disappear into the twigs. Yet it's also a comfort that you don't find little brown fleas among the Lapp dogs in the northern Lappmarks.

When it's quite cold, it also happens that the Lapps make the tent smaller, more close-fitting, to more easily get it warm. Nor do you select the campsite with particular care, when you only intend to stay there a couple of days. And so we were, for the whole Christmas period, quite uncomfortable. Large granite boulders stuck up through the snow inside the tent, and we had to arrange our bedding between them or on them as best we could.

Meanwhile the days grew lighter and lighter, and on Epiphany we saw the sun for the first time this year. The tents lay on a hillside below the forest, and in front of them was a large mountain plateau with small, tree-covered island-hills. When we unsuspectingly came out in the morning our eyes were dazzled by the strong rays. The sun was a pale green slice in the midst of a sea of fire. Wherever you turned your eyes, you saw green suns, and the snow sparkled and flashed. A certain holiday feeling spread quickly through the camp, and everyone told each other the news.

The children played excitedly the whole morning outside the tents. They went to the market, pulled one another on skis, as when a reindeer is harnessed to a skier. They romped in the snow to their hearts' content until Elle burst out in dismay, "Oh, my goodness, it's a *bassi* [a holy day]. Imagine if Stallo came!"

The joyful mood ebbed considerably. A little afterward the game was discontinued.

The next day we were to move on again. A couple of ravens had crossed over above and notified us with their "runk, runk" that brother wolf was in the vicinity or, in any case, would be there soon. It was so cold that the Lapps shrank from trekking, but we had to go. The tents were taken down, the sleds stood ready, only the fires burned and the coffee kettles waited for those who were bringing the reindeer.

Finally they arrived, recognizable as a white cloud that moved low across the snow in the clear air. It was the animals' warm breath that condensed around them in the cold. Slowly the gray patch with its cloud passed over the great expanse of snow. At the apex of the herd was Nikki on his long skis with the leader on a rein after him; he steadily repeated the long drawn-out *cus, cu-s*.

After the leader came the followers and the whole herd, encircled by herders and dogs. They stayed some distance away, and the draft reindeer were captured. As soon as the herd came into view, the older children set out with all the reins in a loop over their shoulders.

As all the reindeer were captured and roped together, the children pulled them in the direction of the sleds. The people who would be in the lead and would drive the herd went ahead of them, while the others began to harness the reindeer and put the caravan in order. Little Nilsa tended to be the most eager to fetch and harness the draft reindeer, but this time, when he arrived with the draft reindeer and the harnessing had begun, he suddenly began to cry from the cold and shouted, quite despairingly and bad-temperedly, *In mon leat lengeme, in, in!* "I won't harness, I won't!" Inga smiled and took over the work, while Nilsa went to the fire to thaw out his humor and his toes.

It was already twilight by the time we departed. The icy cold soon bit through all our clothes, since it was also mixed with wind. We sat quietly in the sleds. The snow shrieked and whistled. The sounds cut into the deadly stillness in the air. No one uttered a word; everyone was trying to cope with his own sensations of cold. I believed, by the way, that it was only me who froze so badly; for instance, I saw a young woman stop her sled and nurse her baby in the middle of the migration. But I also saw Sara dig out a large shawl from a sled and put it around her head and neck, so she at least couldn't have been too warm, I thought. When we told stories about the trek later in the tent, I realized all the Lapps had very likely been quite frozen.

Sara even said, "Well, I was so freezing that when I saw Marja nursing the baby, I thought, If it had been my child, he could have just starved to death. I couldn't have nursed in such cold."

After that migration I developed a fever with strong rheumatic pains and had to stay in bed for several days. The Lapps said, quite frankly, "You'll probably die now." But since I myself had no such premonition, I took the situation in good humor and asked them merely to build up the fire so as to get the cold out of my body. Quite without result I took all the medicine I could lay my hands on, both from my own pharmacy and from Sara's little store, though I didn't experiment with dried seeds, which perhaps was wrong of me.[21] Fortunately, the next trek was to Vittangi, where there was a doctor.

The journey there was certainly agonizing. All the same, it was cheering to drive the last stretch down to the river and see the lights from the farmhouses that lay in a long unruly row. We stopped a little ways from the farm lying farthest away, where Nikki was accustomed to board. The flames from the open fireplace shone through the window. The puppy and I were last in the string to go inside. He was unsure where to turn—there was no tent after all and I almost couldn't walk. Usually the puppy chose to follow the others' tracks, but Sara and the children had disappeared into the house before the rear party arrived. There stood the puppy. His people had been swallowed up in a big black hole that now opened up to swallow him. The dark entryway appeared quite unpleasant, especially for a little dog that had never seen a house before.

Suddenly fear grabbed him and he lost his head. He ran for his life across the snow and would surely have been overcome by cold in the course of the night if he hadn't been caught. I limped after him sweating in agony and got hold of the little chap, whose heart banged wildly in fear as we went inside.

For my part I was happy about the stay at the farm among the kindly Finns, where I grew quite well again with the doctor's help. But for the puppy it was and remained a strange "tent"—you couldn't pilfer the food, couldn't get up on the bed, couldn't feel any warmth from the fire. You were forced to stay down on the floor where it was hard and cold. But the strangest thing was probably the cat. Such a being the puppy had never seen before. When he'd looked at the fantastic animal in dumb bewilderment for some time, Tji-Tji (a sort of pet name for small puppies) tried to see if it could play. With a sharp little yap and leap he bumped his clumsy front paw invitingly just in front of the puss. The result was unexpected and terrifying: a hiss, a pair of fiery eyes, and a sharp cuff.

The puppy sneezed and stared crestfallen after the cat, which, with a bound, was up on the cornice above the stove. The furry little bungler looked foolish; it was exceedingly hard to get on in this strange world.

The very young Lapp children also found the room remarkable; they didn't experience the same hardships as the dog, but they looked straight up in the air and burst out, *Dat lea imaš goahti, goi i leat reahpen.* "This is a strange tent. It has no smoke hole."

A number of Lapps lodge for longer or shorter times in the farmhouses during the hardest part of the winter. They are mostly young mothers with small children. The men are usually out with the reindeer, and some of them live in a tent with relatives or acquaintances in the vicinity of the herds. There were no infants with us, and therefore the family moved quickly to the forest a half a dozen kilometers from Vittangi. But almost every day someone from the camp went in to town on some errand or another. Sara had been commissioned to sew several pairs of Lapp shoes for the farmers, and in the bitter cold she preferred to be in the Finnish farm during the days that she sewed. Now it was light and clear; the snow glittered and shone like sun on a windowpane, wherever you turned your eyes.

One day when I came near the farm after a short stroll, I saw some Lapps and dogs come down the frozen river with a small herd of reindeer, a *čora* (group of forty to fifty animals), just the number we'd expected they would be bringing (some of the Lapps had gone back after the trek here to collect the reindeer that remained behind). They walked remarkably quietly, which surprised me a little; however, I went inside without paying further attention and announced that the reindeer we'd expected had come. When Nikki trudged in shortly afterward, he vehemently denied that a single reindeer had arrived. At which I became a little miffed, since I was certain of my facts.

Sara listened to us and then she said, half-whispering to me, *Ulddat*.

I yielded to this explanation and she added, "If you'd understood these were Uldas, you should have gone nearer and cast your knife or even a sewing needle at them. Then you would have been able to own the reindeer. At any rate you'll become rich, since you both see and hear Uldas."

The Lapps value having attractive animals in the herd. White reindeer or white reindeer with dark patches are considered ornamental. The Lapps are of the opinion that the underground beings have very pretty herds, which to a large extent consist of white reindeer, very tame and powerful. Therefore, it's worth stealing them when the Uldas are so good as to show their herd to someone or another. To be friends with the underground beings means comfort for the herd and other luck in life. If you have many white reindeer, you can gratify your desire to be clad in white in winter. It was particularly common in the northern Lappmarks to have white furs. Among the Lapps in Kautokeino only the women wore white furs. In the Torne River district, furs were mainly dark, but furry white boots and furry white gloves still are part of the finest costumes.

Life at the Finnish farm became, in spite of all its conveniences, monotonous. I longed for the tent and smoke hole with its stars that were mirrored in the black coffee in the morning. And one fine day when I'd become well again, when a group of Lapps came trekking by on their way south, Sara and I went with them. I was allowed to sit in the sled together with the young wife. Her powerful reindeer pulled both of us with ease along the smooth roadway. The sun shone, the snow sparkled white on all sides, and the conversation was lively. It was something besides sitting around twiddling your thumbs in a farmhouse. And how joyful it was to return home to the tent. There are those who say, half-scornfully, that the Lapp has no home, but those people don't understand the situation; in every meaningful way, the tent is his home. Certainly, the tent is moved from place to place, but the tent is always the same, inside and out. As soon as it is set up, the fire lit and the things taken inside, everything is in its old place and you continue with your daily tasks that you gave up a few hours ago.

You are home.

XVII

By happy accident, in March my wish to go to Karesuando was ful-filled. This was around Márjjábeaivi, Mary's Day (March 22), the great Lapp fair. In Karesuando during the holiday I met many Lapps and wanted to go with them on their spring migration into Norway, which would soon begin. The Talma Lapps, with whom I'd been staying up to now, were in fact heading back to the same tracts of land where they'd been in the autumn, which would be a little humdrum. Here, on the contrary, were new people, new conditions, and new territories. After arranging to spend the whole spring with a family, I went back to Vittangi to pack up my few belongings. It wasn't at all easy to say farewell to the people and dogs I'd lived with for nearly nine months, in hard times and good.

The Karesuando Lapps' spring migrations began that year in April. When the snow crusts over, in either March or April, the reindeer don't have food, with the exception of a little beard lichen they can snatch off trees. So they find their way up to the high mountains, where the wind and the sun together have thinned the snow earlier than in the forest. This migration to the high mountains generally takes place quickly and at night, when the layer of ice on the snow bears people and caravans.

"In the spring we are like flying birds, we don't leave a trail," say the Lapps, and in the course of a few days they trek many kilometers.

The family I'd negotiated my way into consisted of the husband, Heikka; wife, Gate; and an eleven-year-old girl, Rauna. The last two had been in Kare-suando for a while, and I went with them from there out to a small Finnish farm where we would meet the husband and begin the migration to the high mountains.

In the small dairy room, which is always found next to the main room, lived the old parents of the Finns; we stayed with them. It was as full of people as the main room. There were six of us—in the other room, countless. Besides that, the cow had calved that day, and since it was too cold in the stall for the newly born calf, she was brought in and placed in a corner by the fireplace.

Soon there was a big discussion among the children as to what the little heifer should be called; the name chosen was Puolankukka—Ligonberry Flower.

We also increased our animal population in the main room with two tiny, still blind puppies. The Lapps' old dog had been injured during the birth, so when Gate left Karesuando, she took along both the puppies, swaddled in a fur, and asked the farmer to put down their mother. It was difficult for Rauna to leave the dog, but each time she began to talk about it, Gate gave her a sharp reprimand, so she pushed her feelings away and kept the crying down.

It was a great deal of work for Gate to care for the two little mewling puppies. At the tip of a small horn she had sewed a teat of leather, but it wasn't easy to get them to suck the milk. They needed a gentle massage on the stomach, too, and were tickled with a stick to keep their bowels moving.

Two old Lapp women were lodging there, one of them "old as the sky," blind and quite deaf, the other animated and easy to understand. Each of them had their sled inside the main room; it served as a bed at night and a resting place during the day. The liveliest of the two old women was amusing to talk with; her husband had been a great bear hunter, but finally a bear had killed him. He'd been careless enough to go after an "angry" bear (a bear provoked by an unsuccessful attack). That led to his death. It was however, not easy to get her tell the story; she was eager to refresh herself by hearing something new and therefore asked me about everything touching myself.

The Lapps' first questions were always my age; if I was "rich"; if I was married or thought of getting married. An unmarried man or woman who reaches maturity is a nuisance to them. "Old maids" are highly unusual. There's always a particular reason or other when a girl remains unmarried.

The next questions generally have to do with what Denmark looks like and what it produces. That it has no mountains awakens great surprise. Next they ask whether tobacco, coffee, and rice grow in Denmark. They know that wheat and other sorts of fine grain grow there. Danish flour they know from Norway as the best, but they find it strange all the same to have that confirmed by a real Dane. All this and much more she wanted to know about. "It's so easy to talk with you. Some people are so difficult to talk with; it's like pulling a sled full of stones over dry ground."

I asked her if it wasn't difficult in the beginning to give up life in the mountains and stay in one place.

"Yes, the first year was quite hard. I couldn't sleep at night, and spring and autumn, when the Lapps were moving past here, it felt completely wrong. I used to go up on the hill nearby look around. We Lapps have the same nature as the reindeer. When it's spring, we yearn for the high mountains, and when it gets to be winter, we long to come down into the forests."

The second old Lapp woman, the blind one, wasn't enjoyable to talk with by reason of her deafness, but she herself was very talkative and almost always angry about something or other. Very miserly, she'd given a reindeer leg away in a bout of kindness. There was, however, not much meat on the leg, and the person to whom she'd given it had let her know. Now there was hell to pay. It was impossible to stop the stream of words coming from the old lady, or get through to her. "She talks as long as her mouth is warm."

A little after the storm of words, the door to the room where I was alone for a moment opened, and a small wrinkled hand grasped the frame; then came the staff and finally the blind one herself. She closed the door carefully after herself and went over to the open fireplace and stretched her hands over the coals to warm them. Afterward the thin gray figure folded itself over the staff and shrank like a soft little bat down on the floor in front of the fire. The worn old fur was as wrinkled and gray as sun-dried earth, the same color as her face and hands. The thin wisps of hair hung loose under the faded red cap; her face, in the manner of the blind, was turned upward. The live coals from the fire cast a faint glow over her one side and over the narrow doorway's worn red paint. Up on the chimney mantle was a small wooden box, where green grain grew a few centimeters high. This green blanket seemed so alive in the dark, golden-gray room with the faded red colors.

Suddenly the little gray Lapp-mother began to speak in sibylline tones. She tossed out oaths about present-day gluttony and lack of respect for food. "They throw the bones wherever they want, without chewing off all the meat first. There's a price to pay for that. Once, when the Son of God wandered here on earth and passed by a Lapp community, he saw a discarded leg with meat on it and said, 'In this place I'm going to reduce their daily bread.'"

She resembled a ghost, a spirit who cursed the living, and it was quite a relief when she got up and went into the main room.

When I came in soon afterward, the little gray mummy lay in the sled. Her bedding consisted mainly of rags and scraps of fur. She was too stingy to use anything better, and when it was suggested to her that as a well-to-do woman she should have nicer bedding, she answered that her scraps were made of silk. At the same time, she stroked them lovingly, as if she touched the finest of material. Perhaps the old lady believed it herself. She had been blind half her life, and they said she would soon be a hundred years old. Reality could not correct the fantasy.

We remained at the farm a couple of days until Heikka came with the reindeer. It was blowing cold that Saturday afternoon. The sleds were packed up and we set out for the mountains. Now our journey would take us toward the Norwegian border, together with the highest "high people."[22] We had only one driving sled, and Gate, Rauna, and I took turns sitting in it while Heikka led the string with the baggage sleds.

When we'd gone some distance, Heikka stopped and went off. From somewhere or other he had gotten a good store of pine to burn. He came back with it and put in the sled. From his wanting to trek a long way carrying firewood, I understood we were going so high up that we had to conserve fuel.

The string glided slowly upward, steadily over the snow to the high mountains. Everything was so strangely shapeless and unreal that night. We went forward in a numb white-gray darkness that could never lighten. A sharp wind blew around the top layer of fine snow; in circles and streams it glided over the endless expanses. No other sound was heard than the fine crunching of the snow and the footsteps of the reindeer. Something soft, half unseen, once came brushing closely past, rapid and ghostlike up from the mountain slope. It was a pair of white foxes.

The tracks of the string immediately drifted over, and in front there was no track. We were alone that dead white night. Heikka stopped a moment to fix something with the string. Gate sat down in the snow to light her pipe. The snow began to drift around us. It would be easy to become obliterated.

Suddenly an unpleasant howl, mixed with a kind of bark, sounded somewhere out in the snowy darkness. "The fox is howling. That warns of evil," said Gate. "If the fox allows itself to be heard when a Lapp *siida* is on migration, there will be one less in the *siida* when it treks back down in the autumn."

At length Gate was able to light her pipe. Heikka grumbled and Rauna ventured a small remark about the old dog they had left behind. Then everyone was silent again, and the string glided farther hour after hour. Finally, it began to lighten in earnest; the horizon grew visible, and the sun rose, miraculously. The ptarmigans played in the snow all around without bothering about us. All the silly uneasiness of the night vanished, and over at the edge of the mountains some small rounded dark peaks came into view. These were the tents of the *siida* that had migrated before us. No smoke rose yet; all the same, Gate with her fine sense of smell could be aware of the tents before we'd seen them.

The sun was completely up when we reached the *siida*. The reindeer were let loose. They moved slowly among us in the still, light morning hour and grazed on some snow-free spots.

Gate sat down in the snow and enjoyed her morning smoke in peace and quiet. Heikka rustled about, setting up the tent, and Rauna lay down to sleep in a sled. Without haste we raised the tent and brought in the bedding, after which we slept for a few hours.

It was quite true, as the Talma Lapps said, that up here their tents were smaller. It was partly that the tents were smaller and partly that the tent frame was slighter and not so carefully shaped, though the construction was completely the same. However, the tent was big enough for us four.

It was a Sunday morning (April 24) when we arrived at the *siida*. The sun shone over all this white wilderness, and sometime during the evening joiking sounded from the tents out over the lonely world of the high mountains.

The Lapps' joiking sounds as if it was learned from nature itself; it resembles the wind moving in withered grass and shrubs. It reminds you of water babbling and insects buzzing when there's quiet joiking, barely audible, during handiwork. But it can also be hoarse and violent in its expression, like a gale in a forest, like ravens croaking and storms howling. I have not heard joiking so often but I have heard both sorts, and always it's made me think of the sounds that are heard in the forests and mountains.

The Lapps up here have preserved their sense of color and love of everything that gleams and glitters. Silver, brass, and glass pearls were not banished from their clothes. Large silver buttons decorated both men's and women's belts; even quite young children had silver buttons on their belts. Silver was regarded as an amulet among them, something that would protect the children from being switched by the underground beings, who can't abduct children wearing silver with a hallmark. The underground beings don't have hallmarked silver and therefore can't substitute a child's button to exactly match. Otherwise, all their clothing is the same.

There were many young children in the *siida*. I grew to be especially good friends with seven-year-old Ingaš, the daughter of our foreman. Her father had become a widower a few years earlier and could not get over his grief. The very youngest, who had cost the mother her life, was being cared for on a Norwegian farm (it's almost impossible to have an infant along during the migrations when it has no mother to nurse it). The foreman had many grown sons and daughters, but the small brown girl was his favorite. The two were always to be seen, hand in hand, when they were together. He was melancholy that he would soon be without the child for several years, when her schooling began. He told me that if I wanted to teach Ingaš to read and write during the time I was with them, he would give me a tame, strong reindeer to borrow during all the migrations, so I could avoid walking so much. The old foreman was quite rich and the owner of many kinds of reindeer.

Unfortunately, neither he nor I could keep our promises. There was far too little calm during the frequent treks to practice any proper teaching (in contrast, there would be a good opportunity to teach the children in the tent during the winter and summer, when the Lapps are in one place for some months), and as for the tame, strong reindeer, its pace was just so-so. It was tame in all respects, but strength it had not. The whole herd starved unmercifully this spring and all the treks were the purest misery. We managed the first couple of moves since the reindeer had a little weight on them from the winter grazing down in the forests, though that also had been bad this year. But as time went by and it seemed like it would never become spring, the animals' energy was sapped to an alarming degree.

We didn't stay long at Nælgge-oaivve. The snow lay thick and white everywhere, and we had to find a better place. It was a long, tough trek over white mountains. Beauty there was plenty of—the sun shone, and the mountain's cleft resembled clear water with a glossy stripe of sun. Then the sun disappeared behind a mountain for a few hours while we continued wandering in a night light as day.

The endless white snowfields without a single bare patch were a sad sight for the Lapps and reindeer. The Lapps stopped and deliberated briefly, and the foreman went up a hill, with little Ingaš by the hand, to look out over the territory. No snow-free spots could be discovered, near or far, and therefore it was no use to set up camp yet. Tired and dispirited we moved forward into all that pitiless white. What use was all the beauty, with pale green ravines, golden colors, and the splendid winding trail of colorful strings and Lapps? It was such a horrible disappointment for them that no mountain slopes showed dark patches. The Lapps looked discouraged. At long last, the caravan stopped and the reindeer were unharnessed. Here the snow was thin in places, but under it was only sand and withered brush. The herd hungered miserably.

The tents stood high up on a hill, from which there was a broad view into "the forbidden land"—Finland. The only border was the river that lay thick with ice, underneath the ridge, and the reindeer can't respect a frozen river as a state boundary. Over there grew lichen, "as thick as hair on a reindeer pelt," and naturally the starving animals crossed the river. The herders were on their skis day and night, in part to collect the herd, which spreads out when hungry to find nourishment, in part to bring back the reindeer from the other side of the river. If they were caught over there, the Lapps were fined, with every tenth reindeer.

It was a strenuous time for both herders and dogs, without much rest. Occasionally a herder came home snow-blind; his eyes watered painfully, and he couldn't tolerate the slightest bit of light. But when the blindness passed, after one or two days, he had to set off again. Remarkably enough, they didn't protect their eyes with anything but an ordinary little oilcloth visor bought and sewn onto their own cloth caps. In earlier times, some placed a piece of birch bark up under the front of their cap, as a sort of screen. The Lapps don't use snow goggles of any kind. Nor are ordinary modern dark glasses popular, partly because they break easily and they're rarely dark enough to do any real good. But the most important obstacle for glasses most certainly has to do with the Lapps' aesthetic sense. Sara could sit there failing to thread her needle time after time when she sewed, and when I advised her to get some glasses, she answered, "I actually have some glasses, but I don't want to use them, because then I'd be as ugly as a foreign gentleman [*fasti dego hearrá*]."

The dogs also do badly in spring—the skin comes off their feet and legs. They can come home bleeding. They have to take time off work until their legs get better.

The sharp cold was with us day after day, without the slightest sign of spring. It was almost unpleasant, with the high, transparent frost sky that steadily poured its cold down on this part of the globe, without so much as a cloud to warm it when you knew it was spring and fertile in other places. The reindeer wandered here and there, looking worn out. They scraped the snow away, but it was incomprehensible they could keep alive with the little to be found. There was no point in moving on; the grazing wouldn't be any better. If a thaw didn't come, the herd would thin out badly and there would be many reindeer who "wouldn't hear the cuckoo in summer."

On the 8th of May, it was still persistently winter. Every day we had a driving snow so fine that not a hint of spring was to be found in the air, only sharp dead winter cold. Our playful little offerings to the Haldas didn't help.[23] They even got coffee with reindeer milk that was poured for them near the stones in the vicinity of the kitchen space.

On the 9th of May we had to trek farther, for each move must bring us a little closer to the spring in Norway. It was good to know that the reindeer cowherd was safe in the old calving place. We were coming afterward with baggage and the freely ranging herd.[24]

The trek was painful now because of the reindeer's wretched condition. Already some had fallen and could not go farther; they had to be unharnessed and left behind, while the men went into the herd that followed close by in order to capture new draft reindeer. The richest had more animals to harness, but the reindeer were tired and couldn't be exchanged for new ones.

Heikka had to work hard with his strings, changing the sleds around, lighter and heavier, after seeing the different reindeer's staying power. And then in addition he had to thrash the tired animals on their legs and help them over obstacles by taking hold of them himself.

The calming *hai hai* sounded continuously when a reindeer sank down into the snow and needed to get on its feet again. Once, while Heikka stood pushing and striking a reindeer that remained lying down unusually long, Rauna, who had been watching with a pained expression on her face, exclaimed, "Don't hit it anymore, it has tears in its eyes!"

Her mother, who also was working hard with her string, answered sharply, "That doesn't help. Our eyes are also watering from exertion and misery—and we're going on."

Sometimes, a long string of six or seven reindeer could all fall, so that they all lay down at once. When they are already weak in the legs and one falls, the others can't withstand the yank of the connecting reins, but are pulled down.

The Lapps cursed and swore and protested that their life was a dog's life. "We used to be able to drive our sleds like lords here and now we have to struggle forward in this miserable way."

One of the men herding the stray reindeers had lain down on a hill while the reindeer rested. He looked over Finland close by: it was easy to guess his thoughts—a Lapp is almost always thinking about reindeer. They're in his dreams at night and his thoughts during the day. They demand all his talents and energies and give him in return all the necessities of life. They're his sorrow and joy, his pride and worry; his personal wealth rises and falls depending to the state of his reindeer.

Over there to the east on the other side of the river, the lichen was gray and heavy; there he and the animals could find strength and courage. Over to the west behind the white mountains was spring and grass. But all the goodness was blocked by state boundaries, behind which lurked legal statutes, which were just as incomprehensible to the Lapp as to the reindeer.

It was completely forbidden to go east; to cross the border meant heavy losses. The western border wasn't closed in that sense, but inside it were settlers in the old dwelling places of the Lapps. They were now the masters while the Lapps were the unwelcome, importunate foreigners who were supposed to pay damage compensation because the reindeer grazed the places they were accustomed to from time immemorial. Perhaps it was not the worst thing in the world, but the case had a psychological aspect that gnawed deeper. The Lapps felt insecure and friendless over there, where before they and their relatives had been at home. Once they had longed for spring and summer as a joyful time. Now they were approaching obstacles and were worried and depressed.

Dejected and tired we reached Virko-kårsa, where we were to set up camp. When the tents were up and we'd slept a few hours and had morning coffee, our spirits rose somewhat. Here the grazing was a little better for the reindeer, and so we stayed quite a long time in the same place.

MAY.

The sun is up almost the whole day, the stars are gone and the moon is about to disappear in the light sky, but at the moment we're having the most horrible snowstorm. The tent doors flap open to the sky and the smoke flows around in thick clouds so your eyes run. We wait endlessly for spring up here. Not many yearlings will get to Norway this year if we don't get a serious thaw soon. And all the same, it's not as bad as 1906, when almost all the young animals died. Then there was weeping and heavy spirits in the tents; even children five years old understood the grief. Gate told the story of how one day, when little Ingaš was alone in the tent, she heard her pray: "Dear Father in Heaven, let the mild wind [*láfu biegga*] blow, so the little calves can live and we can be saved."

"That same day, a thaw came," Gate added.

Our old foreman, Ingaš's father, was rarely here in the evening. Tired and in a hurry, he lay down in front of the fire; his eyes wept and grew red as a reindeer stomach filled with blood, *dego mállečoavji*. He is on skis night and day, and when he finally attempts to sleep a little, his arms and legs ache and sleep doesn't come. They have a huge job preventing the reindeer from going into Finnish territory and from streaking over to Norway, and now, when the herd is hungry and therefore spread out, it's almost impossible to keep it together. The way of it here is that the rich Lapps work hard and the poor have it easy—they take reindeer herding more lightly, because they think: let the rich men labor; after all, the largest part of the herd is his. Since the Lapps never pressure one another, each one remains the other's problem: how much work he'll do for the common good.

In the evening, after Gate had boiled us a strong brew of tea, she grew so stimulated that she started telling some frightful stories of the dog-Turk—

half animal, half human with a dog's head and tail—that eats people. When she was finished, she said, "Well, there are many kinds of people in the world. The year before, a man came to Karesuando. He was wearing clothes of seal-skin, and his trousers were sewn in a strange fashion. He said that human flesh tasted wonderful when the poison was drawn out, and he ate reindeer meat raw. A woman from Karesuando grew frightened when one day she saw him walking with her granddaughter. She thought fearfully that perhaps he might eat her girl."

I questioned her a little more closely about this modern cannibal who had walked around openly in Karesuando. "Well, he had dark blood, dark skin, a big nose, and black 'crooked' hair." Suddenly I realized that it was Knud Rasmussen. He had been up there at that time and he had taken his Eskimo clothes to show to the Lapps. This is how easily myths spring up.

Here they can still tell stories. Sometimes in the evening a group gathers, both young and old, in the tent. If Gate is in the mood, it's not long before Stallo, the underground beings, ghosts, dog-Turks, and more throng forward. Each one has something to recount and add, but Gate is one of the best of the storytellers; she smokes her pipe and with calm dignity expresses everything in a way that makes it alive and real. The listeners lie and sit around the fire and follow the narrative with deep interest and rapt attention, often interrupting to ask about details. It can be midnight before the thin tent door rattles after the last guest.

MAY 14.

Winter, protracted winter. Everyone wants a thaw, everyone predicts a thaw; but in spite of "silk clouds," a west wind, sacrifices to the Haldas, and so on, it remains spring. How will it go with the herd? Oh, you wicked gods, Russians, and Norwegians!

But the children take what winter pleasures they find. They gather at the top of one or another suitable hill and the playing begins. Even small children of three or four go along, though it's not as fun for them since they can't participate on their own in the playing. It ends with them crying about being cold until one of the bigger children brings them home to the tent, where they're consoled and warmed by a father or mother.

The older children can continue playing, on the other hand, in the bitterest cold. They practice skiing either in the usual fashion or by making a toboggan. They do this by putting two skis tightly together and squeezing on as many as can fit, one behind the other. The downward trip begins, almost always ending with the whole flock tumbling off in the snow, and the skis, liberated from their load, setting a course out into the blue. When they ski in the usual way it's amazing to see the confidence with which the little ones treat the large skis. Few of them have children's skis that fit; most often it's a half-destroyed pair that the grown-ups passed on to them. Sometimes they only have one ski, but that only increases their skill.

Here, as in other places, children's play is often simply a repetition of the grown-ups' work. Naturally, they prefer to play "reindeer"—preferably the whole herd. The smallest children are the calves; some are draft reindeer, and the wildest are the untamed bulls, and so on, until the herd is represented. Both girls and boys participate in the game. Lassos whirr, and when a really wild bull is captured, a fierce battle is fought. Imaginary dogs are commanded. If a puppy happens to be along, it joins in eagerly of course.

They also have a number of games, *stálostallat* and *saeibástallat*, and others. The first consists of children stationing themselves at certain intervals and pretending to be dry tree stumps. One is Stallo, and he comes to fetch wood to burn and overturns the submissive tree stump. If the "stump" doesn't quietly allow itself to be chucked about, Stallo goes after his ax, whereupon all the children take off running. Stallo then captures one, who takes over his role. The tent is a free zone. *Saeibástallat*, the tail game, consists only of only children walking in a long line holding the backs of one anothers' clothes. The first one will then try to grasp the last one's "tail."

MAY 18.

The weather begins to be milder. Heikka predicts a thaw. I believe in his predictions. The reindeer are managing a little better now, that's quite a relief to hear.

A few days ago we got the puppy back from its foster mother. As a puppy is growing up, the Lapps regard him with a certain anticipation, to see how he's developing, if he has the something that will make him a good reindeer dog. It's a good sign if he bites and pulls at the layer of twigs on the ground; if he's eager and barks a lot. Besides that, he should have a high projecting forehead, be well supplied with dewclaws and have a small *bahtaráigi* (anus). It's best if his legs aren't too short or too thick, because then he's too heavy and not fast enough on the snow. But he can't be too thinly furred either, since then he won't tolerate the cold. One thing observed with particular anticipation is whether the ears come to stand straight up in the air and don't get too large.

It's regarded as particularly ugly if a dog has *luŋkebealjit* ("droopy ears"). If a puppy shows signs in that direction, they try to discourage it by constantly straightening up the ear with a little lengthwise pressure. Some also make a small cut in the ear, but whether these methods help is more than uncertain. (In the southern Lappmarks it's held that if the puppy's eyes are picked open too early, he will become clairvoyant). A fine dog mustn't have a large head either. The Lapps never lift a puppy by its neck. They maintain that will hurt him a great deal. Nor must a puppy be teased too much, so as not to become vicious.

Some Lapps break the eye teeth of small puppies to stop them biting and tearing as puppies tend to do, but other Lapps maintain that it wounds a dog for life if you break its teeth as a puppy. A Lapp dog won't stand being clipped either. A girl in Jämtland clipped her dog, which was so shaggy that he couldn't do his work, but the dog "was never a dog again." He lost his energy and staying power. A puppy must not be spoiled, must not sit on laps, or get too hot. Nor must you talk too much with the puppy or with a grown dog— that will make him demanding. You must not give a dog attention or ask others about a dog. If you spoil him then he'll "become insulted" when you occasionally don't have time or interest for him.

MAY 22.

Today we have our first spring day, warm and delightful. I've lazed on a snow-free spot near the tent, enjoying the warmth and sounds of spring. It's the first time this year I've heard a brook running, and now the birds begin to arrive. The golden plover is here, for example. With its sorrowful whistle, it recalls the moors and lonely places at home in Denmark. The Lapps predict changes in the weather from its call.

Snow still lies everywhere, but there are definitely open spots, and the reindeer move calmly over the mountain slopes, grazing. The sky is true spring blue: bright white clouds spread slowly up above; the smoke from the tents slips quietly out of the smoke hole and fades into the blue sky. The Lapps move around outside the tents and occupy themselves with their spring work: they repair skis and sleds; they dry meat by bringing it to the *suonjir*, a scaffold of three birch trunks with crooked branches, placed together at the top. Outside the tents of the rich a lot of meat hangs in many scaffolds. Outside some tents stands a very small *suonjir* with only a few pieces of meat on it, often gifts, from those who have much.

The children play, and snatches of conversations are heard here and there from the tents. Sunday is in the air, even though it's not the Sabbath. It's as if something really joyful has happened. Rauna is in the midst of laying fresh twigs on the floor of the tent. I hear her chop snow and ice away from the sleeping places. We'll rest softly now.

MAY 23.

The beautiful day yesterday ended in driving rain; it was the first time this year and quite pleasant. The Lapps felt that way too. They visited one another, drank coffee, and spun thread from sinew. The chatting came very easily while the rain pattered down on the tent cloth and the bushes. But of course the rain has its unpleasant side too; for if there's suddenly far too strong a thaw now, it could be difficult to leave here with the sleds and to travel the distance to the next place from which we'll move with the pack reindeer, there where the Lapps left their summer belongings last year. When we went to sleep in the evening far past midnight, it stormed so the tent was almost torn off its poles. The door flapped wide open. Now there was a whirling snowstorm. The stiff squall whipped down through the narrow valley, the wind shrieked and cried, but I lay warm under the covers and enjoyed the storm. Sleep was impossible.

Hallodagat. ASCENSION DAY.

We're finally going to move on. I've had a great deal of work to waterproof my things, meaning I had to pack up books, camera, and other vulnerable items so that water can't easily soak through. Now that it's truly spring, rivers and brooks have broken up; it's flowing and streaming around us from all sides, and the youngsters come running, tear open the door and shout inside, *Gula got johka šoavvá.* "Hear how the water roars."

During the night a new stream formed that made a channel right through the foreman's tent. Today they had to move to a dry place. The innocent little trickle of water that quietly murmured past our tent has now swollen to a thundering river with splashes of foam. Drop by drop, the yellow water has cut deep furrows and curves in the snow and is in places a couple of meters deep. The children measure with ski poles. The water makes noise day and night, and we have a storm so that the tent cover flaps around our ears. The desolate white quiet of the high mountains is replaced by the most vivid unrest. The sun shines and the clouds chase after one another high and low, the air and water are in motion, and the migratory birds are arriving with all their sounds. The sudden violent thaw is both a pleasure and a misery.

JUNE 5.

It is cold as the devil, now that we've ascended higher. We move incessantly, and conditions in this uncharted region aren't pleasant. There was an oozing, drenching rain the day we left Virko-kårsa. It was strenuous for the reindeer to drag the heavy sleds over the soaking earth and through heavy snowmelt. Everyone had to help; some led the reindeer while others assisted the reindeer in pulling. The caravan went through deep and shallow snow, though streams and dammed spots, some of which resembled small ponds. Fortunately, shoes and leather trousers were watertight; only the outer clothes became wet and heavy and when we came higher up, they froze stiff in the wind. Then came an endless moraine with large round granite boulders. Everyone understood what it would mean to bump over them with heavy sleds.

Heikka almost wept from exertion and irascibility; he swore so that the ground shook and ended angrily with a *Hearrá sivdnit, dat lea váivi.* "Lord, how hard it is." And in the middle of everything, the puppy had to be comforted. Now that he'd grown somewhat larger he wasn't enjoying himself too much in the narrow casing at the tip of the sled. He was jolted and bumped by the sled and often was almost suffocated with heat. When he expressed himself too loudly, he had to be attended to and quieted so that he wouldn't scare the reindeer. But it was even worse when, at a very critical moment, he rolled out of the sled as it was just about to overturn in a stream, and the jolt spilled him out of his narrow casing. There wasn't much time at such a moment to show humane consideration. The puppy was fished out, berated, and once again stuffed in the casing; when he cried he was punished, good and proper. As the difficulties increased, patience wore out.

Finally the rain stopped; it began to freeze—a big gray sky low over the desolate gray landscape. A pair of honking wild geese came flying low, quite near us. A cold wind blew, and the children, who had gone some way ahead, had made a fire. In passing we warmed ourselves at their bonfire. The night was past, yet here there's almost no difference between night and day. It's light the whole time.

Since both reindeer and people were so tired after the night's work that they couldn't stand any longer, we rested a couple of hours in a ravine at the foot of a steep mountain. The reindeer were tethered where they found lichen.

Here on the mountainside was shelter, and the sun suddenly began to shine. Many fires were lit; flames and smoke rose up between the great boulders. Those who had time lay down immediately to sleep in the sun after having eaten and drunk coffee. The reindeer were frequently moved; afterward we continued with the same drudgery as before.

Some of the strings of the caravan had been much delayed by mishaps; others had an easier time and they took the lead. Once, when we passed a large rock, we saw one of the *siida's* small boys sitting next to it, sleeping, with his father's dog as guardian. He had grown tired along the way, but his mother, who was in the lead, couldn't take him up in her string, and had therefore left the boy sleeping there by the rock and ordered the dog to stay with him until the father, farther back, could take him along. When Gate saw the lad sitting there, with his head resting on his arms, sleeping deeply, she said that it was very careless to leave a child like that—that is, by the side of a big rock. He could easily be exchanged by the Uldas.

At length, past noon, people and reindeer were so tired that we had to set up camp, even though the site was very bad, both wet and stony. We rested until the evening of the next day; that is to say, the reindeer rested. The Lapps didn't have time. They had to be among the herd; there wasn't an abundance of people when most of the young folk were with the herd of reindeer cows in Norway. The women had their work to take care of: the small children needed to be bathed as usual; some skins had to be tanned; sewing and food preparation went on as usual.

The herd so strongly craved fresh grass now that we had to move quickly. Many times I saw the reindeer stand looking over the mountain borders, and if the Lapps and dogs hadn't been nearby, they would have gone straight for the country of spring. The Lapps maintain that they can smell the grass; for her own part, Gate asserted the same during the migration.

Yet it's not impossible that a sensitive nose really could catch the scent of spring when a mild west wind came, as it did now when we'd had several days of thaw.

Just before we were to move out, while the men went to capture the draft reindeer, a little late-born calf came into the world. The children told me the news and pulled me in its direction. The mother lay in the lee of the wind to protect the little, licked-clean calf. Its lifespan would be short, however. Some reindeer cows that haven't been separated out in time always follow the stray herd; they calve in accidental places along the route during the migration. Yet such calves are exposed to far-too-great exertions and bad weather and attacks from dogs (the stray herd must be guarded by dogs, and the Lapps can't prevent the dogs from occasionally killing a calf), so not many calves can survive the migrations.

By evening, we were again ready to continue. The route went steadily upward, the wind grew stronger, and the snow squalls thicker; you couldn't keep your eyes open. Yet it was a relief for the reindeer that there was snow here: the sleds weren't so heavy to pull. We went over many rivers that were neither dangerous nor impressive since they were thick with ice; but on the ice ran a rather deep stream of green water. It was slippery treading in the rushing water, knowing it was deep under the ice. But the Lapps sought out the best wading places; otherwise, the ice broke through wherever they wanted to go.

The reindeer shrank from going in, and even the puppies didn't dare try. The Lapps often had to run a long distance to capture the puppies, who continued alongside the river to find a better crossing. The dogs barked, the children cried, the reindeer stumbled, and a sled overturned in the middle of the water, yet everyone got to the other side without greater mishaps.

It is a certain sign we'll soon set up camp when someone pulls out by its roots a juniper bush that he or she passes and either carries it or sticks it down in the baggage. Up here there's nothing else to burn than juniper bushes, which are small, and some twigs. It is quite difficult to collect enough for a serviceable fire, and therefore you take what you come across along the way, toward the end of the day's trek, to have a little something for the first coffee pot.

Here, on a barren hillside, among barren mountains and under a barren sky, we stayed a couple of days. Now it's summer—so it says in the almanac; there's a biting cold frost in the wind and last night was a snowstorm. It's true that the sun was large and red in the sky the whole day, but it apparently only had enough warmth for itself—in any case, it didn't share any with us.

Whitsun Saturday.

Another move. This time it went easily, that is to say that the driving conditions are quite fine: hard snow and clear, sharp frost, occasionally with snow flurries. Heavy smoke-blue clouds tumble around and dump snow over us. The first part of the move usually goes easily, but as it turns into night, you have to fight off sleep. The move always happens at night because of the driving conditions. During the day the snow doesn't support either people or the caravan. So if something needs to be fixed and there's a short stop, some one always lies down on the snow to rest. With your head on your arms, you rest soundly, and it's possible to fall asleep for a couple of minutes before the caravan starts up again. Besides sleepiness, you're also plagued by thirst that you have to satisfy with snow if there's no water to be had.

We go steadily toward the border, and the other day when we came up on a mountain plateau with the caravan, Gate called to me, "There you see the big sea mountains."[25] She pointed to some massive but jagged and wild mountain peaks ahead, which extended up through the clouds, so the sun shone on the snow up there. Deep blue shadows showed where ravines were to be found. The Lapps said, "Yes, we're going over the mountains; there, between the peaks, is our passageway, a place where we can see the dark forest under us as a hell and the steep mountain above us as a heaven." I was reminded of what the Talma Lapps said when they heard I wanted to trek with the Karasuando Lapps into Norway: "Then you'll probably be killed, because up there the migration paths are so dangerous."

Tomorrow it's Whitsun. I'm freezing, *dego dihkki*, "like a louse." My feet are cold, *dego beatnaga njunni*, "like a dog's nose." The snow drifts down and there's not a single spark of spring to warm the heart with.

JUNE 12.

Vuoi, vuoi, what weather we've had now for many days. It rains and storms. It's to the point of it being difficult to keep my spirits up; still, the other day I was, almost against my will, the cause of a bit of cheer in the tent. I hadn't been in the mood to speak more than necessary, but suddenly I felt like repeating all the oaths I'd learned during the difficult moves and paraded them all out at once. It was so surprising and unexpected for the Lapps that they broke into laughter and cried, "Listen to what she's learned, but she can't do it right, because she mixes men's and women's oaths together."

During this time our diet changes for the better. The Lapps go fishing in the ice-covered lakes, but it's only the less well-off who have time for this not-quite-safe sport. The ice is quite uncertain now that the weather is thawing. All the same, both children and grown-ups fish as soon as the opportunity presents itself; for everyone it's a welcome change to eat the fine mountain fish, which taste equally delicious boiled or broiled over the fire.

One day in the middle of the migration, Heikka gave me his string to lead while he went fishing to a lake a few kilometers off. When, after several hours, we'd arrived at the tent site and had set up the tent, Heikka came with a big bundle of magnificent red-bellied and silver-backed fat salmon trout, a catch he was proud of.

Rauna immediately began to remove the guts and cut them up into suitable pieces for the stewpot. I attempted the small suggestion that they should be scraped a little and washed. "Washed! The fish that has just come out of the water is clean, I suppose?"

While eating I was informed that it was *sáivoguolli*, that is, fish from a *saivo* lake, a sort of holy lake, which the Lapps believe has a double bottom. The fish are very fat but particularly difficult to capture. The slightest noise or conversation scares them away. Heikka had, however, always been lucky at getting fish from the *saivo* lakes; he had a quiet presence and spoke little. The tools for fishing are very simple—an ordinary, purchased fishhook with a line tied to the ski pole. As bait they use a piece of yellow and red cloth (of the sort they use to trim their tunics) until they've caught the first fish. Then they take a little piece of its red skin from the belly as bait.

The days pass in fog and rain, but it's more springlike than snowy and frosty, even though it's not much more comfortable. We all wish for, yearn for, a trace of brighter weather, and no one is supposed to throw any muck or twigs from the floor on the fire inside the tent; that keeps the bad weather here, they say. The dank, close fog, which surrounds us like a wall, is oppressive and freezing. Your fingers almost freeze off when you want to gather a few twigs to make yourself slightly comfortable in the tent. Most of the day there's no fire, only when there's some food to be prepared or coffee boiled is the fire lit, and those who want more warmth have to create it themselves. Here in these desolate places there's not one tree or the hint of a forest.

A young Lapp from another *siida* has been here a couple of days. He joiks steadily at his work, but Gate won't allow joiking in her tent, so it's quite difficult to get hold of some of his words; even the melody I unfortunately can't note down.

The Lapps have many old joiks that have to do with the migrations over the border in spring. They can vary as regards to the text, but the main content and even the melody is the same.

Boares heargi manná Stuoranjárgii.
Boares heargi njoallu juohke geaḍggi Veadjemáttaváris
vai eallá badjel másealggi mannat,
vai nealgi ii jovssa gaskkas.

The old draft reindeer goes to the big headland.
The old draft reindeer licks each stone on Veadjematto mountain
to get over the ridge of mountain,
so that hunger won't overtake it on the way.

Áldu manná—čoarvi skállá—
Stuoranjárgii—boares áldu.

The reindeer cow walks—the antlers jingling—
To the big headland—the old reindeer cow.

Boazu njunnohallá mearravuvddiin
ja njolggásta mearravuovdái, go haksá rási
ođđa čorvviid dahkanáigge,
Ja guolgga muhttá mearravuvddiin
ja ođđa guolgga bidjá nala— — —
ođđa čorvviin vara njammet čuoikkat.

The reindeer sniffs the coast forest and runs to the coast forest
when it smells grass under the waxing crescent moon
In the coast forest it changes its coat and puts on a new coat— — —
At the crescent moon the mosquitoes suck blood.

JUNE 15.

Here where we now have the tents, it's haunted. The Haldas cry at night;
Gate has heard them. There's something so eerie in the wind along the moun-
tainsides. Several Lapps have laid their bones in the area. An old Lapp died
in a snowstorm and so did a girl who was guarding reindeer in a snowstorm
in the autumn. The girl's father also "vanished." The poor widow went mad
with grief and is no good for anything anymore.

JUNE 16.

No, now the weather has gone completely crazy. I believe it's culminating
today: storm and hail, rain and snow. If it we hadn't placed large granite boulders all around the walls of the tent, it would have flown up into the sky. The
pole structure inside is braced up and, to hold the whole thing to the ground,
heavy stones hang in leather thongs down from the tent frame. We stayed in

our skin bedding as long as possible in the morning. Even though the wet sleeping sacks weren't particularly comfortable, it was far worse to get up and be thoroughly pelted by rain and hail. In such weather there's not much light in a Lapp tent. It was difficult to make a fire; everything glistened with moisture. In such a storm the heat vanishes, but the smoke stays inside in a stuffy thick cloud. The door flies open and claps against the tent like something possessed. The tent cloth, which is wet and heavy, flogs the tent frame. The rain falls down through the smoke hole, so the water drips into your face. When the tent cloth doesn't even keep the wet weather out either, you might as well give up and bow to your fate. One person swears, another talks about the Gospel; another says it's "death weather"; "a sinner is dying now."

Heikka mutters, "Well, if it's so bad here, the road to heaven is clear. The best thing is to take a leap up there right away."

At present we share the tent with a young married couple who have two small boys. The man has put on his rain hat and begun to make us coffee. It's a humane task, yet anything but comfortable and easy. The rain puts out his fire, the smoke burns his eyes, and he's soaking wet. The coffee raises our spirits a little, but our mood can't persist in the storm. Only the two small boys and the puppy don't allow themselves to be bothered. The boys throw their lasso at the coffee kettle, and the puppy entertains himself with the cleaning whisk. The smallest of the boys is a little nipper who can walk on his own so well that he can escape from the tent in an unguarded moment and land in a soft snowdrift or in a puddle of water where, eagerly and thoroughly wet, he splashes around until he's missed and brought inside by his mother to the fire and dry clothes. He is, on the other hand, not so advanced when it comes to fluent speech. The child can't utter a single understandable word yet. All the same, he can imitate, with astonishing fidelity, all the sounds of the reindeer herd, the herders' commands to the dogs, and the dogs' sharp barks when they're working. He's caught everything, down to the curses expressed in hoarse voices. We often break out in laughter when he suddenly reproduces in sound the whole lively picture of reindeer, herders, and dogs that he sees by the tents immediately before every move. The only word he can pronounce understandably is *ce, gov, hu!*—the reindeer herders calming cry to the dogs. We call him therefore mostly *ce gov!*

During this period, the Lapps go frequently to look at the lakes and rivers to find a passable migration route. All the streams have now become rivers, and the ice on the lakes is more than uncertain. We should have actually have moved already, but the weather has been too bad.

Wednesday before midsummer—
Kåbmejaure (Ghost Lake).

This time we were traveling—for the first time this year—with pack reindeer. It was not a little tiring, in part because the reindeer go faster than when
they pull a sled and in part because the track was so difficult, whether we
walked in deep watery thaw or through willows. Most of the time the path
sloped up. However, the weather was good—still and overcast. The sun wasn't
far off, but it looked so threatening; the whole time it hid behind some ugly
clouds, from where it sent wild fiery rays down over the big sheer sides of
Päldsa Mountain. The dark violet clouds were a colorful background for the
many intense red and yellow colors of the Lapps. Up here they have the beautiful custom of putting on their finest clothes for the migration moves: silver
belts, clean scarves and caps, clean aprons and shoe bands. That lends the
whole caravan a certain inner and outer festivity that is quite bracing.

I led the string the whole way. It's actually quite a diversion, being so close
to reindeer; it's so beautiful, for instance, to see the whole landscape in the
reindeer's eyes, as in a black concave mirror. The Lapps also know this mirror
and look in it, but they see more than I do. They can see omens inside. If the
reindeer suddenly grows shy, and if you can't see a reason for it, the Lapp looks
into its eye and can often get an explanation. That was how Heikka once saw,
in the black mirror, a Lapp of his acquaintance come along with reindeer and
sled. Suddenly the Lapp lay down in the sled, and immediately the sled took
on the appearance of a corpse-sled. Heikka understood from the omen what
was going to happen, and a short time later the Lapp died.

All things considered, it's unpleasant here. Not far away a young Lapp died
last autumn. The *siida* needed to move, but the dying man remained behind
in a tent, along with his father and a couple of other Lapps. His struggle with
death lasted several days, and since then, it had become unpleasant to pass
by the place where he died. The reindeer were frightened, and sounds were
heard. Because of that, the Lapps want to change their migration route during
the autumn so as not to go by this particular spot.

Now we have only one move left, the last and the worst. The Lapps say that
we will walk a whole day without stopping; we'll try to keep up with the reindeer, for if they get into Norway without being watched closely, the devil is
loose. And to follow the reindeer now that they're just at the border of the
grassland is almost impossible without having wings.

Strange to think that there on the other side of the mountains it's summer,
such a rich summer with green colors and warm air, and here on this side we

haven't even seen a green shoot. Here we've had hard winter for nine months. How I understand the Lapps' longing for summer and a little rest after cold, dark, and hardships for all these months. In the morning we'll begin a new trek that even the Lapps dread. For example, when Rauna, on one occasion or another complains about anything that's difficult, her mother will often say to her, "You have nothing to complain about, as long as you're not still 'in front of the mountains.'" (Vare-ouddan, a place on the last migration route where the mountains are very wild and dangerous.)

XVIII

EARLY IN THE MORNING THE LAPPS BEGAN to get ready for the last move, from Kåbmejaure. A departure with pack reindeer is always more colorful and more troublesome than when you travel with sleds; these are already packed, and you only have to harness the reindeer.

Although all the loads are completely ready and have been weighed by hand so that the loads are precisely as heavy on either side of the reindeer, there's still much to do. Thick saddle blankets, which consist in the best case of reindeer skins folded once, must be placed on the reindeer. You can also use clothes or a felt for the saddle blanket. Reindeer must have a thick and soft pad for their burdens, since they get sores from rubbing particularly easily. Pack reindeer should be harnessed with painstaking care, and only when the harnesses are pulled into shape and tested should the loads be carefully hung over the reindeer. All of this would have gone quite easily if all the pack reindeer were patient and easy to handle, but that was far from the case. They knew what all this was about and they would have preferred to have nothing to do with the whole business. They kicked and moved restlessly, turned obstinate, and wouldn't step forward.

Only the old, gentle animals that were used to carrying the children stood still and were conscious of their responsibility. All the Lapps were busy and anxious. One of the younger men got into trouble asking his wife several times about different things. She answered brusquely, "You ask questions like you just arrived in a foreign country this evening."

She was busy seating her children on the reindeer. With the little one in the cradle, it's no problem. The cradle is merely hung off the packsaddle like a normal load. It's harder for those who are a little bigger. The three-year-old was packed sitting up in a chest and tied in gently. Afterward the child was hung on the side of the reindeer, naturally with an equivalent weight on the reindeer's other side. The children who are too large to be seated in such a way must ride. The wooden pommels on the reindeer to be ridden are especially made for this; they are so long at the highest end that the child can grasp them firmly.

The young Lapp who joiked so well was still in our *siida*, and he helped getting the caravan in order. He was a fellow undeterred by anything, and when the reindeer refused to move forward too many times, he swore and carried on until red flames came out of his head. His curses were colorful, lengthy, and emphatic. Gate reproached him for his dangerous invocation of the Evil One, just before the difficult trek. It would be better if he asked God to help us. But the fellow thought his supplications just as effective. "Our Father only did what He wanted to anyway."

Finally, later in the morning, the caravan set off into the desolate gray landscape, which rose steadily the whole time. Almost immediately, we had to take a detour; that is, we were supposed to cross a river, but the rivers at that period were so deep and rapid that they could only be crossed over natural snow bridges. However, the bridges were the first thing that these particular rivers had destroyed, and the Lapps had no other alternative but to go up to the source of the river and ford it there. We went the whole way up over the mountainside in mud and between willows. There was now water everywhere. This detour delayed us considerably, and it was many hours before we reached the large ravine in the mountains where we'd have our first rest.

The reindeer were unharnessed, the children unpacked, a big campfire flamed up—here there was enough brushwood. The Lapps and dogs gathered around the fire. Up along the mountain slopes lay some clouds, and from high up came avalanche after avalanche. After the thundering noise you saw something like a white waterfall, which headed out over a mountain edge up near the clouds. A pair of the women took only a short rest. They went in front in order to walk at a slightly more comfortable pace. The caravan went quite quickly, with the object being to arrive as soon as possible. The route was long, and you could meet with accidents. I saw an advantage in accompanying those who went in front, something I must say I later regretted.

One young woman had two reindeer: one carried the baggage, and the other reindeer, completely white, carried the cradle with her youngest child. Along with the young woman was a somewhat older, rather delicate woman with her little girl. In a sack she had two puppies. We were also given a large number of children between the ages of seven and nine. When we came through the ravine to its entrance, high, high up, a deep, wide valley lay under us, quite filled with clouds. On the other side, some sharp mountain peaks far away projected up through the clouds. Before we went down into the valley the young woman stopped and nursed her little one in the cradle on the reindeer. Afterward we started down the mountain slope, which was very steep. The children, who weren't yet tired, naturally ran everywhere they wished. Using their poles, they tried out the ground through the snow and quickly disappeared into the white cloud. We, on the other hand, went a bit more carefully and called out now and then, so as not to lose one another in the dense fog, where we couldn't see our hands in front of our faces. Down at the bottom of the valley we found one another safe and sound, and the women sat down a while to rest. The clouds were just over our heads like a lid. We couldn't see anything and were a little uncertain which path to take. It was hard to orient ourselves, and cold inside this white clamminess surrounding us. "If we only had the dogs now to chase away the clouds," they joked.

We continued up to the opposite side of the valley and came upon a track, which we followed. It was a sled track sliced into loose dirt and melting snow. A sick person had been transported by this means the long, difficult way into Norway. The women knew who the sick person was, a middle-aged women from another *siida* who'd grown ill here during the spring stopover in the mountains. During all the moves she'd been driven in a sled. Now, when the route could only be traversed by pack reindeer, it was strenuous beyond measure to carry a sick person. We lost the trail during a long stony stretch and had again to search for the way forward.

Then suddenly our voices were drowned in a crashing thunder from a river. When we came right up to it, we could barely shout to each other. How were we going to cross this foaming, roaring monster, rushing white deep down between two sheer boulder walls? The women went a distance along the bank until they found a passable snow bridge, the kind formed in winter from snow and frozen spray. In spring the water wears the bridge thin. I shuddered at the thought of going over a not very wide bridge that looked anything but solid. Under it the river boiled at furious speed. The delicate woman now began to relate every possible story she knew of death and disaster in these parts. It wasn't exactly cheering and I asked her to stop. We had a great deal of trouble with the puppies. When the woman grew tired of carrying them on her back or in her arms in a sack, they were placed on one of the reindeer, but naturally they cried and barked and frightened the reindeer, so once more they had to be carried. They certainly tried to walk for very short stretches, but at that pace we didn't get far, so they were stuffed into the sack again.

When we came up to a mountain plateau, the women began to sniff. They smelled smoke. A little later we actually stood in front of an abandoned campfire where the ashes were still warm. We found a piece of ski and the remains of the original fire, and by scratching around in the snow we got a handful of twigs and relit the fire. The younger of the women made coffee while I dried the shoe-hay. I had worn holes in my shoes, and they were no longer waterproof. An hour after we left the place with the fire, we again arrived at a large river that had to be crossed over a snow bridge. This was unusually thin, probably only about twenty-five centimeters thick and not at all wide either.

The women considered hard whether to go over it. They threw stones on it to test its ability to hold us, but since there were a number of reindeer tracks that weren't too old, they ventured out on it. There was no other possible alternative. Over we would go. The young woman went resolutely in front with her reindeer and we followed her. The children didn't know enough to entertain any sort of anxiety. They toddled along blithely with their far-too-long poles.

Just as we were walking through a very wet spot under a hill, one of the boys shouted as he pointed with a grubby little finger, *Gea, gollerássi, ale duolmmas!* "Look at the yellow flowers, don't step on them!" There were actually two tiny little buttercups in full bloom on a small clump of green leaves, the only flowers and green things we'd seen in all the months in the Swedish high mountains, and this was June 20th!

At long last the caravans caught up with us. I felt safer having more people accompanying us and was no longer so afraid when we had to go over the snow bridges. The children were very tired, though their endurance was incredible. We'd probably at that point been underway about a dozen hours. Now one or another of the children cried from tiredness and was therefore permitted to sit up on a reindeer when the track was level and smooth.

In the middle of the night—but in full daylight—we came to the worst place, where we were meant to see the forest under us like a black hell and the mountains over us like a heaven. The caravan divided up; most chose a stonier route that would take a little longer down to the tree line. They soon disappeared out of sight. However, the young man with whom we'd shared a tent wanted to follow the mountainside quite high up. This was probably a little shorter, and my hosts went with him. None of the others dared run the risk of going up there with pack reindeer. It was, all things considered, seldom that anyone dared venture there, and it could only be attempted at all if we could go that night in very deep melting snow. The mountain was so steep that if a reindeer or person stumbled it was useless to try to save them. And if one of the reindeer in the string stumbled, it would pull the whole string down.

Everyone walked silently and carefully forward; no one looked around; everyone had to take care of themselves and tread closely in the track of the person going before. The worst, I found, was that the abyss far down sucked at me so strongly that I literally had to shore myself up on that side with the pole. It was lucky, as far as I was concerned, that the clouds lay under us and made it impossible to see to the bottom of "hell." When a puff of wind tore holes in the cloud cover below, it was like gazing into a well, and I felt dizziness approaching.

It was close to early morning when we met up with the other strings on a great barren plateau where we were to rest. It blew cold up through the mountain ravine; thick dark clouds rose from where we'd been. How desolate it was here, desolate as it was before the time of man. How, in this biting cold, would summer come this year? The great hot campfire, consisting of twigs and juniper bushes, reconciled us a little to the difficult conditions. Moreover, the worst was behind us; the rest of the journey would be comparatively easy. Yet how tired everyone was. It helped in the meanwhile to get something to eat. Some had even found ptarmigan eggs, a rarity, along the way. They were carried carefully in hats and boiled in the coffee kettle.

Now and then an avalanche sounded, and we saw the snow foam down over the mountain some distance off. The Lapps said that most avalanches fall toward early morning; therefore, they rarely walk in the dangerous places in the morning. Yet this time they had to because of the delay with that first river and having to detour around it.

Once more the loads were placed on the tired reindeer and we continued. For the first while we went forward in melting snow and slush, over streams and smaller hills. But then we began to feel the downward slope more and more. There wasn't a trace of spring in the air yet; a sharp wind iced our tired limbs, while we plodded steadily forward in silent dullness. A slightly feeble woman had gotten tired; she allowed the others to go ahead and sat down on a stone, attempting to build a fire.

Gate and I came over to warm up a little, but her fire wouldn't get going, so we went on. An old woman from our *siida* returned back along the migration route. She'd lost her *suoidnefierra* (the large bundle of shoe-hay that was supposed to last the whole summer). Now she was out searching and asked if we'd seen it. No, it was and remained lost, to her great sorrow.

Gradually, as we descended, the air grew warmer and our spirits rose. Gate told me that on a small hill near the migration route that you could find "thunderstones." They were little round blood-colored stones that fell down from the sky during a thunderstorm, and if they struck a person, he died. But otherwise, they were good for sickness. If you had a painful spot you should press a *bajángeaðgi* (thunderstone) on it; then you were cured. That's what her old mother-in-law said. When we came to the small hill, we went up and found a whole slew of the miraculous stones. They were little pebbles the size of sparrow eggs and peas.

Toward afternoon, the descent grew very rapid. We came to small birches that had true green leaves, and before we knew it, we were walking on soft moss; the birches grew larger, the forest floor lush, and the birds sang. Gate pointed up toward the mountainside and said, "Look, the reindeer." Yes, indeed, the herd was coming—with antlers thrown back and white tail stumps in the air, the reindeer raced forward. The dogs ran in front and barked furiously. The herders shouted and ran as fast as they could. But it was useless; the reindeer had the scent of grass in their nostrils. Now nothing could stop them. A little red calf was visible in the group, along with its mother. It was the only one of them born during the migration that managed to survive to the spring.

All the winter cold from the mountains melted on the path through the forest. The transition from somber, deathly cold to soft, lush summer warmth with living sounds and colors was completely intoxicating. It began to rain, but it was gentle, friendly summer rain, which almost seemed like a caress. Gate pointed down into the valley, where smoke from a Norwegian farm rose up in the air over the green grass roof.

We had reached the Sea Kingdom. Now the short summer of the Lapps and the reindeer would begin.

Heikka, who had gone in front, had already set up the tent when we came down. We sat inside on fine soft grass. Now we'd arrived and could nod, smiling, to the *siidas* that came after us.

Siida after *siida* trekked down from the mountains; reindeer, breathing heavily, advanced with their loads, led by strong young men and women. After them came the old people, their frail, wrinkled hands grasping their staffs. Their backs were bowed and their steps small. The children were tired too and were walking with the old people.

As Lapps and reindeer come migrating now, so have they migrated for a thousand years, the same route with the same goal, with the same blissful feeling of again reaching the Sea Kingdom after a long winter in the high mountains.

XIX

IT'S SUMMER, HOT, TREMBLING SUMMER. The sun glints and sparkles like little bolts of lightning on all the glossy leaves and blades of grass; the brook behind the tents is gilt-edged with buttercups. You can't imagine the pleasure of walking on soft turf after long months of only having snow, ice, and stones under your feet. All the winter stiffness of soul and body relaxes; all the senses awake. The young people exchange glances and secret smiles. The children play; the adults rustle about airing out clothes and bedding in the sunshine, or sit near the tent with their sewing or tanning. The tents are empty; everyone works outside.

When we were trekking up in the desolate high mountains, in the middle of discomfort and effort, a small thought underneath still shone brightly: the Sea Kingdom! When we arrived there, life would be bright and cheerful again. The Sea Kingdom is a wonderland both for Lapps and reindeer, and the little calves that come into the world in the green grass valleys don't know what hardship is. It's not strange that the Lapps love the summerland and can't live without it, in fact; from time immemorial they've gathered strength and courage there to withstand the ice-cold winter, the dark, and all the hardships with which their lives are so richly supplied.

That the Lapps can't live without Norway is no cliché. For all the nomads along the whole Swedish side of the border, it's more or less necessary to travel with the reindeer into Norway for a longer or shorter time, and even if the Lapps don't officially move over the border everywhere with their reindeer, the reindeer themselves go there without permission and must be brought back. But for the most northerly of the Swedish Lapps, it is of vital importance that the reindeer cows can get into Norway early enough that the calving in May can take place there in mild weather and in peace. If they are forced to stay in the Swedish high mountains during the calving, the lives of the calves are at risk. In part they succumb to cold and storms; in part they perish, if they're quite small, moving with the herd over the dangerous mountain borders. In any case, the reindeer need grass in summer. The warm winds from the Gulf Stream that give Norway green grass and an early spring turn to ice-cold winter storms over in the Swedish high mountains, and the stony earth there isn't covered with soft grass. The gray lichen grows only sparsely over sand and gravel. But even if the lichen was found in great quantities, so that the reindeer didn't need to lick every lichen-covered rock, it wouldn't be enough. The reindeer can't live off lichen when it's summer-dry. They need greenness and grass.

Unfortunately, the fondness of neither the reindeer nor the Lapps for the "Sea Kingdom" is returned by the "Sea People." Particularly in recent years the expectant joy of spring during the migrations has come to be mixed with uncertainty and fear, and this puts a great damper on the delights of summertime. I myself was infected by the same mood; I too longed immeasurably for Norway, yet at the same time felt, like the Lapps, uneasy about setting foot in that promised land.

As soon as we entered Norway, a number of Lapps experienced severe bad luck, which unfortunately tends to repeat itself every year in the same area: they lost dogs from poison that had been set out. Of course, this poison is set out in a completely lawful manner and only to capture foxes and other small carnivores. But the farmers shouldn't be allowed to place poison on the Lapps' travel route during the migration period. Several dogs are lost in this way every year; besides the grown dogs, I heard of two large puppies belonging to a widow in our *siida*. If you knew how difficult it is to raise puppies in a Lapp tent in winter and to take them along on the migrations, you would understand the Lapps' sense of loss and anger and spare them such disappointment. But perhaps the Lapps themselves bear some of the guilt for this being repeated year after year. They never complain to the right people. When I reproached them about this, they answered, "What's the use? Who cares how it goes with us?"

We stayed in Elfkroken a few days, that's to say, the tents and the family members who weren't herding the reindeer. The reindeer and their herders went to the district's usual summer grazing fields in Tromsdalen. During these days it was burning hot. The transition from winter to summer was far too abrupt, and everyone from the Lapps down to the puppy and me were limp from the heat—some of that was simple tiredness after our exertions. "You're just as worn-out as we are, just as brown, thin, and lined, but you'll see, it will become better quickly here where we can rest and enjoy ourselves."

The children seemed least affected by the trek; they ran around and played and took care of themselves. Yet here in Norway they were strangely shy, as if they walked in foreign surroundings. If I asked them to go with me into the forest to fetch a bundle of willow I needed for tanning some skins, the oldest ones immediately said, when I wanted to cut a branch, "Leave them alone! Those are the *dáža*'s [Norwegian's] trees, you mustn't touch them!" Or, "Don't go there, that's the *dáža*'s grass."

The children didn't dare go too far away from the tents without the company of grown-ups. They were afraid of everything: afraid of the dogs that didn't resemble their own; afraid of everyone who wasn't wearing Lappish clothing. If we walked along a country road and met a farmer, right away they stepped behind me to protect themselves. This terror of everything foreign and foreignly dressed is something the Lapps and their children experience strongly; it's much greater than commonly believed. It's found particularly in children and such adult Lapps as come in relatively infrequent contact with other people. This fear is of course easily understood. Their history is full of murderous attacks, fleecings, and robberies that they've been subjected to from neighbors and foreign bands of thieves. They still tell, vividly and graphically, multiple stories of the unpleasant exploits of the Russian Čudernes.[26] More mythic but no less horrifying are the countless tales of the man-eating Stallos, though these stories often have a strong touch of the comic. And until comparatively recently there have been painful clashes with the settlers. It's a known fact that these, in many cases, have cost Lapps their lives. The Lapps must always yield or be overcome. Following their way of life has meant never being able to gather forces enough to defend themselves.

All this can well bequeath a certain nervous fear for later generations, and the solitary life in the wilderness can only increase it. But on their own turf the Lapps don't know fear. The people who can't be made to feel afraid when nature manifests itself in all its sinister might in the high mountains, who aren't afraid of wild animals and all sorts of dangers, grow small and fearful when they meet a unfamiliarly clad person of another race.

The Lapps here had their summer home in Tromsdalen, where their turf huts stood waiting for them.[27] When we had rested ourselves well and the reindeer and their herders had moved on, we also departed. The women and children and those who could be spared from reindeer herding took the easiest way to Tromsø, with the steamship that traveled on the Balsfjord. Some, those who didn't wish to travel that way or hadn't the means, continued along the reindeer's path, even though it was long and difficult.

We'd rented a pair of horses to carry the small amount of baggage we had. The pack reindeer were far off and might be needed as replacements. Those of us who were departing by steamship left on the most beautiful dawn to walk, chatting animatedly, along the excellent country road. Generally, the Lapps don't enjoy walking on a true country road: "It's so boring."

"Yes, now we can walk leisurely down into the valley. Up until this road was built, it was our old migration route with reindeer. But now it's forbidden to come here, and that's why the reindeer and herders have to trek way up there," and they pointed up at the steep, sky-high mountains, where the snow still lay and where you saw water pouring down into ravines and emerging from ledges. "Up there it's dangerous for people and reindeer, and we lose many calves that fall and die."

When we landed in Tromsø everything was a colorful bustle. There are probably always onlookers in a little town when the steamer ties up, but there were unusually many here. You can well understand that the Lapps, with their bright colors and rather peculiar get-ups can lure people down to see them. It's harder to understand why the curiosity should be expressed in loutishness and scorn, sneering catcalls, slurs, and impudent stares. The Lapps had prepared me for this beforehand: "When we come to Tromsø, you'll see how they stare at us, as if we were wild animals. They also call after us. What would they think if we did the same to them?"

Only when we were installed in the large pleasant turf hut up in the valley did we feel free and comfortably at ease. Now there was no difference between night and day. The sun shone around the clock. All that suggested nighttime was the glowing light and the long clouds hanging low. We went about when we felt like it, no matter what time of day it was. The children could go out at midnight to gather angelica and come home to the tent from the mountains toward dawn. They then began to eat and make coffee before they lay down.

In Tromsdalen we shared a turf hut with our old foreman and his children, but there was lots of room, partly because the hut was very large, and partly because the grown sons almost always were out with the herd. If they returned to rest, they preferred to sleep on the hill outside the tent. Like their dogs, the Lapps spend as little time as possible indoors during the summer.

A turf hut is certainly a cozy place to live in. When it's hot outside, it's both cool and airy if it's well built. Of course, if you cook any food it easily becomes too warm, but fortunately, in summer there's not so much food preparation as in winter. You eat less, and milk and dried meat play a large role. It's rare to use much fuel, only dry wood gathered in the forest. I've never seen the Lapps fell a living tree for burning during their stay in Norway in the summer. Accusations against them for wasting wood are completely exaggerated and unjust.

One morning a farmer came into the hut. He was hot and worked up as he talked about the reindeer having done a great deal of damage to his fields and destroying a potato patch of his. Now he'd come as quick as possible to the Lapp's foreman, so he could be compensated.

Only the women were home, however, and so he soon went away again. I was sorry for the man and said a few words about how tiresome it was that the reindeer couldn't be kept from the farmer's fields. It must be exasperating, even if you were compensated, to see your work destroyed. The women freely conceded that, but they knew no more than I did. When the foreman came home and heard about the damage, he grew quite unhappy and said, "It is solely my fault. I sent both my sons out to the reindeer and gave them instructions about the places where the reindeer usually wanted to move down and asked my sons to pay special attention to them, but the reindeer had never gone down by this particular farm so I believed there was no reason for my sons to be on guard—you can't be everywhere at once. And now the reindeer have gone down just there—so it's my fault."

On the day fixed, the authorities, Lapps, and farmers met at the farm. The sworn men, who had surveyed the damages, estimated ninety crowns, but now, fortunately or not, it had rained a little in the intervening week and the trampled-down grass had sprung up. The farmer encouraged us, nine-strong, to inspect the small field of grass. Here and there lay a couple of reindeer hairs, and you could see faint signs of a reindeer bed in a few places.

The Lapps said, "All of us are trampling things down and doing far more damage than the reindeer has done. Let's move away from here." They walked lightly and carefully on their toes in the fine soft grass with true feeling for its worth. The whole scene reminded me strongly of the story of the Molbo people and the stork in the cornfield.[28]

I spoke a little with one of the three assessors, the only one who looked amiable. He said, among other things, "They say the cows won't graze where the reindeer have gone, but that's not true. I've seen the opposite many times on my own property."

During a short break in the negotiations—the Lapps naturally weren't going to pay ninety crowns, whether the damage amounted to ten crowns or one, just like that—the young man who was conducting the investigation and represented the authorities asked if we shouldn't, for our own interest, take a look at the damage (it was with his encouragement, by the way, that I was present on this occasion). We took a look at the potato patch that was supposed to be the most damaged. Here and there I saw prints left behind by a reindeer hoof, but not a single broken potato shoot. When I asked my escort if he could discover any "damage," he shrugged his shoulders and answered no, whereupon without saying anything further, we returned to the room where the uncomfortable negotiations resumed.

The new Lapp foreman was, in spite of his quiet demeanor, not as compliant as our old, always agreeable foreman had been in these sorts of cases. He didn't want to pay the ninety crowns. The whole day had almost gone before they settled on a sum around half of that. Thus, the Lapps gave in. But the foreman said later, "We've paid a fine, because the reindeer have gone where they shouldn't go, but we haven't paid compensation, for there was no damage."

It was evening when I returned home with the Lapps to Tromsdalen, and the shadows were lengthening. We were tired and in low spirits. It had been a painful experience, yet the Lapps were pretty well hardened against such things, which were the order of the day for them in Norway. Even if not all "punishment" stories are as unjust as this one, it is still painful to witness how a "higher" civilization makes itself guilty, to put it mildly, of inhuman treatment of a peaceful and valuable people.

"We're like a strange dog that you kick away, but the king probably doesn't know how we're treated," said the foreman when we had been walking silently a long time.

Down in the valley lay the Lapps' small green homes; you could mistake them for rounded tussocks of grass if a fine coil of smoke hadn't risen from some of them. At the end of the valley lay the mountain with its snow-packed kettle depression, and the river ran shining bright between the green hillocks deep in the valley bottom. In the sunshine and quiet, all of it resembled a prehistoric landscape from a dream.

On a hill near the turf hut stood a reindeer corral. It was only used when the Lapps received instructions to bring some reindeer down to satisfy the curiosity of tourists from foreign countries. This was almost a nuisance for them, but they complied as well as they could with the request. The earnings were small, when you considered the handsome fee they had to pay one of the *dáža* for the use of the farm, while they themselves had a lot of trouble getting the reindeer down from the mountains in warm weather. Nor did it do the animals good to stand around in a corral in the burning sun without food or water; normally when it's warm and still, they stay up on the patches of snow.

All the same, in Norway you hear sharp comments about the Lapps' laziness and their living off tourists. Regrettably a form of tourism has developed: that is, the less well-off and the completely poverty-stricken make and sell small things. The women sell little pouches, dolls, and other toys, while the men offer objects made of antler. Most often these are meager and badly crafted items; in many instances they're completely warped versions of Lappish handiwork. But tourists want to have things cheap, and they have no understanding of what they buy or any ability to judge the value of the work. When the

bad craftsmanship is often the same price as the good, you can quickly understand how that soon demoralizes the craftsperson.

Some of the well-off Lapps who don't admire this industry can still find it
necessary to sell objects, such as duplicates of silver spoons and the little silver-
plated pipe. They can't enjoy such things in peace because of the tourists, and
since the latter prefer to have used objects, lately the Lapps have tended to
smoke "tourist pipes" before they come to Norway. The tourist-buying mania
knows no decency; they buy the strings of pearls from a girl's neck; they buy
silver buttons from a woman's belt and everything precious they clap their eyes
on. If the Lapps' everyday clothes were more tempting, the tourists would buy
them off their backs. If you reproach the Lapps for selling things, they answer
that it's difficult to avoid the foreigners' insistence. Often the tourists pay so
well that the temptation is too great.

When the tourists gather around the corral, taking photographs and ges-
ticulating, the atmosphere seems filled with exclamation marks. The whole
business is a repellant marketplace. The Lapps go around with small bundles
of wares; bargaining and buying goes on while the reindeer stand there drowsy
and hungry after having run themselves ragged around the corral, frightened
of the confusion and all the strange people.

The children, who look like miniature adults, enthrall the tourists, who
feed them candy and money. It's remarkable that so-called cultivated people
can't conduct themselves with more dignity and true understanding. It's as if,
for the foreigners, the Lapps are only a flock of curious and "sweet" animals.

Many of the Lapps don't like this life. One day I saw a young Lapp walk
around with a small sardonic smile, looking at the French group and the
Lapps' own trading.

"I don't suppose you have anything to offer for sale, Anda?"

"No, I'm keeping this for myself."

At least, some Lapps think like this, and therefore they try to get back to
the turf hut as soon as they've been paid for the reindeer skin or antlers
they wanted to sell. But the hut is no secure haven. The braver of the tourists
make so bold as to venture inside the hut; the others, afraid of the smell and
the animals, among other things, fill the doorway opening; and the more
nimble youth even crawl up the sides of the hut and peek through the smoke
hole. Decent people are unfortunately too few; the group is represented by
other sorts.

Not all children like the advances and money of the strangers. Rauna and
her friend almost always disappeared when there were tourists in the offing,

and didn't return into view until it was evening and the valley, with its green hillocks and its inhabitants, was itself again.

When the strangers' visit is over and done with, the Lapps immediately slip into the days' work, and no one speaks about the foreigners, the sales, or anything connected with the whole hullabaloo. The reason for this indifference lies primarily in a true lack of interest and then perhaps in something quite unconscious—the sense of being humiliated. The tourists are full of indelicate questions and remarks. They don't attempt to disguise their abhorrence for closer contact, both with the tent and the people. The tourists' grimaces of disgust and scorn don't escape the Lapps either. "Many of the foreigners believe we are heathens."

This last wounds them particularly, which isn't odd considering they're deeply religious. They treat one another with a delicacy and helpfulness not always found in our society, yet they're unfamiliar with any kind of sentimentality. If the poor have no draft reindeer, the rich loan them some. If they have no tent, the better-off share theirs. It never happens that they can't be reconciled, given that they live right under one another's eyes day and night, and share fires and fuel and the narrow space. Gossip about tentmates is deeply despised and therefore doesn't take place. That sort of thing falls into the category of "tent sin." Their readiness to help is something all mountain travelers can certainly attest to. You'll never ask in vain for shelter and a bed for the night. At farms and among "better people," on the other hand, you can be turned away when you arrive tired and asking for a night's lodging. Among the Lapps you'll always be certain of getting correct information about the route, and they will guide you if they see it's necessary, even though they don't really have time—almost never do they have sufficient manpower.

There's no place you feel more secure, with your life and belongings, than in a mountain Lapp's tent out in the wilderness. And there are few places where you'll be met with such good manners and refinement in your dealings with people. Harmony rules, from their quiet, graceful movements to their calm, well-balanced composure. Along with that, they understand the fine art of conversation. In a few words, without banality, they can with warm humor, find exactly the right thing to say. Their liveliness and intelligence almost always turn a longer stay in a tent into a festive experience. In spite of the Lapps' great sense of humor, you need never be afraid of being laughed at, if in some comic way you offend the custom of the tent.

I'll remember my whole life the reprimand I received from Sara, when I once laughed at a gentleman's complete inability to move around in the tent.

"You must not laugh at a stranger. What will he think, he who doesn't understand our language?" This is culture, the Lapps' own culturedness, which they haven't learned in our schools or with the assistance of civilization.

Their aesthetic sense and feel for nature are also things they haven't learned from us. They love nature in the same way that the plants love sun and air and the earth that nourishes them. The Lapps put up their tents in the most beautiful places in the terrain, and they have done that from ancient times. The prehistoric settlements are sought out and used even today. That they really are the same is proved by the Lapps being able to point out what are plainly old tent sites in the immediate vicinity of their settlements; that is to say, the strongly rounded hollows in the earth, of which a very large number are still to be found, always two or three or more together, just like the tents still in the *siida*. I was shown many such ancient tent sites, both in Tromsdalen and in Elfkroken.

The Sea Kingdom, the summerland, is the Lapps' old country, "the grass-green valleys are the calves' mothers," and the calves are the herds' survival and the future, the Lapps' existence. You understand right away what the calves mean when you hear the tenderness with which all Lapps pronounce the word *ruksemiessi*, that is, "red calf or newborn calf." Its skin also clothes their small children, and when they gently stroke the fine soft fur, they're caressing both the child and the calf.

Unfortunately, the time of rest and pleasure in the Sea Kingdom is short; the grass dies back, the reindeer want to go up into the mountains again to eat lichen, and the Lapps must follow them. They joik, "When the night darkens in the coastal forests, the reindeer yearn for the high mountains." So beautifully do they understand how to express themselves in words, and beautiful is the whole life of the Lapps, closely entwined with nature.

Each stone, each lake, each mountain shape is a message from kinsfolk and tells a tale of their sorrows and joys, terrors and struggles, love and enchantment—a tale of oppressive darkness and burning sun, storms and death. Over the mountains drift the shadows of the clouds and the sheer radiance of the sun. It's wild and lonely up there where the Lapp lives, and he can only find his way forward because he, in the tradition of many generations, has been given knowledge of all that the mountains are. And he knows the movement of the clouds, the voices of the animals, and the voices that come from the earth and the air. His eyes can see what others cannot see; he can name what other people don't have a clue about.

He sleeps on the snow most nights of the year; but he is a migratory bird who moves his living places spring and fall. He follows the reindeer; he settles

down where they find fodder and puts up his gray tent where it's beautiful
and where he can see far and wide. His best friends are the dog and the fire.
He doesn't bother large-scale industries with his requirements; from the reindeer he gets almost everything, both food and clothing. In this society, life is
similar for rich and poor; it is just as hard for both, just as insecure and just
as beautiful. The Lapp loves beauty and understands it. His music is the voice
of nature; the sigh of the wind over the wilderness, the echo of the mountains
and the heavy fall of the rivers. His own voice is wild and intoxicating. When
he works with his reindeer herd, the barking of the dogs and the rushing of
the animals incites his voice and his very being into an ecstasy just as wild and
primordially beautiful as his mountains.

The Lapp's life is like his surroundings, hard and dangerous as mountains
and storms, beautiful and joyful as the northern lights in the winter sky and
the golden nights of the midnight sun.

Just like the wild animals of the wilderness, he has fear in his blood, fear of
the "dark-clad people," fear of nature's magic, fear of solitude—but he also has
the easy disposition that lives and enjoys what the moment presents. His
speech is like clear running water through which life glimmers with shiny
pictures, which wrap affectionately and truly around everything that they take
in. His limbs are lithe and healthy; he has endurance when he runs and walks,
like a wolf and a bear. In the winter he prefers to dress himself in white like
the hare and the ptarmigan.

You, who close the borders and take the earth from him, do you know what
you do?

You force this proud child of the mountains into a poverty-stricken life in
a shack. Eyes that are used to follow stars moving across the sky in watchful
nights, you want to coop up under a solid roof, lungs used to breathing the
air of the high mountains are supposed to breathe the sickness of the low-
land people. The limbs light as a bird's and the quick feet that are used to
feeling the skis spring and sing under them, used to running for miles with
the reindeer in the mountains and moors—the strong elastic tendons will be
weakened by idleness. The slender practiced hands that are used to grasping
the thin lasso and with a sure cast capturing the animal wanted from "the flock
of birds" will laboriously turn the topsoil in a wretched field.

He whose pride and joy and only property on the earth is the "silk-haired"
reindeer herd, which "spreads itself like sunbeams over the mountains," he
is to have his reindeer taken and to be given cows and sheep instead. The
mind that enjoys listening to and telling "sagas," that lives trustingly with the

mysterious beings of the wilderness, that mind is to be crammed with "knowledge." He who joiks all his feelings, he who sings of the animals and nature, frees himself through song in sorrow and pleasure—you wish to staunch the flow of the ancient, vibrant sources in his soul with the dross of civilization.

Let the nomads live their own life, the way they have for thousands of years and the way that suits them. Let them be productive in their own way, for in that way they create the values that entitle them to live side by side with their neighbors.

Notes

INTRODUCTION

1. "En danske Lappe-Dame," Tromsø newspaper clipping, undated and unidentified, but certainly from the summer of 1908. Emilie Demant Hatt papers,
Nordiska Museet Archives, Stockholm.

2. The Sami, an indigenous people of Scandinavia, Finland, and the Kola Peninsula of Russia, number at least eighty thousand, with the majority living in Norway
(twenty thousand in Sweden). Although the Nordic Sami now live everywhere in
Fennoscandia, including the capital cities, those who still own reindeer and speak
Sami are concentrated in the north of Sweden, Norway, and Finland. Their name
for themselves has always been Sami. Until the last few decades, however, they were
known as Lapps and also referred to themselves in that manner when writing
and speaking to a larger public. For more on language issues, see the "Translator's
Notes." Here, in the introduction, I use "Sami," which is both noun and adjective and
refers both to the people and their language, but "Lapp" when quoting from older
sources and Demant Hatt's work.

3. Sápmi is the Sami word for their ancestral homeland, an area that encom-
passes the Kola Peninsula in Russia, the northernmost part of Finland, the coastal
and inland areas of northern Norway, and the inland part of northern Sweden. Lapland today corresponds to no set territory, but both Sweden and Finland call parts
of their northern provinces Lapland. During the time that Demant Hatt was living
in the north, the historic and common word for the area was Lapland. She also
refers at times to southern "Lapmarks," to include her travels and research in southern Sápmi in later years.

4. Johan Turi, *Muitalus sámiid birra/En bog om lappernes liv*, edited and with an
introduction by Emilie Demant (Stockholm: A.-B. Nordiska Bokhandeln, 1910).
The first English version was translated from the Danish by E. Gee Nash (London:
Jonathan Cape, 1931). In 2010 *Muitalus sámiid birra* was published in a new Sami
edition based on the notebooks, edited by Mikael Svonni (Karasjok, Norway:
ČálliidLágádus–Authors' Publisher, 2010). A new English translation by Thomas A.

DuBois, from the Sami, was published as *An Account of the Sámi* (Chicago: Nordic Press, 2011).

5. Emilie Demant Hatt, *Med lapperne i højfjeldet* (Stockholm: A.-B. Nordiska Bokhandeln, 1913). EDH's book, like Turi's in 1910, was typeset and printed by Græbes Printing in Copenhagen under her supervision; the pages were then sent to Stockholm to be bound and distributed as part of a series produced by Hjalmar Lundbolm, The Lapps and Their Land.

6. Yngve Åström, *Hjalmar Lundbohm* (Stockholm: LTs Förlag, 1965).

7. Information on the districts and routes comes from Ossian Elgström, *Karesuandolapparna* (Stockholm: Åhlén & Åkerlunds Förlag, 1922); Ernst Manker, *The Nomadism of the Swedish Mountain Lapps: The Siidas and Their Migratory Routes in 1945* (Uppsala: Hugo Gebers Förlag, 1953); and Lars J. Walkeapää, *Könkämävuoma-Samernas renflyttningar till Norge* (Tromsø: Tromsø Museum, 2009).

8. Walkeapää, *Könkämävuoma-Samernas renflyttningar till Norge*.

9. Ibid.

10. Letter, June 30, 1908, Emilie Demant Hatt papers, Danish National Archives, Copenhagen.

11. See Ivar Bjørklund, *Sápmi: Becoming a Nation* (Tromsø: Tromsø Museum, 2000), for a short history of forced "Norwegianization" after World War II.

12. Gerda Niemann, "Sol och sommarglädje bland Lapplands fjäll," in *Svenska Turistföreningens Årsskrift* (Swedish Tourist Association's Yearbook) (Stockholm: Wahlström & Widstrand, 1904), 321–44.

13. Ellen Kleman, "Till Lapplägret vid Pålnoviken," in *Svenska Turistföreningens Årsskrift* (Stockholm: Wahlström & Widstrand, 1908), 285–94.

14. K. B. Wiklund (1868–1934) wrote several books about the Sami, including an educational series for the children of the reindeer herders, *Nomadskolans läsebok 1–3* (1917–29). He was one of the translators of the Swedish version of *Muitalus sámiid birra*. He also read and corrected the Sami orthography of *With the Lapps in the High Mountains* and *Lappish Texts*.

15. K .B. Wiklund, "Lapparna, deras lif och kultur," in *Svenska Turistföreningens Årsskrift* (Stockholm: Wahlström & Widstrand, 1903), 15–44.

16. Letter, June 30, 1908.

17. Knud Rasmussen, *Lapland* (Copenhagen: Gyldendal, 1907). For more on Knud Rasmussen and his early views of "nature's children," see Kirsten Hastrup, *Vinterens hjerte: Knud Rasmussen og hans tid* (Copenhagen: Gads Forlag, 2010).

18. See Barbara Sjoholm, "How *Muittalus Samid Birra* Was Created," *Scandinavian Studies* 82, no. 3 (2010), 313–36, for a full account of the process of the writing and production of *Muitalus*. See also Kristin Kuutma, "Collaborative Ethnography before Its Time: Johan Turi and Emilie Demant Hatt," *Scandinavian Studies* 75, no. 2 (2003), 165–73.

19. Letter, March 14, 1908. Hjalmar Lundbohm to Emilie Demant, Nordiska Museet Archives. All correspondence from Lundbohm to Demant Hatt is to be found at the Nordiska Museet Archives.

20. Letter, January 5, 1913. Hjalmar Lundbohm to Emilie Demant.

21. Letter, April 17, 1908. Hjalmar Lundbohm to Emilie Demant.

22. "For længe siden" ("Long Ago"), Nordiska Museet Archives.

23. Johan Turi and Per Turi, with the cooperation of K. B. Wiklund, *Lappish Texts*, ed. E. Demant-Hatt (Copenhagen: D. Kgl. Danske Vidensk. Selsk. Skrifter. Række 7, hist. og filos. Afd. IV. 2, 1918–19). The original Sami was corrected by Wiklund, translated into Danish by Demant Hatt, and then translated into English by Gudmund Hatt. It appeared in a bilingual Sami–English edition.

24. Gudmund Hatt, *Arktiske Skinddragter i Eurasien og Amerika: Et etnografisk Studie* (Arctic Skin Clothing in Eurasia and America: An Ethnographic Study) (Copenhagen: J. H. Schultz Forlag, 1914).

25. Gudmund Hatt, "Notes on Reindeer Nomadism," *Memoirs of the American Anthropological Association* 4, no. 2 (1917), 75–133; "Rensdyrnomadismens Elementer," *Geografisk Tidsskrift* 24 (1918), 241–69.

26. Demant Hatt's collection at the National Museum of Denmark numbers around two thousand objects.

27. Oluf Olufsen, in *Geografisk Tidsskrift* 22, 1913; H. P. Steensby, *Berlingske Tidende*, December 21, 1913; Christian Engelstoft, *Politikken*, December 21, 1913; K. B. Wiklund in *Fataburen* 1914 (Stockholm: Nordiska Museet, 1915), 125–27.

28. Gudmund Hatt, in an unpublished memoir sketch of Emilie's life, written after her death in 1958, Danish National Archives. Boas may well have been interested in Demant Hatt's collaboration with Turi, having himself worked with George Hunt on numerous projects, including *Kwakiutl Texts*, which lists both Boas and Hunt on the title page. Note also that Demant Hatt titled her next book with Turi *Lappish Texts*.

29. See Henrik Gutzon Larsen, "Gudmund Hatt," *Geographers: Biobibliographical Studies*, vol. 28, ed. Charles Withers and Hayden Lorimer (London: Continuum, 2009), for the fullest account to date in English of Hatt's career, including his downfall after World War II on the basis of writings and radio talks said to have supported the Germans.

30. Bertel Engelstoft, "Malerinden Emilie Demant Hatt," *Samleren* 6 (1943), 117–19.

31. Sjoholm, "How *Muittalus Samid Birra* Was Created."

32. For more on the history of Danish anthropology, see Ole Høiris, *Antropologien i Danmark* (Copenhagen: Nationalmuseets Forlag, 1986); Esther Fihl, *Exploring Central Asia*, vol. 1 (New York: Thames & Hudson, 2002); and Hastrup, *Vinterens hjerte*.

WITH THE LAPPS IN THE HIGH MOUNTAINS

1. EDH uses the Danish word *telt* at times for the communal tent but most often the Dano-Norwegian word *kote*. The Sami word is *goahti* (pl: *goaðit*). A smaller tent, used by herders or on migrations, is only referred to by its Sami name, *luovvi*. The large tent, constructed of birch poles, was covered by two wool blankets. The door, also of cloth, was fastened by wooden pegs, but often left open.

2. A conservative Lutheran revival movement begun in the 1840s by Lars Levi Laestadius, a Sami Swedish botanist and pastor in the Lutheran church. The movement was widespread in the north of Scandinavia, and the Sami and Finnish settlers were some of the strongest adherents. The church is still active, particularly in Scandinavia, Russia, and North America.

3. *Kofta* is the Swedish word EDH uses throughout her text; the Sami word is *gákti*. A dress or tunic of wool with sleeves and a split in the neckline, often embroidered, it was the summer garment of the Sami, worn with a belt. In the part of Sápmi where EDH traveled, *koftas* were blue.

4. The *boaššu*, in addition to being the tent's kitchen, was once used to mean both the back door of the tent and the tent's rear corner, once sacred and accessible only by certain family members at certain ritually prescribed moments. In earlier times the sacred drum was kept there. In EDH's time the only reference to this heightened ritual function is when Nikki brings in a dead reindeer killed by wolves on Christmas Eve.

5. Stallo or Stállu: a mythological ogre or bogeyman with cannibalistic tendencies, often outwitted by the Sami. EDH's note (12): *The meaning here is probably that he lifts you by the belt to see if you're fat enough.*

6. *Siida*, which I've left untranslated throughout, is a reindeer pastoralist community composed of families. A core concept in Sami culture, with roots back to prehistory, *siida* is historically specific, once referring to a group of people who lived together in tent villages, made migrations together, and had shared hunting and fishing rights in delineated territories. In modern times *siida* is translated into Swedish as *sameby* or "Sami village," and is a political term. Sweden is divided into fifty-one *samebys*, each of which has specific grazing and migration areas. *Siida* also has a larger meaning, continuing today, of home, security, extended family, and community.

7. Reindeer herding and husbandry had long been what was called "intensive," in that Sami *siidas* owned small groups of reindeer, which they used for many purposes: food, clothing, objects carved from bone and antler, and so forth. The Sami also milked the cows and made cheese. In the early nineteenth century a different model of reindeer herding emerged, called "extensive." *Siida* members owned large herds, numbering in the thousands of animals, and they were more likely to be slaughtered for meat and furs, which were sold for cash. The district of Jukkasjärvi

had been primarily based on the intensive model until Sami from Norway, forced south because of state border closings and in need of pasturage, brought their extensive herding techniques into the district. The Turi family and their *siida* came originally from Kautokeino, Norway, and had herds of many hundreds of reindeer. They continued to do some milking, particularly in autumn.

8. In Danish the word for reindeer (*ren*) is the same word as for clean (*ren*).

9. The concept of "nomad schools" for the children of the reindeer pastoralists was under much discussion during the time that EDH was in Swedish Lapland. At its heart was the issue of whether to take children from their parents and continue to educate them in boarding schools, as had been done for some two hundred years, or to create "nomad schools" for the children in the tent encampments. The issue of Sami education was primarily discussed in terms of the reindeer-herding Sami. Other Sami children in Sweden attended state-run schools alongside the majority population. The Swedish government passed the Nomad School Reform law in 1913, and nomad schools operated until the 1940s (it's worth noting that this law was opposed by the Sami in their national assembly of 1918 as offering substandard education). In *With the Lapps* EDH makes no mention of "Nilsa" and "Elle" attending school seasonally in Jukkasjärvi, where many Sami children studied.

10. The Torne River, which flows from Lake Torneträsk to the Gulf of Bothnia, was traditionally home to both Swedes and Finns. Pre-1809, when Finland was ceded to Russia, the river valley was part of Sweden. The village of Jukkasjärvi, long a Sami residence, received its first Finnish settlers in the seventeenth century. Some of the Finnish settlers EDH speaks of were long-time residents in Sweden and some were newcomers to the area. Agriculture in the mountainous areas north of Jukkasjärvi was, as EDH notes, very difficult. The Finnish settlers and Sami *siidas* of the district had conflicts but many mutually beneficial arrangements. The Sami provided reindeer meat in exchange for boarding with the Finns on occasion and camping in their vicinity, such as in Kattuvuoma, where they kept permanent storehouses.

11. *Liitkutuksia*, the Finnish word for movement, was part of the Laestadian tradition from the church's beginnings and was sanctioned by Laestadius as a positive expression of religious fervor. Some believe that *liitkutuksia* is akin to the ecstasy of Shamanic trance or has its origins in the older spirituality of the Sami.

12. EDH's note (31): *A circular enclosure of birch trunks and branches, in which the Lapps have the herd when they are to be either milked or separated,* ratken. *For the latter use, smaller enclosures are constructed outside the large corral. The reindeer to be separated are chased inside so that they can be set apart until the whole separation process is over, and each owner can leave with his flock. Such a reindeer corral is 75–100 meters in diameter and is preferably situated central to several* siidas. *It is particularly from autumn to close to Christmas that the large separations take place. The herds are easily*

mixed together when they come back over the border in the autumn, since many siidas
have the same migration route.

13. Joik, noun and verb, comes from the Sami word *juoigat*, to chant. The joik
(sometimes spelled yoik in English) is a traditional form of singing unique to the
Sami, though similar in some ways to the chanting of Native Americans. Traditional joiking had no accompaniment and was often spontaneous and improvised,
yet many joiks were also handed down and shared in communities. The subjects
were often reindeer, animals, people, and nature. They were not so much about a
person as meant to evoke that person. Not all joiks have words or only words. Many
are mainly vocables or include vocal sounds as refrains. The joik, once almost in
danger of dying out, is now once again a vibrant, evolving part of Sami culture. The
following is EDH's original note (42) on joiking:

> *An old woman in Jämtland told me that in her youth, when they guarded the rein-*
> *deer, they passed time during the long winter nights by joiking. When the wolves*
> *left them in peace and the herd rested, the young people gathered around the bonfire*
> *and taught each other joiks. You wanted to know as many as possible; there it was*
> *very welcome, when one person could teach the others joiking from other parts. In*
> *this way the melodies diffused. Also, when the reindeer herder walked alone with*
> *the herd, he or she joiked. "The reindeer were once so tame that guarding them was*
> *easy; you could do handiwork. We did band weaving and spun sinew thread and*
> *during the long nights, when the weather was good, we joiked. At night, home in*
> *the tent, when mother lay there unable to sleep, she began to joik. She joiked about*
> *the reindeer, that God would bless them, so they must flourish. She joiked about*
> *whatever occurred to her." That the Lapps joiked in the tent at night, when they*
> *couldn't sleep, was quite common. In Härjedalen during the summer I woke one*
> *night to an old woman lying there singing.*
>
> *The Lapps don't only joik songs about individuals; they joik about everything*
> *possible; very often they improvise joiks in an instant. The old seventy-year-old*
> *Lappish woman in Jämtland said, "But it's soon thirty years since I joiked, and if*
> *I try now, no words come. In those days when I was young and went among the*
> *reindeer at night, the words came of themselves. We also had a certain song for*
> *grief, but many joiked in a wicked, ugly way as well. If anyone here started joiking,*
> *the young people would laugh."*
>
> *In Härjedalen and Jämtland, they no longer joik, but in Västerbotten joiking*
> *is still quite alive and flourishing. In the northern Lapmarks it is equally as alive,*
> *but only secretly, and it will scarcely be long before Laestadianism completely chokes*
> *it out. The "truly old" joiks are known by very few Lapps up there, and the next*
> *generation will have totally forgotten them. It is therefore gratifying that in Sweden*
> *now the serious study and valuing of the Lapps' old songs and melodies has begun.*
> *Mr. Karl Tirén is traveling through all the Lapmarks and collecting a rich and*
> *beautiful harvest of Lappish poetry and music.*

The seventy-year-old woman EDH mentions here is almost certainly Märta Nilsson, who, with her husband Nils Nilsson, hosted EDH in their tent for three months in the summer of 1910, in Glen, Jämtland. Karl Tirén (1869–1955) was a man of many talents—a painter and gifted violinist as well as a conductor on the northern railways of Sweden. Tirén first began to collect joiks through transcription; by 1913 he was using the new technique of wax cylinders to make recordings in the field. His scholarly work, *Die Lappische Volkmusik* (Stockholm: Acta Lapponica), appeared in 1942.

14. The winter outer garment of the Sami is called a *beaska* and is a parka or tunic worn over other clothes. Here and there, EDH calls it a *beaska*, but often she just calls it a fur. The women's version is longer than the men's and usually belted, more like a dress or a coat. I have translated it as both fur and fur parka.

15. Uldas (*ulddat*) are supernatural beings, often quite beautiful, who will increase a reindeer herd or protect it if they are given a sacrifice. However, they are also known for stealing babies and children to raise as their own.

16. A string of reindeer and sleds, called a *rajde*, was generally composed of five to seven animals, harnessed and strung together. In winter migrations most of the animals were draft reindeer pulling cargo sledges or boatlike sleds covered on top (EDH calls these latter sleds *pulks*. They were also used by individuals driving a single reindeer. In Swedish they are *akjas*. The basic Sami word for such sleds is *gieres*.) At other times of the year, the string included pack reindeer or, when the snow had melted, only pack reindeer. Often a family had two strings: one was led by the woman of the household and the other by the man. I have used "caravan" to refer to many strings.

17. Reindeer eat a limited diet. In summer they graze on a few species of grasses and herbs; in autumn on mushrooms; and from November through May on lichen, specifically *Cladonia rangiferina*, sometimes called reindeer moss, which they dig for through the snow with their front hooves.

18. EDH's note (46): *Cus or cissa means urine. Some reindeer are very greedy for urine, a quality the Lapps value highly, since such animals like to seek out the camp and remain tame. The word is therefore used to coax the herd when leading it.*

19. EDH's note (54): *Snow crust (Lappish cuoŋo), called in Swedish isskorpe, is created on the snow in the spring when the sun thaws the top layer during the day and this freezes to ice during the night. The reindeer can't break through the ice crust with its hooves and get down to the lichen. When the ice crust occurs over a couple of days, the reindeer are suddenly without food, with the exception of a little beard lichen they can snatch from the trees. Then they head rapidly for the high mountains, where a combination of sun and wind in some places—on mountain peaks and south-facing slopes—has thinned out the snow enough that the reindeer can scrape through. When the ice crust occurs, the Lapps must in hot haste make ready to move in order to follow the reindeer.*

20. Holger Henrik Herholdt Drachmann (1846–1908) was a Danish poet and dramatist. Bjørnstjerne Martinus Bjørnson (1832–1910) was a Norwegian writer and a 1903 Nobel Prize in Literature laureate.

21. EDH's note (65): *The seed has from ancient times played a large role in Lappish beliefs and medicine. Sara actually had a little dried seed in a cloth, but in truth she didn't offer me this remedy. The Lapps are beginning to lose faith in the effect of old remedies and more and more use medicine from a pharmacy. Instead of their own "doctors," in most cases of illness they seek out true doctors if they are found nearby.*

22. EDH's note (67): Badjeolbmot, *the high people,* the mountain Lapps call themselves to show that they live higher up in the mountains than other people. Among themselves, they don't call themselves Lapps but sápmelaččat or sámit (*in the singular,* sápmelaš or sámi).

23. Like *Uldas, Haldas* are supernatural beings found in Sami folklore. The term is related to the Finnish *haltija* and can refer to enticing female spirits, sometimes with a tail, known in Swedish and Norwegian folklore as well. They are by-and-large protective spirits, guarding pathways, property, or particular places.

24. The freely ranging herd (*löshjord* as EDH calls it, using Swedish here) is the greater part of the herd left after the reindeer cows have been separated out to be driven over the Norwegian border to the grasslands to calve. The two herds are kept separated, and the freely ranging herd is kept from traversing the border as long as possible so as not to have all the reindeer coming across at one time and possibly trampling the hay in the meadows.

25. EDH's note (74): *The Lapps call Norway* Mearrariika, *the Sea Kingdom or just* mearra, *the sea, and, instead of Norwegian mountains, Norwegian tobacco, Norwegian bread, Norwegian people and so on, they only say sea mountains, sea tobacco, sea bread, and sea people. Gate, for example, had a grown daughter who had been raised by farmers in Norway, and she always called her* mu mearra-nieida, *my sea daughter.*

26. Čúđit in modern Sami. Also Chudes and Tsudes, possibly connected with Russian or Finnic tribes in the past. The etymology is varied, but the general meaning is "enemy." By the time EDH was writing, the Čúđit were part of folklore, evil-minded intruders in Sápmi who needed to be repelled by means of cunning or magic.

27. Turf huts, *goađit,* were permanent structures of birch trunks and branches and clay or dirt wattle, covered by turf. They were shaped like rounded tents with a smoke hole and wooden door. EDH refers to them as *tørvekoter,* turf tents.

28. The Molbo people are ridiculed in Danish folktales as extremely stupid people. The story EDH refers to is one of the best known. A farmer fears that a stork is eating his corn and wants to drive it away, but decides that his big feet will flatten more of the corn if he goes into the field. So he takes down a gate and hires eight men to carry him on it into the field to drive the stork away. Thus, his feet never touch the ground.

Further Reading about the Sami and Sápmi

http://www.emiliedemanthatt.com. A website about Emilie Demant Hatt maintained by Barbara Sjoholm.

http://archive.org/details/medlapperneihj00dema. The full text of the original Danish edition of *Med lapperne i højfjeldet* from the Internet Archive.

Beach, Hugh. *A Year in Lapland: Guest of the Reindeer Herders.* Seattle: University of Washington Press, 2001.

Gaski, Harald, ed. *In the Shadow of the Midnight Sun: Contemporary Sami Prose and Poetry.* Kárášjohka, Norway: Davi Girji, 1996.

Helander, Elina, and Kaarina Kailo, eds. *No Beginning, No End: The Sami Speak Up.* Circumpolar Research Series No. 5, published in cooperation with the Nordic Sami Institute, Finland, 1998.

Kulonen, Ulla-Maija, Irja Seurujärvi-Kari, and Risto Pulkkinen. *The Saami: A Cultural Encyclopaedia.* Helsinki: SKS, 2005.

Lehtola, Veli-Pekka. *The Sami People: Traditions in Transition.* Fairbanks: University of Alaska Press, 2004.

Manker, Ernst. *People of Eight Seasons.* New York: Crescent Books, 1972.

Paine, Robert. *Herds of the Tundra: A Portrait of Saami Reindeer Pastoralism.* Washington, D.C.: Smithsonian Institution Press, 1994.

Turi, Johan. *An Account of the Sámi.* Translated by Thomas A. DuBois. Chicago: Nordic Studies Press, 2011.